BIG IDEAS MATH®
Modeling Real Life

Grade 2
Volume 2

Ron Larson
Laurie Boswell

Erie, Pennsylvania
BigIdeasLearning.com

Big Ideas Learning, LLC
1762 Norcross Road
Erie, PA 16510-3838
USA

For product information and customer support, contact Big Ideas Learning at **1-877-552-7766** or visit us at ***BigIdeasLearning.com***.

Cover Image:
Valdis Torms, bgblue/DigitalVision Vectors/Getty Images

Copyright © 2022 by Big Ideas Learning, LLC. All rights reserved.

No part of this work may be reproduced or transmitted in any form or by any means, electronic or mechanical, including, but not limited to, photocopying and recording, or by any information storage or retrieval system, without prior written permission of Big Ideas Learning, LLC, unless such copying is expressly permitted by copyright law. Address inquiries to Permissions, Big Ideas Learning, LLC, 1762 Norcross Road, Erie, PA 16510.

Big Ideas Learning and *Big Ideas Math* are registered trademarks of Larson Texts, Inc.

Printed in the U.S.A.

ISBN 13: 978-1-64727-973-8

3 4 5 6 7 8 9 10—25 24 23

One Voice from Kindergarten Through Algebra 2

Written by renowned authors, Dr. Ron Larson and Dr. Laurie Boswell, *Big Ideas Math* offers a seamless math pedagogy from elementary through high school. Together, Ron and Laurie provide a consistent voice that encourages students to make connections through cohesive progressions and clear instruction. Since 1992, Ron and Laurie have authored over 50 mathematics programs.

> Each time Laurie and I start working on a new program, we spend time putting ourselves in the position of the reader. How old is the reader? What is the reader's experience with mathematics? The answers to these questions become our writing guides. Our goal is to make the learning targets understandable and to develop these targets in a clear path that leads to student success.

Ron Larson

Ron Larson, Ph.D., is well known as lead author of a comprehensive and widely used mathematics program that ranges from elementary school through college. He holds the distinction of Professor Emeritus from Penn State Erie, The Behrend College, where he taught for nearly 40 years. He received his Ph.D. in mathematics from the University of Colorado. Dr. Larson engages in the latest research and advancements in mathematics education and consistently incorporates key pedagogical elements to ensure focus, coherence, rigor, and student self-reflection.

> My passion and goal in writing is to provide an essential resource for exploring and making sense of mathematics. Our program is guided by research around the learning and teaching of mathematics in the hopes of improving the achievement of all students. May this be a successful year for you!

Laurie Boswell

Laurie Boswell, Ed.D., is the former Head of School at Riverside School in Lyndonville, Vermont. In addition to authoring textbooks, she provides mathematics consulting and embedded coaching sessions. Dr. Boswell received her Ed.D. from the University of Vermont in 2010. She is a recipient of the Presidential Award for Excellence in Mathematics Teaching and later served as president of CPAM. Laurie has taught math to students at all levels, elementary through college. In addition, Laurie has served on the NCTM Board of Directors and as a Regional Director for NCSM. Along with Ron, Laurie has co-authored numerous math programs and has become a popular national speaker.

Contributors, Reviewers, and Research

Big Ideas Learning would like to express our gratitude to the mathematics education and instruction experts who served as our advisory panel, contributing specialists, and reviewers during the writing of *Big Ideas Math: Modeling Real Life*. Their input was an invaluable asset during the development of this program.

Contributing Specialists and Reviewers

- **Sophie Murphy**, Ph.D. Candidate, Melbourne School of Education, Melbourne, Australia
  Learning Targets and Success Criteria Specialist and Visible Learning Reviewer

- **Linda Hall**, Mathematics Educational Consultant, Edmond, OK
  Advisory Panel

- **Michael McDowell**, Ed.D., Superintendent, Ross, CA
  Project-Based Learning Specialist

- **Kelly Byrne**, Math Supervisor and Coordinator of Data Analysis, Downingtown, PA
  Advisory Panel

- **Jean Carwin**, Math Specialist/TOSA, Snohomish, WA
  Advisory Panel

- **Nancy Siddens**, Independent Language Teaching Consultant, Las Cruces, NM
  English Language Learner Specialist

- **Kristen Karbon**, Curriculum and Assessment Coordinator, Troy, MI
  Advisory Panel

- **Kery Obradovich**, K–8 Math/Science Coordinator, Northbrook, IL
  Advisory Panel

- **Jennifer Rollins**, Math Curriculum Content Specialist, Golden, CO
  Advisory Panel

- **Becky Walker**, Ph.D., School Improvement Services Director, Green Bay, WI
  Advisory Panel and Content Reviewer

- **Deborah Donovan**, Mathematics Consultant, Lexington, SC
  Content Reviewer

- **Tom Muchlinski**, Ph.D., Mathematics Consultant, Plymouth, MN
  Content Reviewer and Teaching Edition Contributor

- **Mary Goetz**, Elementary School Teacher, Troy, MI
  Content Reviewer

- **Nanci N. Smith**, Ph.D., International Curriculum and Instruction Consultant, Peoria, AZ
  Teaching Edition Contributor

- **Robyn Seifert-Decker**, Mathematics Consultant, Grand Haven, MI
  Teaching Edition Contributor

- **Bonnie Spence**, Mathematics Education Specialist, Missoula, MT
  Teaching Edition Contributor

- **Suzy Gagnon**, Adjunct Instructor, University of New Hampshire, Portsmouth, NH
  Teaching Edition Contributor

- **Art Johnson**, Ed.D., Professor of Mathematics Education, Warwick, RI
  Teaching Edition Contributor

- **Anthony Smith**, Ph.D., Associate Professor, Associate Dean, University of Washington Bothell, Seattle, WA
  Reading and Writing Reviewer

- **Brianna Raygor**, Music Teacher, Fridley, MN
  Music Reviewer

- **Nicole Dimich Vagle**, Educator, Author, and Consultant, Hopkins, MN
  Assessment Reviewer

- **Janet Graham**, District Math Specialist, Manassas, VA
  Response to Intervention and Differentiated Instruction Reviewer

- **Sharon Huber**, Director of Elementary Mathematics, Chesapeake, VA
  Universal Design for Learning Reviewer

Student Reviewers

- T.J. Morin
- Alayna Morin
- Ethan Bauer
- Emery Bauer
- Emma Gaeta
- Ryan Gaeta
- Benjamin SanFrotello
- Bailey SanFrotello
- Samantha Grygier
- Robert Grygier IV
- Jacob Grygier
- Jessica Urso
- Ike Patton
- Jake Lobaugh
- Adam Fried
- Caroline Naser
- Charlotte Naser

Research

Ron Larson and Laurie Boswell used the latest in educational research, along with the body of knowledge collected from expert mathematics instructors, to develop the *Modeling Real Life* series. The pedagogical approach used in this program follows the best practices outlined in the most prominent and widely accepted educational research, including:

- *Visible Learning*, John Hattie © 2009
- *Visible Learning for Teachers*
  John Hattie © 2012
- *Visible Learning for Mathematics*
  John Hattie © 2017
- *Principles to Actions: Ensuring Mathematical Success for All*
  NCTM © 2014
- *Adding It Up: Helping Children Learn Mathematics*
  National Research Council © 2001
- *Mathematical Mindsets: Unleashing Students' Potential through Creative Math, Inspiring Messages and Innovative Teaching*
  Jo Boaler © 2015
- *What Works in Schools: Translating Research into Action*
  Robert Marzano © 2003
- *Classroom Instruction That Works: Research-Based Strategies for Increasing Student Achievement*
  Marzano, Pickering, and Pollock © 2001
- *Principles and Standards for School Mathematics*
  NCTM © 2000
- *Rigorous PBL by Design: Three Shifts for Developing Confident and Competent Learners*
  Michael McDowell © 2017
- *Universal Design for Learning Guidelines*
  CAST © 2011
- *Rigor/Relevance Framework®*
  International Center for Leadership in Education
- *Understanding by Design*
  Grant Wiggins and Jay McTighe © 2005
- Achieve, ACT, and The College Board
- *Elementary and Middle School Mathematics: Teaching Developmentally*
  John A. Van de Walle and Karen S. Karp © 2015
- *Evaluating the Quality of Learning: The SOLO Taxonomy*
  John B. Biggs & Kevin F. Collis © 1982
- *Unlocking Formative Assessment: Practical Strategies for Enhancing Students' Learning in the Primary and Intermediate Classroom*
  Shirley Clarke, Helen Timperley, and John Hattie © 2004
- *Formative Assessment in the Secondary Classroom*
  Shirley Clarke © 2005
- *Improving Student Achievement: A Practical Guide to Assessment for Learning*
  Toni Glasson © 2009

Focus and Coherence from

Instructional Design

A single authorship team from Kindergarten through Algebra 2 results in a logical progression of focused topics with meaningful coherence from course to course.

FOCUS
A focused program dedicates lessons, activities, and assessments to grade-level standards while simultaneously supporting and engaging you in the major work of the course.

The **Learning Targets** in your book and the **Success Criteria** in the Teaching Edition focus the learning for each lesson into manageable chunks, with clear teaching text and examples.

Learning Target: Write related addition and subtraction equations to complete a fact family.

Laurie's Notes

Preparing to Teach
Students have heard about time and the language of time. Most students do not understand time or know how to tell time on an analog clock. In this lesson, students are introduced to telling time to the hour. They learn about the hour hand and telling time as o'clock.

Laurie's Notes, located in the Teaching Edition, prepare your teacher for the math concepts in each chapter and lesson and make connections to the threads of major topics for the course.

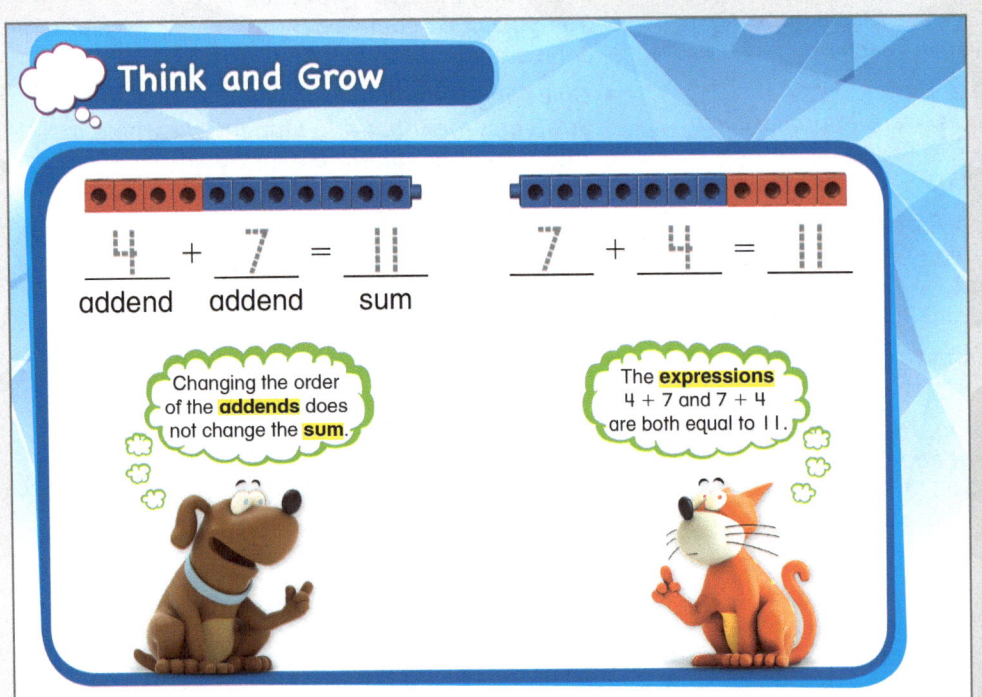

Think and Grow

$4 + 7 = 11$ $7 + 4 = 11$
addend addend sum

Changing the order of the **addends** does not change the **sum**.

The **expressions** $4 + 7$ and $7 + 4$ are both equal to 11.

a Single Authorship Team

COHERENCE

A single authorship team built a coherent program that has intentional progression of content within each grade and between grade levels. You will build new understanding on foundations from prior grades and connect concepts throughout the course.

The authors developed content that progresses from prior chapters and grades to future ones. In addition to charts like this one, Laurie's Notes give your teacher insights about where you have come from and where you are going in your learning progression.

Through the Grades

Kindergarten	Grade 1	Grade 2
• Represent addition and subtraction with various models and strategies. • Solve addition and subtraction word problems within 10. • Fluently add and subtract within 5.	• Solve addition and subtraction word problems within 20. • Fluently add and subtract within 10. • Determine the unknown number to complete addition and subtraction equations.	• Solve addition and subtraction word problems within 100. • Solve word problems involving length and money. • Solve one- and two-step word problems. • Fluently add and subtract within 20.

One author team thoughtfully wrote each course, creating a seamless progression of content from Kindergarten to Algebra 2.

	Grade K	Grade 1	Grade 2	Grade 3	Grade 4	Grade 5	Grade 6	
Number and Quantity	**Number and Operations – Base Ten**				**Number and Operations – Base Ten**		**The Number System**	
	Work with numbers 11–19 to gain foundations for place value. Chapter 8	Extend the counting sequence. Use place value and properties of operations to add and subtract. Chapters 6–9	Use place value and properties of operations to add and subtract. Chapters 2–10, 14	Use place value and properties of operations to perform multi-digit arithmetic. Chapters 7–9, 12	Generalize place value understanding for multi-digit whole numbers. Use place value and properties of operations to perform multi-digit arithmetic. Chapters 1–5	Understand the place value system. Perform operations with multi-digit whole numbers and with decimals to hundredths. Chapters 1, 3–7	Perform operations with multi-digit numbers and find common factors and multiples. Chapter 1 Divide fractions by fractions. Chapter 2 Extend understanding of numbers to the rational number system. Chapter 8	Perfor rationa Chapte
				Num. and Oper. – Fractions	**Number and Operations – Fractions**		**Ratios and Proportional Relation**	
				Understand fractions as numbers. Chapters 10, 11, 14	Extend understanding of fraction equivalence and ordering. Build fractions from unit	Add, subtract, multiply, and divide fractions. Chapters 6, 8–11	Use ratios to solve problems. Chapters 3, 4	Use pr to solv Chapte

Think and Grow

$37 + 14 + 23 = ?$

Remember, you can add in any order.

One Way:

Another Way:

If you can, make a 10 to help you add.

Throughout each course, lessons build on prior learning as new concepts are introduced. Here you are reminded of rules and strategies that you already know to help solve the addition problem.

vii

Rigor in Math: A Balanced Approach

Instructional Design
The authors wrote each chapter and every lesson to provide a meaningful balance of rigorous instruction.

RIGOR
A rigorous program provides a balance of three important building blocks.
- **Conceptual Understanding** Discovering why
- **Procedural Fluency** Learning how
- **Application** Knowing when to apply

Conceptual Understanding
You have the opportunity to develop foundational concepts central to the *Learning Target* in each *Explore and Grow* by experimenting with new concepts, talking with peers, and asking questions.

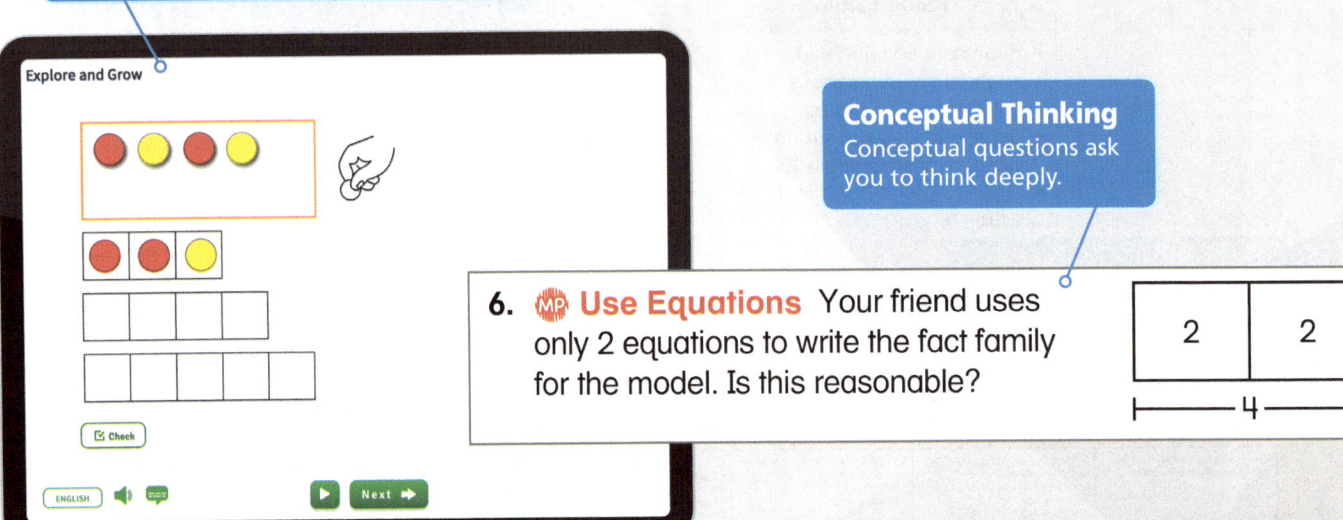

Conceptual Thinking
Conceptual questions ask you to think deeply.

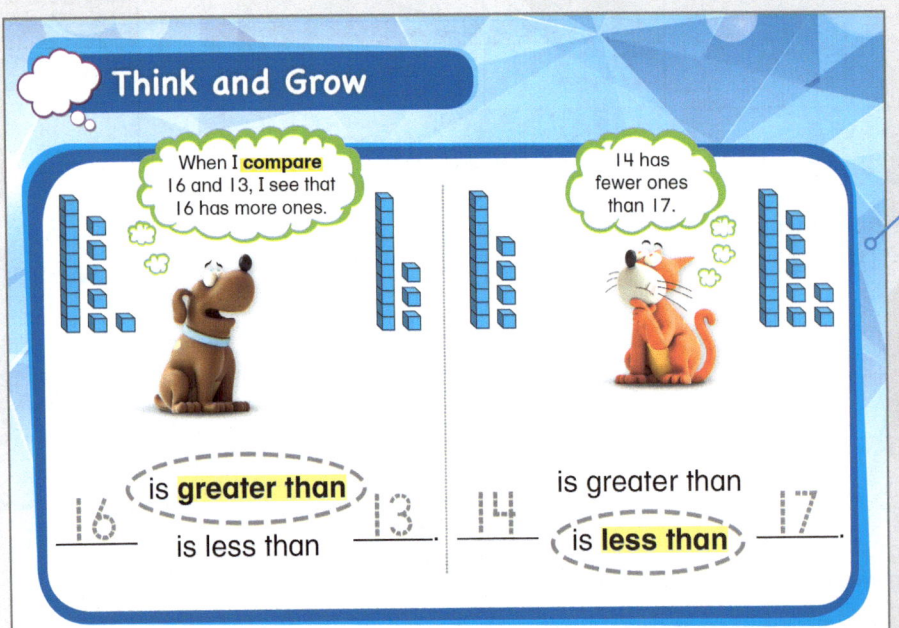

Procedural Fluency
Solidify learning with clear, stepped-out teaching in *Think and Grow* examples.

Then shift conceptual understanding into procedural fluency with *Show and Grow*, *Apply and Grow*, *Practice*, and *Review & Refresh*.

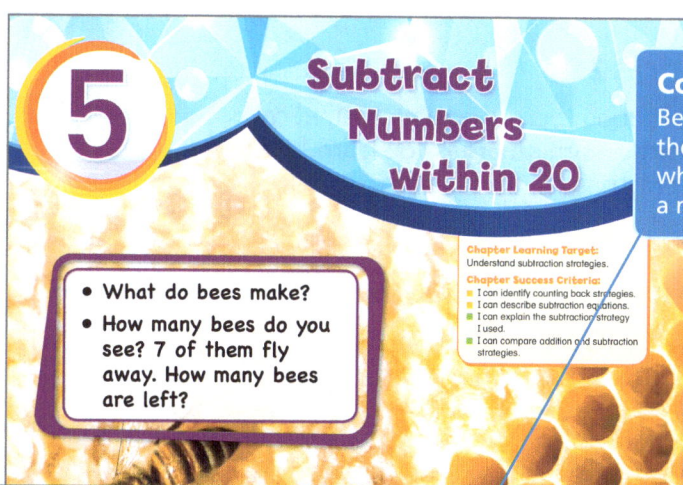

Connecting to Real Life
Begin every chapter thinking about the world around you. Then apply what you learn in the chapter with a related *Performance Task*.

Daily Application Practice
Modeling Real Life, Dig Deeper, and other non-routine problems help you apply surface-level skills to gain a deeper understanding. These problems lead to independent problem-solving.

1. You keep track of the number of honeybees and bumblebees you see.

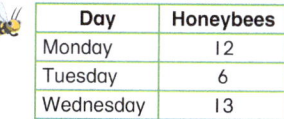
Day	Honeybees
Monday	12
Tuesday	6
Wednesday	13

Day	Bumblebees
Monday	5
Tuesday	14
Wednesday	

a. How many more honeybees did you see on Monday than on Tuesday?

_____ more honeybees

15. **Modeling Real Life** Your magic book has 163 tricks. Your friend's magic book has 100 more tricks than yours. How many tricks does your friend's magic book have?

_____ tricks

16. **DIG DEEPER!** You have 624 songs. Newton has 100 fewer than you. Descartes has 10 more than Newton. How many songs does Descartes have?

_____ songs

THE PROBLEM-SOLVING PLAN

1. **Understand the Problem**
   Think about what the problem is asking. Circle what you know and underline what you need to find.

2. **Make a Plan**
   Plan your solution pathway before jumping in to solve. Identify any relationships and decide on a problem-solving strategy.

3. **Solve and Check**
   As you solve the problem, be sure to evaluate your progress and check your answers. Throughout the problem-solving process, you must continually ask, "Does this make sense?" and be willing to change course if necessary.

Problem-Solving Plan
Walk through the Problem-Solving Plan, featured in many *Think and Grow* examples, to help you make sense of problems with confidence.

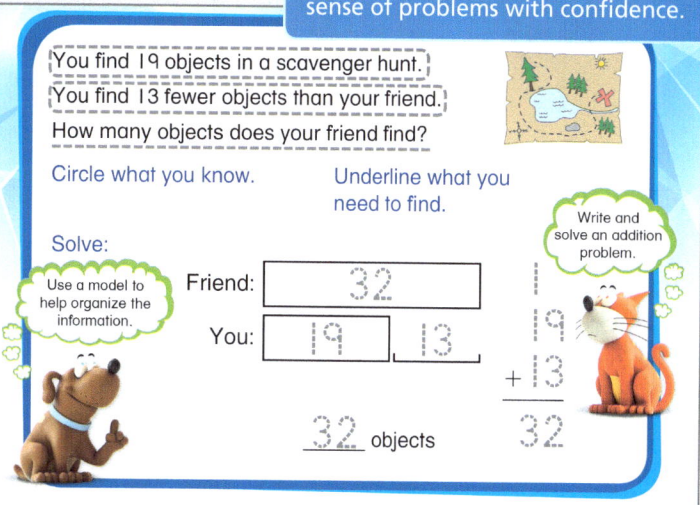

Embedded Mathematical Practices

Encouraging Mathematical Mindsets

Developing proficiency in the **Mathematical Practices** is about becoming a mathematical thinker. Learn to ask why, and to reason and communicate with others as you learn. Use this guide to develop proficiency with the mathematical practices.

1 One way to **Make Sense of Problems and Persevere in Solving Them** is to use the Problem-Solving Plan. Take time to analyze the given information and what the problem is asking to help you plan a solution pathway.

There are 33 students on a bus. 10 more get on. How many students are on the bus now?

Addition equation: _____ students

Check Your Work When adding 10, should the digit in the tens place or the ones place change?

Look for labels such as:
- Find Entry Points
- Analyze a Problem
- Interpret a Solution
- Make a Plan
- Use a Similar Problem
- Check Your Work

5. **Analyze a Problem** Use the numbers shown to write two addition equations.

8   10   2

___ + ___ = ___

___ + ___ = ___

7. **Reasoning** The minute hand points to the 7. What number will it point to in 10 minutes?

Reason Abstractly when you explore an example using numbers and models to represent the problem. Other times, **Reason Quantitatively** when you see relationships in numbers or models and draw conclusions about the problem.

2

Look for labels such as:
- Reasoning
- Number Sense
- Use Equations
- Use Expressions

3. **Number Sense** Which numbers can you subtract from 55 without regrouping?

15   49   33   24

x

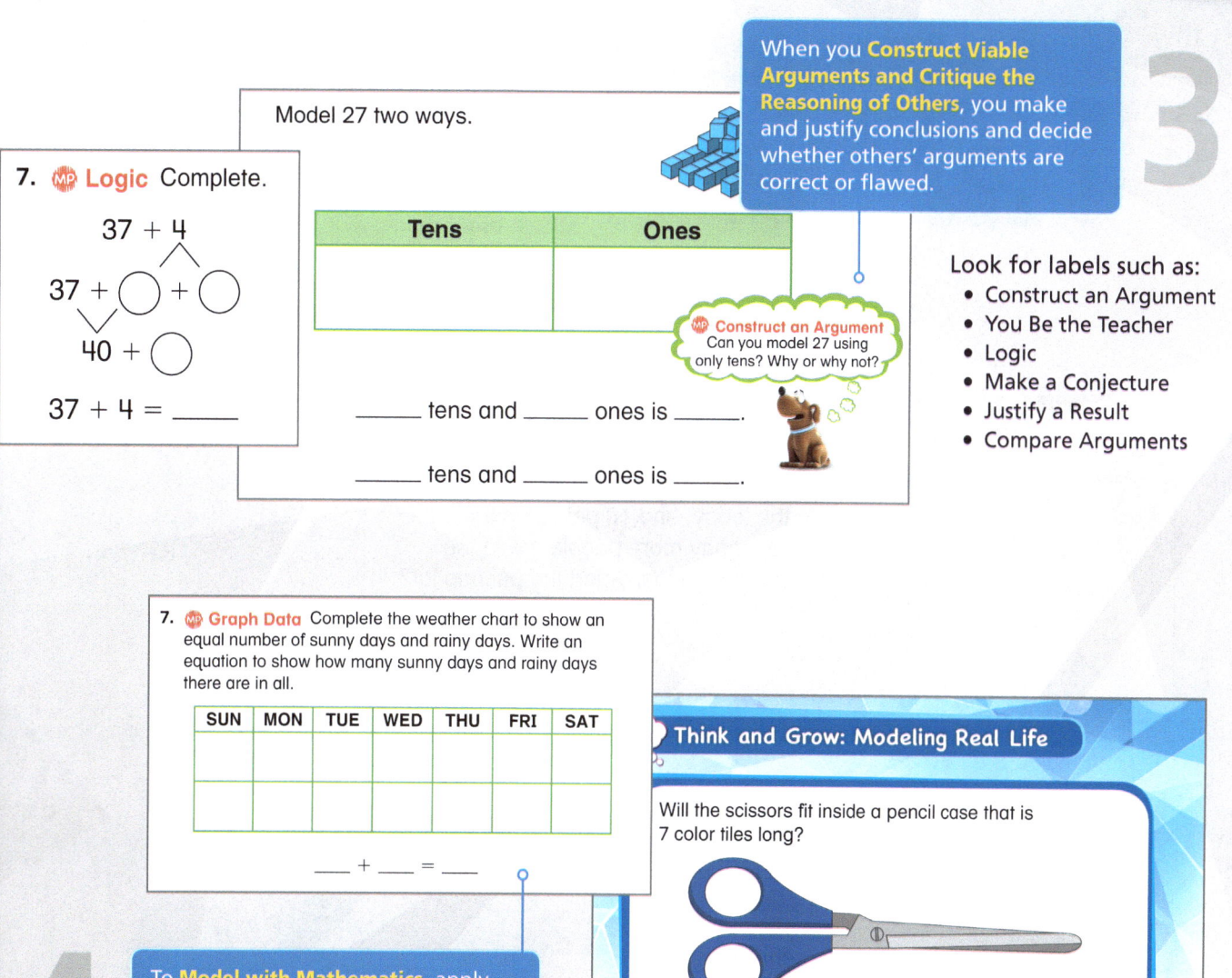

3

When you **Construct Viable Arguments and Critique the Reasoning of Others**, you make and justify conclusions and decide whether others' arguments are correct or flawed.

Look for labels such as:
- Construct an Argument
- You Be the Teacher
- Logic
- Make a Conjecture
- Justify a Result
- Compare Arguments

4 To **Model with Mathematics**, apply the math you learned to a real-life problem and interpret mathematical results in the context of the situation.

Look for labels such as:
- Modeling Real Life
- Graph Data
- Analyze a Relationship
- Does It Make Sense?

BUILDING TO FULL UNDERSTANDING

Throughout each course, you have opportunities to demonstrate specific aspects of the mathematical practices. Labels throughout the book indicate gateways to those aspects. Collectively, these opportunities will lead to a full understanding of each mathematical practice. Developing these mindsets and habits will give meaning to the mathematics you learn.

xi

Embedded Mathematical Practices (continued)

5 To **Use Appropriate Tools Strategically**, you need to know what tools are available and think about how each tool might help you solve a mathematical problem. When you choose a tool to use, remember that it may have limitations.

Look for labels such as:
- Choose Tools
- Use Math Tools
- Use Technology

8. Choose Tools Would you measure the length of a bus with a centimeter ruler or a meter stick? Why?

Use Math Tools How can you use a drawing to help organize the information given?

11. DIG DEEPER! There are 63 people in a theater, 21 people in the lobby, and 10 people in the parking lot. How many more people are in the theater than in both the lobby and the parking lot?

_____ more people

6 When you **Attend to Precision**, you are developing a habit of being careful in how you talk about concepts, label work, and write answers.

Look for labels such as:
- Precision
- Communicate Clearly
- Maintain Accuracy

7. DIG DEEPER! Complete the model and the equation to match.

___ + ___ = 8

Communicate Clearly In the model, what shows the addends? the sum?

5. Precision Which picture shows the correct way to measure the straw?

6. **Patterns** Find the sums. Think: What do you notice?

   4 + 5 = ___

   4 + 4 = ___

   5 + 5 = ___

	Tens	Ones
	□	
	3	8
+	2	4

   38 + 24 = ___

   Structure What step did you use to find 38 + 24 that you would not use to find 31 + 24? Why?

Look For and Make Use of Structure by looking closely to see structure within a mathematical statement, or stepping back for an overview to see how individual parts make one single object.

Look for labels such as:
- Structure
- Patterns

8. **Repeated Reasoning** What other shape has the same number of surfaces, vertices, and edges as a rectangular prism? How is that shape different from a rectangular prism?

When you **Look For and Express Regularity in Repeated Reasoning**, you can notice patterns and make generalizations. Remember to keep in mind the goal of a problem, which will help you evaluate reasonableness of answers along the way.

Find a Rule When you add or subtract 1, what is true about the sum or difference?

4 + 1 = 5

4 − 1 = 3

Look for labels such as:
- Repeated Reasoning
- Find a Rule

xiii

Visible Learning Through Learning Targets,

Making Learning Visible

Knowing the learning intention of a chapter or lesson helps you focus on the purpose of an activity, rather than simply completing it in isolation. This program supports visible learning through the consistent use of Learning Targets and Success Criteria to help you become successful.

Every chapter shows a **Learning Target** and four related **Success Criteria**. These are incorporated throughout the chapter content to help guide you in your learning.

Every lesson shows a **Learning Target** that is purposefully integrated into each carefully written lesson.

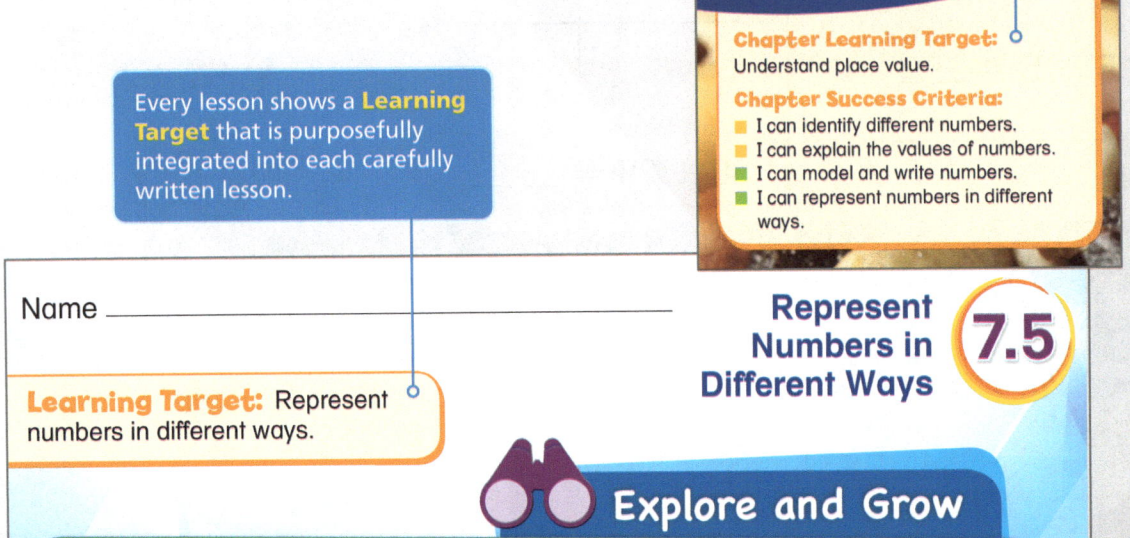

Chapter Learning Target:
Understand place value.

Chapter Success Criteria:
- I can identify different numbers.
- I can explain the values of numbers.
- I can model and write numbers.
- I can represent numbers in different ways.

Access the **Learning Target** and **Success Criteria** on every page of the Dynamic Student Edition.

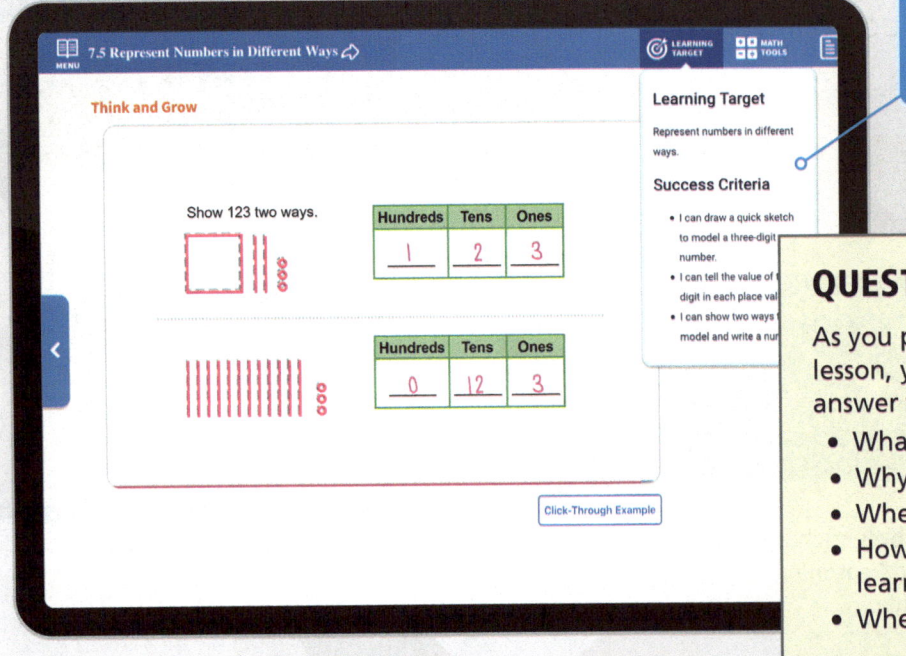

QUESTIONS FOR LEARNING

As you progress through a lesson, you should be able to answer the following questions.
- What am I learning?
- Why am I learning this?
- Where am I in my learning?
- How will I know when I have learned it?
- Where am I going next?

xiv

Success Criteria, and Self-Assessment

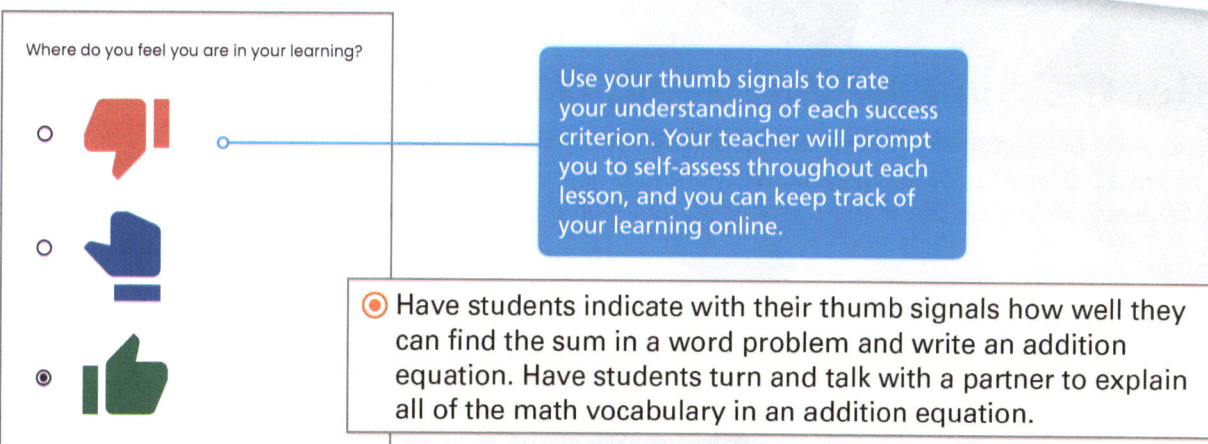

Use your thumb signals to rate your understanding of each success criterion. Your teacher will prompt you to self-assess throughout each lesson, and you can keep track of your learning online.

● Have students indicate with their thumb signals how well they can find the sum in a word problem and write an addition equation. Have students turn and talk with a partner to explain all of the math vocabulary in an addition equation.

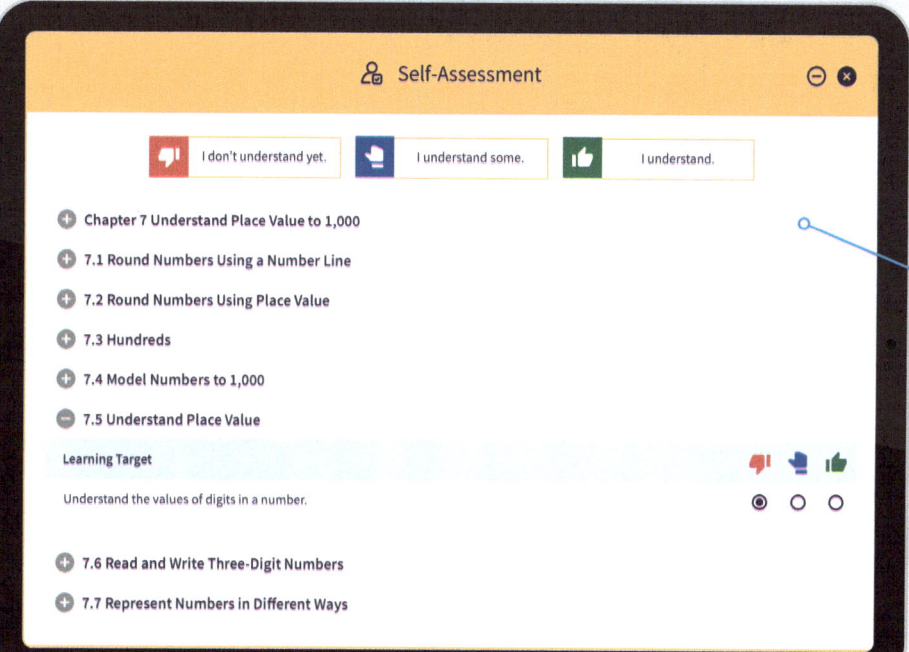

Self-Assessments are included throughout every lesson, and in the **Chapter Review**, to help you take ownership of your learning and think about where to go next.

Ensuring Positive Outcomes

John Hattie's *Visible Learning* research consistently shows that using Learning Targets and Success Criteria can result in two years' growth in one year, ensuring positive outcomes for your learning and achievement.

Sophie Murphy, M.Ed., wrote the chapter-level Learning Targets and Success Criteria for this program. Sophie is currently completing her Ph.D. at the University of Melbourne in Australia with Professor John Hattie as her leading supervisor. Sophie completed her Master's thesis with Professor John Hattie in 2015. Sophie has over 20 years of experience as a teacher and school leader in private and public school settings in Australia.

Strategic Support for Online Learning

Get the Support You Need, When You Need It

There will be times throughout this course when you may need help. Whether you missed a lesson, did not understand the content, or just want to review, take advantage of the resources provided in the *Dynamic Student Edition*.

Use the **Self-Assessment** tool to keep track of your understanding of the lesson's Learning Target and Success Criteria.

Choose **Math Tools** to engage with pattern blocks, digital number lines, linking cubes, and other tools to explore and understand math concepts.

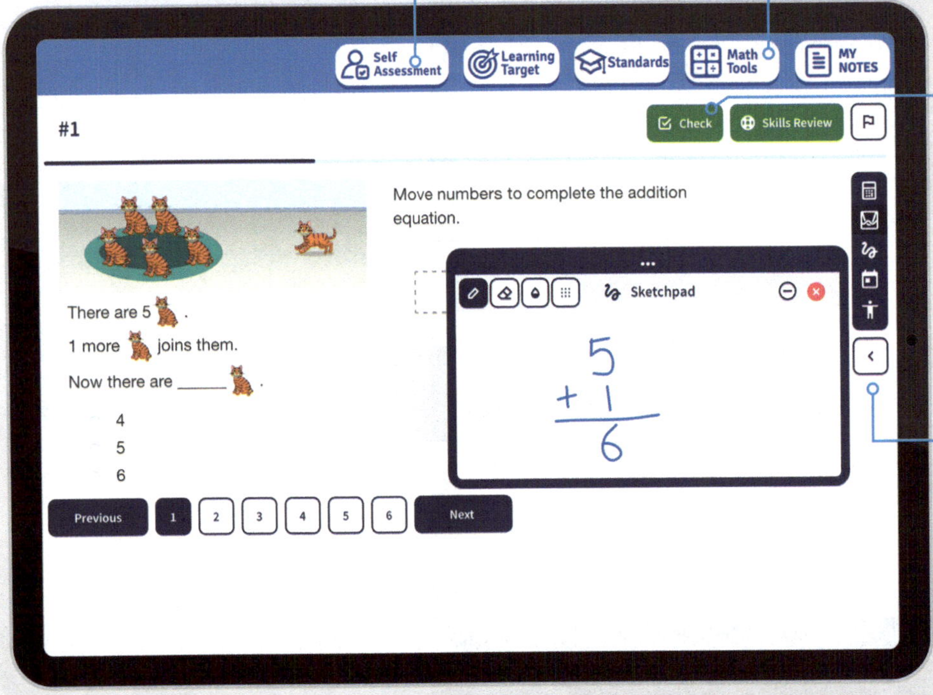

Check your answers to selected exercises as you work through the lesson. Use the **Help** option to view the Digital Example videos.

Use the available **tools**, such as the calculator or sketchpad, to help clearly show your work and demonstrate your math knowledge.

USE THESE QR CODES TO EXPLORE ADDITIONAL RESOURCES

Multi-Language Glossary
View definitions and examples of vocabulary words

Skills Trainer
Practice previously learned skills

Interactive Tools
Visualize mathematical concepts

Skills Review Handbook
A collection of review topics

xvi

Learning with Newton and Descartes

Who are Newton and Descartes?

Newton and Descartes are helpful math assistants who appear throughout your math book! They encourage you to think deeply about concepts and develop strong mathematical mindsets with Mathematical Practice questions.

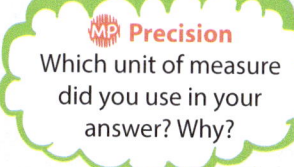

MP Check Your Work
How can you use the addition facts to check that the differences are correct?

MP Precision
Which unit of measure did you use in your answer? Why?

Newton & Descartes's Math Musicals

Math Musicals offer an engaging connection between math, literature, and music! Newton and Descartes team up in these educational stories and songs to bring mathematics to life!

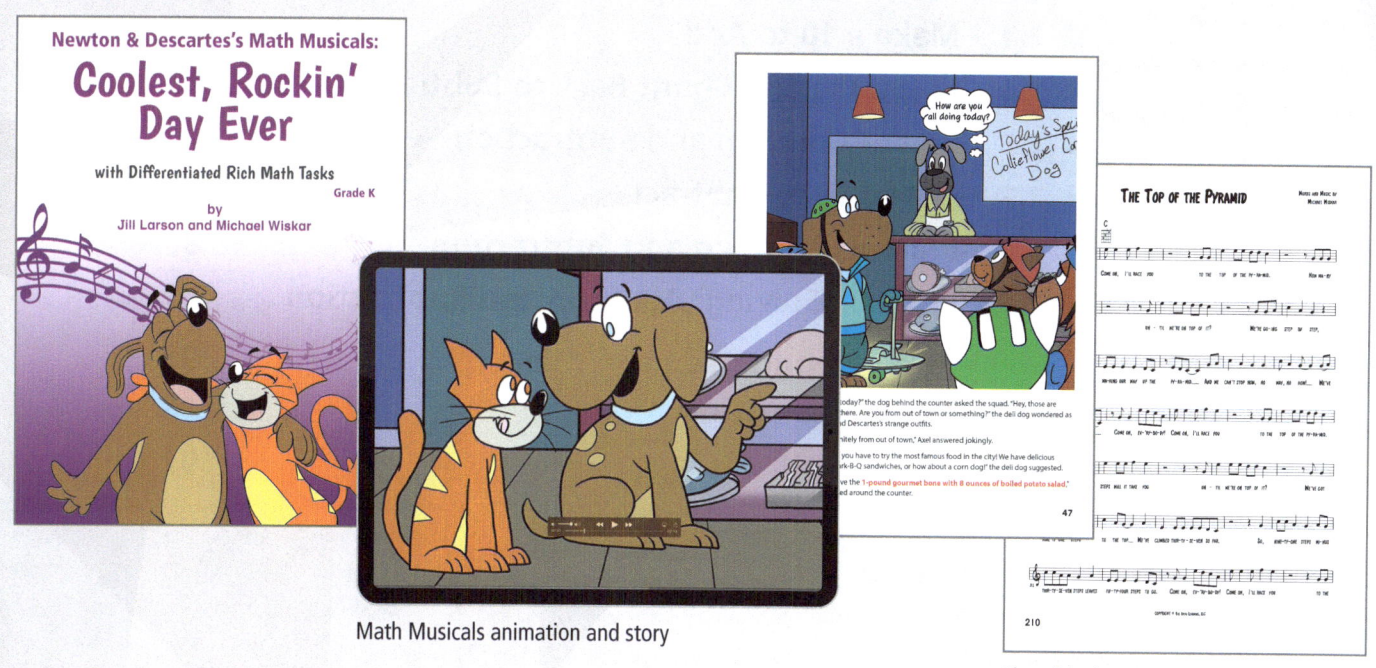

Math Musicals animation and story

Sheet Music

Numbers and Arrays

	Vocabulary	2
■ 1.1	Even and Odd Numbers	3
■ 1.2	Model Even and Odd Numbers	9
■ 1.3	Equal Groups	15
■ 1.4	Use Arrays	21
■ 1.5	Make Arrays	27
	Performance Task: Art Supplies	33
	Game: Array Flip and Find	34
	Chapter Practice	35

Fluency and Strategies within 20

	Vocabulary	40
■ 2.1	Add in Any Order	41
■ 2.2	Use Doubles	47
■ 2.3	Add Three Numbers	53
■ 2.4	Make a 10 to Add	59
■ 2.5	Count On and Count Back to Subtract	65
■ 2.6	Relate Addition and Subtraction	71
■ 2.7	Get to 10 to Subtract	77
■ 2.8	Practice Addition and Subtraction	83
■ 2.9	Problem Solving: Addition and Subtraction	89
	Performance Task: Library Books	95
	Game: Joey Jump	96
	Chapter Practice	97

■ Major Topic
■ Supporting Topic
■ Additional Topic

Addition to 100 Strategies

Vocabulary 102
- 3.1 Add Tens Using a Number Line 103
- 3.2 Add Tens and Ones Using a Number Line ... 109
- 3.3 Use Place Value to Add 115
- 3.4 Decompose to Add Tens and Ones 121
- 3.5 Use Compensation to Add 127
- 3.6 Practice Addition Strategies 133
- 3.7 Problem Solving: Addition 139

Performance Task: Amusement Park 145
Game: Three in a Row: Addition 146
Chapter Practice 147

Fluently Add within 100

Vocabulary 152
- 4.1 Use Partial Sums to Add 153
- 4.2 More Partial Sums 159
- 4.3 Regroup to Add 165
- 4.4 Add Two-Digit Numbers 171
- 4.5 Practice Adding Two-Digit Numbers 177
- 4.6 Add Up to 3 Two-Digit Numbers 183
- 4.7 More Problem Solving: Addition 189

Performance Task: Swimming 195
Game: Solve and Cover: Addition 196
Chapter Practice 197
Cumulative Practice 201

Let's learn how to fluently add within 100!

xix

Subtraction to 100 Strategies

Vocabulary 206
- 5.1 Subtract Tens Using a Number Line 207
- 5.2 Subtract Tens and Ones Using a Number Line 213
- 5.3 Use Addition to Subtract 219
- 5.4 Decompose to Subtract 225
- 5.5 Decompose to Subtract Tens and Ones 231
- 5.6 Use Compensation to Subtract 237
- 5.7 Practice Subtraction Strategies 243
- 5.8 Problem Solving: Subtraction 249

Performance Task: Egg Incubator 255
Game: Three in a Row: Subtraction 256
Chapter Practice 257

Fluently Subtract within 100

Vocabulary 262
- 6.1 Model and Regroup to Subtract 263
- 6.2 Use Models to Subtract a One-Digit Number from a Two-Digit Number 269
- 6.3 Use Models to Subtract Two-Digit Numbers .. 275
- 6.4 Subtract from a Two-Digit Number 281
- 6.5 Use Addition to Check Subtraction 287
- 6.6 Practice Two-Digit Subtraction 293
- 6.7 More Problem Solving: Subtraction 299

Performance Task: Paper Snowflakes 305
Game: Solve and Cover: Subtraction 306
Chapter Practice 307

- ■ Major Topic
- ■ Supporting Topic
- ■ Additional Topic

Understand Place Value to 1,000

	Vocabulary	312
■ 7.1	Hundreds	313
■ 7.2	Model Numbers to 1,000	319
■ 7.3	Understand Place Value	325
■ 7.4	Write Three-Digit Numbers	331
■ 7.5	Represent Numbers in Different Ways	337
	Performance Task: Trail Mix	343
	Game: Naming Numbers Flip and Find	344
	Chapter Practice	345

Count and Compare Numbers to 1,000

	Vocabulary	350
■ 8.1	Count to 120 in Different Ways	351
■ 8.2	Count to 1,000 in Different Ways	357
■ 8.3	Place Value Patterns	363
■ 8.4	Find More or Less	369
■ 8.5	Compare Numbers Using Symbols	375
■ 8.6	Compare Numbers Using a Number Line	381
	Performance Task: Fish	387
	Game: Number Boss	388
	Chapter Practice	389
	Cumulative Practice	393

Let's learn how to count and compare numbers to 1,000!

xxi

9 Add Numbers within 1,000

	Vocabulary	398
9.1	Add 10 and 100	399
9.2	Use a Number Line to Add Hundreds and Tens	405
9.3	Use a Number Line to Add Three-Digit Numbers	411
9.4	Use Compensation to Add Three-Digit Numbers	417
9.5	Use Partial Sums to Add Three-Digit Numbers	423
9.6	Use Models to Add Three-Digit Numbers	429
9.7	Add Three-Digit Numbers	435
9.8	Add Up to 4 Two-Digit Numbers	441
9.9	Explain Addition Strategies	447
	Performance Task: Robots	453
	Game: Three in a Row: Three-Digit Addition	454
	Chapter Practice	455

Three in a Row: Three-Digit Addition

To Play: Players take turns. On your turn, spin both spinners. Add the two numbers and cover the sum. Continue playing until someone gets three in a row.

10 Subtract Numbers within 1,000

	Vocabulary	460
■ 10.1	Subtract 10 and 100	461
■ 10.2	Use a Number Line to Subtract Hundreds and Tens	467
■ 10.3	Use a Number Line to Subtract Three-Digit Numbers	473
■ 10.4	Use Compensation to Subtract Three-Digit Numbers	479
■ 10.5	Use Models to Subtract Three-Digit Numbers	485
■ 10.6	Subtract Three-Digit Numbers	491
■ 10.7	Subtract from Numbers That Contain Zeros	497
■ 10.8	Use Addition to Subtract	503
■ 10.9	Explain Subtraction Strategies	509
	Performance Task: Race Cars	515
	Game: Greatest and Least	516
	Chapter Practice	517

11 Measure and Estimate Lengths

	Vocabulary	522
■ 11.1	Measure Lengths in Centimeters	523
■ 11.2	Measure Objects Using Metric Length Units	529
■ 11.3	Estimate Lengths in Metric Units	535
■ 11.4	Measure Lengths in Inches	541
■ 11.5	Measure Objects Using Customary Length Units	547
■ 11.6	Estimate Lengths in Customary Units	553
■ 11.7	Measure Objects Using Different Length Units	559
■ 11.8	Measure and Compare Lengths	565
	Performance Task: Gardening	571
	Game: Spin and Cover	572
	Chapter Practice	573

Let's learn how to measure and estimate lengths!

xxiii

Solve Length Problems

	Vocabulary	578
■	**12.1** Use a Number Line to Add and Subtract Lengths	579
■	**12.2** Problem Solving: Length	585
■	**12.3** Problem Solving: Missing Measurement	591
■	**12.4** Practice Measurement Problems	597
	Performance Task: Musical Instruments	603
	Game: Draw and Cover	604
	Chapter Practice	605
	Cumulative Practice	607

Represent and Interpret Data

	Vocabulary	612
■	**13.1** Sort and Organize Data	613
■	**13.2** Read and Interpret Picture Graphs	619
■	**13.3** Make Picture Graphs	625
■	**13.4** Read and Interpret Bar Graphs	631
■	**13.5** Make Bar Graphs	637
■	**13.6** Make Line Plots	643
■	**13.7** Measure Objects and Make Line Plots	649
	Performance Task: Art Supplies	655
	Game: Spin and Graph	656
	Chapter Practice	657

■ Major Topic
■ Supporting Topic
■ Additional Topic

14 Money and Time

Vocabulary 662
- 14.1 Find Total Values of Coins 663
- 14.2 Order to Find Total Values of Coins 669
- 14.3 Show Money Amounts in Different Ways ... 675
- 14.4 Make One Dollar 681
- 14.5 Make Change from One Dollar 687
- 14.6 Find Total Values of Bills 693
- 14.7 Problem Solving: Money 699
- 14.8 Tell Time to the Nearest Five Minutes 705
- 14.9 Tell Time Before and After the Hour 711
- 14.10 Relate A.M. and P.M. 717

Performance Task: Public Transportation 723
Game: Flip and Find 724
Chapter Practice 725

15 Identify and Partition Shapes

Vocabulary 730
- 15.1 Describe Two-Dimensional Shapes 731
- 15.2 Identify Angles of Polygons 737
- 15.3 Draw Polygons 743
- 15.4 Identify and Draw Cubes 749
- 15.5 Compose Rectangles 755
- 15.6 Identify Two, Three, or Four Equal Shares . 761
- 15.7 Partition Shapes into Equal Shares 767
- 15.8 Analyze Equal Shares of the Same Shape .. 773

Performance Task: Suncatchers 779
Game: Three in a Row: Equal Shares 780
Chapter Practice 781
Cumulative Practice 785

Glossary A1
Index A13
Reference Sheet A23

Let's learn about money and time!

xxv

9 Add Numbers within 1,000

- What is a robot? What are some things that robots can do?
- You use 220 parts to make one robot and 157 parts to make another. How many parts do you use in all?

Chapter Learning Target:
Understand adding numbers.

Chapter Success Criteria:
- I can identify 10 and 100.
- I can count on from a number in different ways.
- I can explain how to use different counting strategies.
- I can represent numbers in different ways.

Name _____

9 Vocabulary

Organize It

Review Words
edge
flat surface
vertex

Use the review words to complete the graphic organizer.

Define It

What am I?

```
  4  2              3  7
  2 (3)             2 (4)
  3  5  — 10        3  1  — 8
+ 2 (7)           + 2 (4)
```
numbers that help you add mentally

5 − 2 = O   9 − 8 = I   12 − 4 = L   14 − 2 = A
18 − 3 = B   10 − 3 = C   13 − 3 = P   16 − 7 = E
20 − 4 = M   17 − 6 = T

| 7 | 3 | 16 | 10 | 12 | 11 | 1 | 15 | 8 | 9 |

numbers

398 three hundred ninety-eight

Chapter 9 Vocabulary Cards

compatible numbers

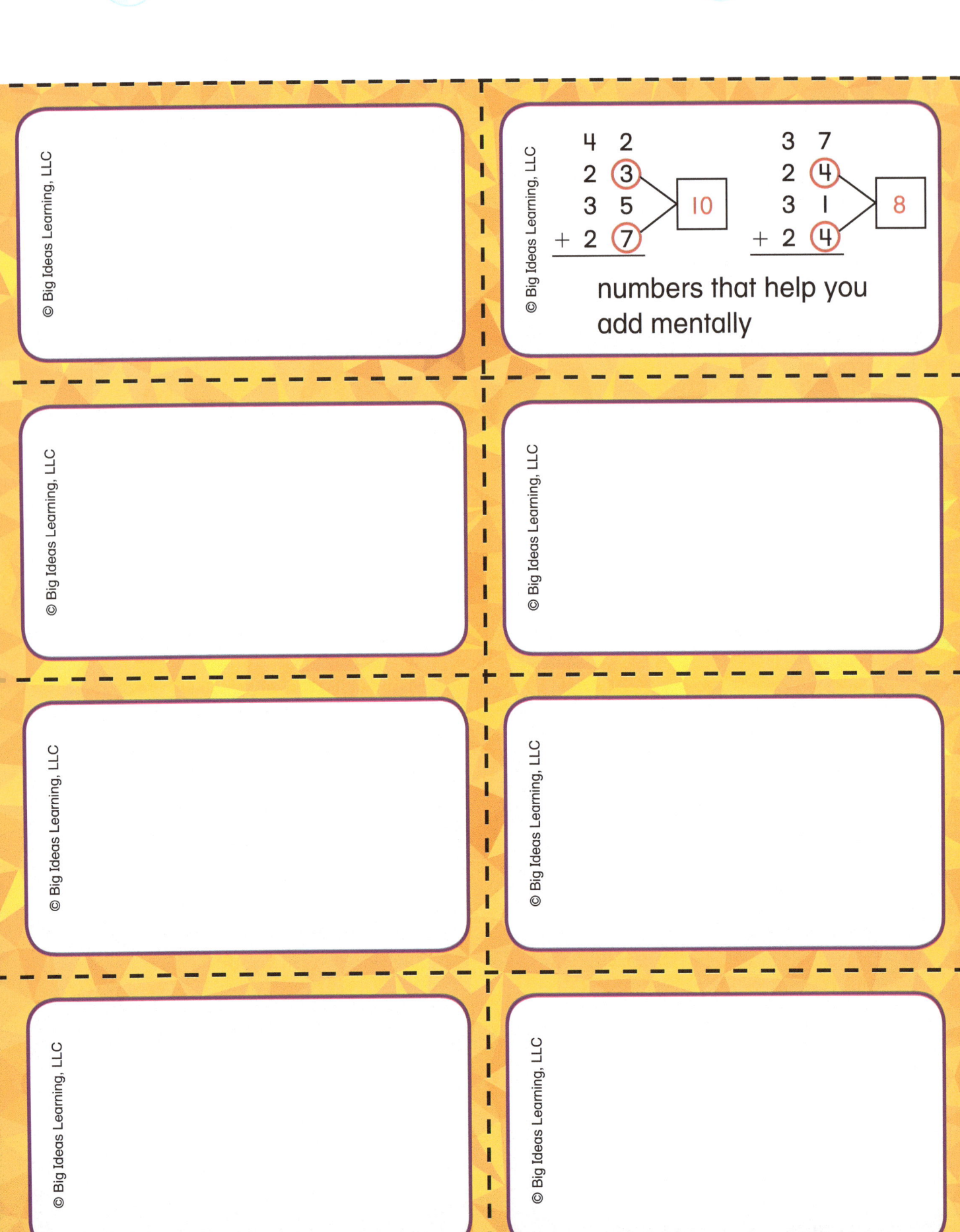

Name _____

Add 10 and 100

Learning Target: Use mental math to add 10 and add 100.

Model 231. Make a quick sketch of your model.

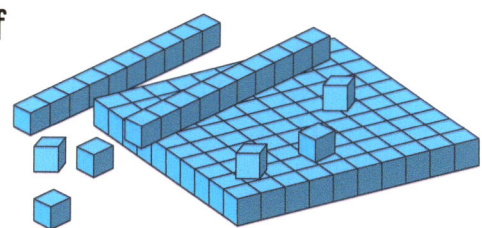

231

Model 10 more than 231. Make a quick sketch of your model.

231 + 10 = _____

Model 100 more than 231. Make a quick sketch of your model.

231 + 100 = _____

Chapter 9 | Lesson 1

Think and Grow

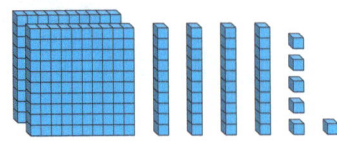
246

$4 + 1 = 5$

$246 + 10 = \underline{256}$

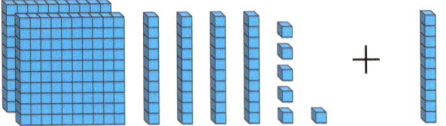

The digit in the tens place increases by 1.

$2 + 1 = 3$

$246 + 100 = \underline{346}$

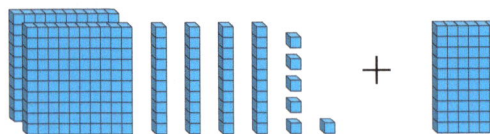

The digit in the hundreds place increases by 1.

Sometimes when you add 10, the digits in the tens place *and* the hundreds place change.

$390 + 10 = ?$

39 tens + 1 ten = 40 tens

So, $390 + 10 = 400$.

Show and Grow   I can do it!

1. $317 + 10 = $ _____

   $317 + 100 = $ _____

2. $168 + 10 = $ _____

   $168 + 100 = $ _____

3. $223 + 10 = $ _____

   $223 + 100 = $ _____

4. $490 + 10 = $ _____

   $490 + 100 = $ _____

Name _____

Apply and Grow: Practice

5. 731 + 10 = _____

6. 674 + 100 = _____

7. 620 + 10 = _____

8. 713 + 10 = _____

9. 564 + 100 = _____

10. 349 + 10 = _____

11. 456 + 100 = _____

12. 802 + 100 = _____

13. 192 + 10 = _____

14. 900 + 100 = _____

15. 349 + _____ = 449

16. _____ + 10 = 791

17. **Number Sense** Use each number once to complete the equations.

312   412   100   322

_____ + 10 = _____

_____ + _____ = 512

Chapter 9 | Lesson 1

four hundred one 401

Think and Grow: Modeling Real Life

You and a friend play skee ball. Your score is 290. Your friend's score is 220. On the last roll, you score 10 more and your friend scores 100 more. Who wins?

Addition equations:

MP Find a Rule
Which digit increases when adding 10? when adding 100?

Compare: _____ ◯ _____

You   Friend

Show and Grow — I can think deeper!

18. You and a friend play a card game. Your score is 420. Your friend's score is 530. In the last round, you score 100 more and your friend scores 10 more. Who wins?

You   Friend

19. You spin the wheel and score 100 points. Your friend scores 335. On the last spin, you score 275 more and your friend scores 10 more. Who wins?

You   Friend

402   four hundred two

Name _____

Practice 9.1

Learning Target: Use mental math to add 10 and add 100.

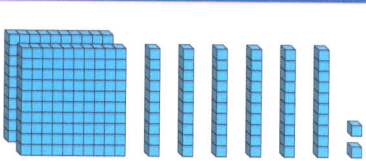
262

262 + 10 = __272__   262 + 100 = __362__

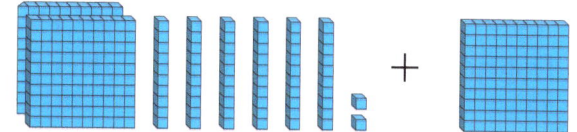

1. 850 + 100 = _____

2. 625 + 10 = _____

3. 704 + 10 = _____

4. 294 + 100 = _____

5. 556 + 100 = _____

6. 471 + 100 = _____

7. 308 + 100 = _____

8. 149 + 10 = _____

9. 690 + 10 = _____

10. 990 + 10 = _____

11. 621 + _____ = 631

12. _____ + 100 = 613

Chapter 9 | Lesson 1   four hundred three 403

13. **YOU BE THE TEACHER** Your friend says that 847 + 110 = 957. Is your friend correct? Explain.

_____

_____

14. **Modeling Real Life** You pick 220 blueberries. Your friend picks 200. You pick 10 more and your friend picks 100 more. Who picks more blueberries?

        You   Friend

15. **Modeling Real Life** You download 100 songs. Your friend downloads 125. Then you download 145 more and your friend downloads 10 more. Who downloads more songs?

        You   Friend

Review & Refresh

16.
```
   5 6
 −   8
 ─────
```

17.
```
   7 3
 −   5
 ─────
```

18.
```
   4 1
 − 2 6
 ─────
```

Name _____

Learning Target: Use an open number line to add hundreds and tens.

Use a Number Line to Add Hundreds and Tens

9.2

Explore and Grow

Show how to skip count by tens five times on the number line.

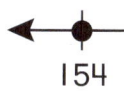
154

154 + _____ = _____

Show how to skip count by hundreds five times on the number line.

154

154 + _____ = _____

Chapter 9 | Lesson 2 four hundred five **405**

Think and Grow

One Way:

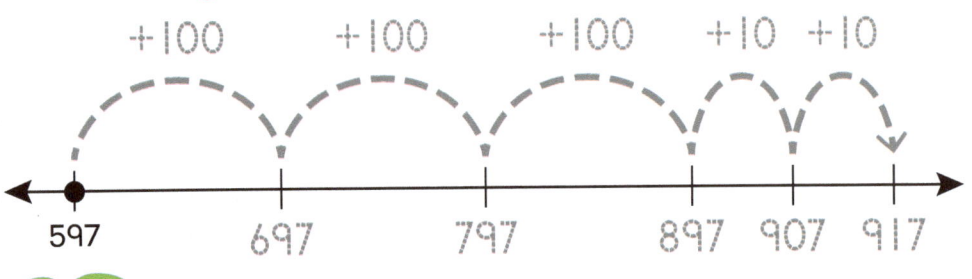

> Start at 597. Count on by hundreds, then by tens.

Another Way:

> Make greater jumps. The sum is the same!

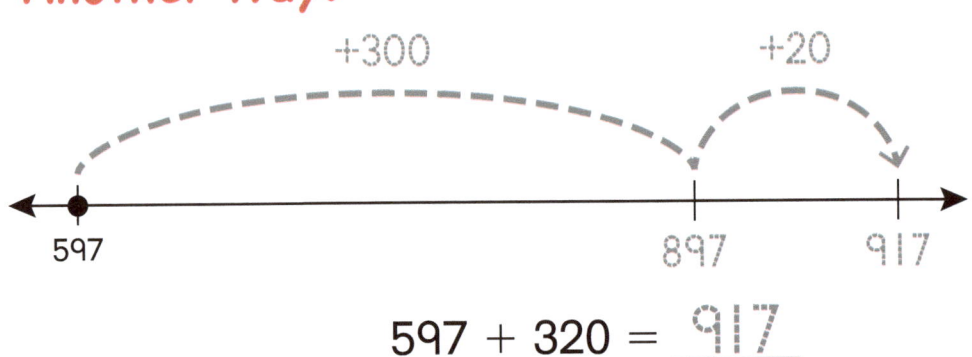

597 + 320 = __917__

Show and Grow — I can do it!

1. 380 + 340 = _____

2. 462 + 270 = _____

406 four hundred six

Name _____

Apply and Grow: Practice

3. 550 + 210 = ____

4. 725 + 160 = ____

5. 469 + 350 = ____

6. **Reasoning** Complete the number line and the equation.

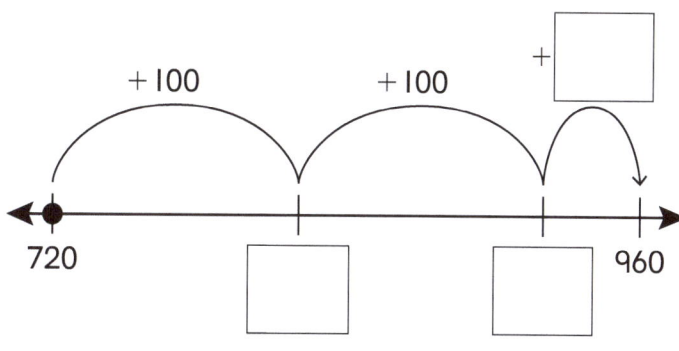

____ + ____ = ____

Chapter 9 | Lesson 2   four hundred seven   407

Think and Grow: Modeling Real Life

A post office has 330 large envelopes and some small envelopes. There are 560 envelopes in all. How many small envelopes are there?

Addition equation:

Model:

⟵─────────────────⟶

_____ small envelopes

Show and Grow   I can think deeper!

7. A postal carrier delivers 280 letters and some postcards. She delivers 390 pieces of mail in all. How many postcards does she deliver?

_____ postcards

8. There are some children and 180 adults on a subway. There are 300 passengers in all. How many children are there?

_____ children

Name _____

Practice 9.2

Learning Target: Use an open number line to add hundreds and tens.

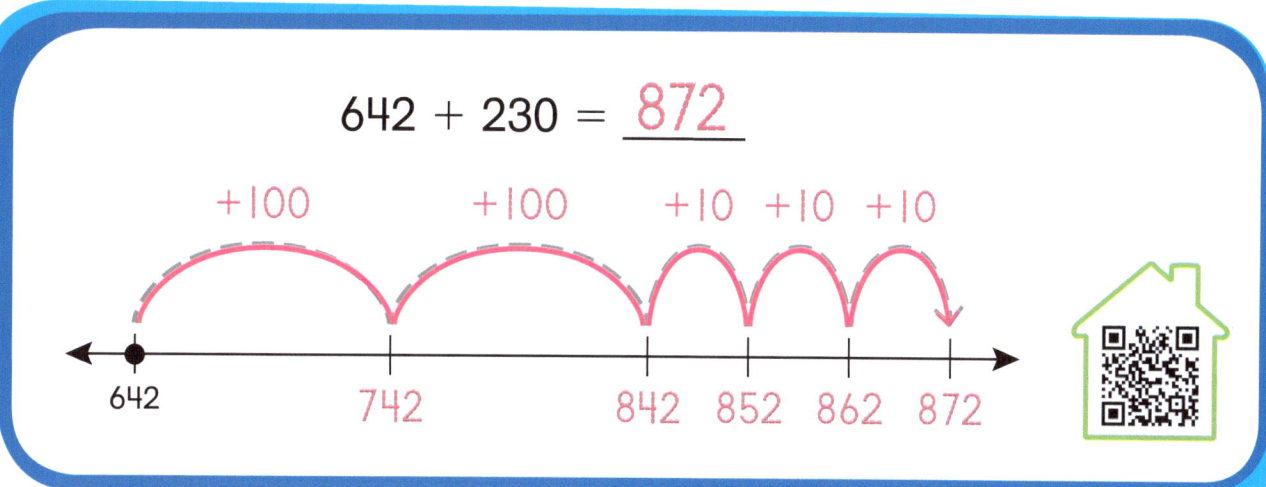

1. 150 + 610 = _____

2. 291 + 450 = _____

3. 553 + 250 = _____

4. **Structure** Write the equation shown by the number line.

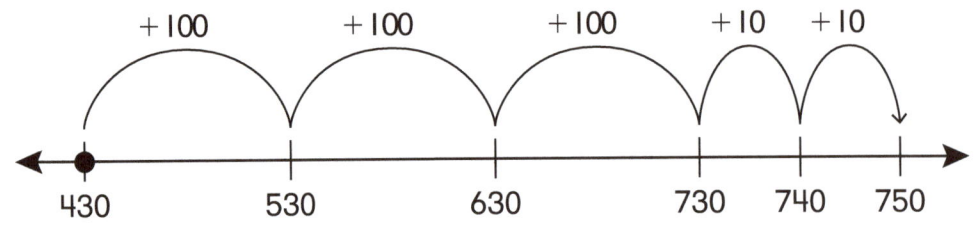

_____ + _____ = _____

5. **Modeling Real Life** A carpenter has 320 nails and some screws. There are 470 nails and screws in all. How many screws are there?

_____ screws

6. **DIG DEEPER!** In Exercise 5, the carpenter buys more nails and screws. Now there are 670 nails and screws in all. Is it possible that the carpenter bought the same number of nails and screws?

_____

_____

Review & Refresh

7. Show 416 two ways.

Hundreds	Tens	Ones
___	___	___

Hundreds	Tens	Ones
___	___	___

410   four hundred ten

Name _____

Learning Target: Use an open number line to add.

Use a Number Line to Add Three-Digit Numbers

9.3

 Explore and Grow

Use each sum as the missing addend in the next equation.

$$425 + 200 = \underline{}$$

$$\underline{} + 20 = \underline{}$$

$$\underline{} + 2 = \underline{}$$

MP Use a Similar Problem How does this help you find 425 + 222?

_____

_____

Chapter 9 | Lesson 3

Think and Grow

Start at 483. Count on by hundreds, then by tens, then by ones.

483 + 224 = ?

One Way:

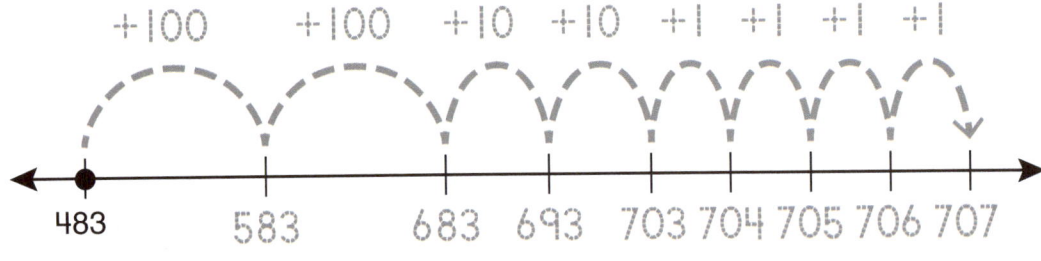

Another Way:

Make greater jumps.

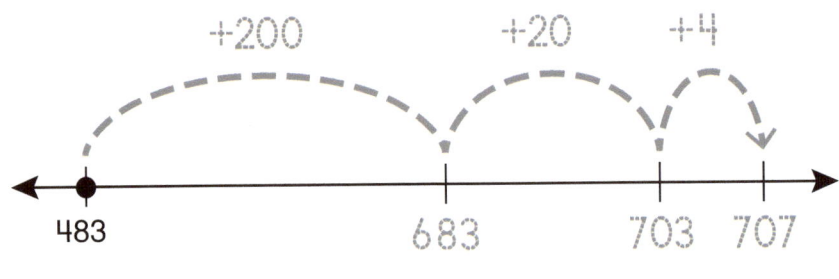

483 + 224 = 707

Show and Grow   I can do it!

1. 371 + 145 = _____

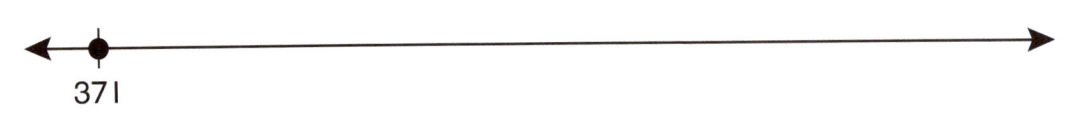

2. 419 + 237 = _____

412   four hundred twelve

Name _____

 **Apply and Grow: Practice**

3. 524 + 312 = _____

4. 645 + 108 = _____

5. 836 + 74 = _____

6. **Structure** Write the equation shown by the number line.

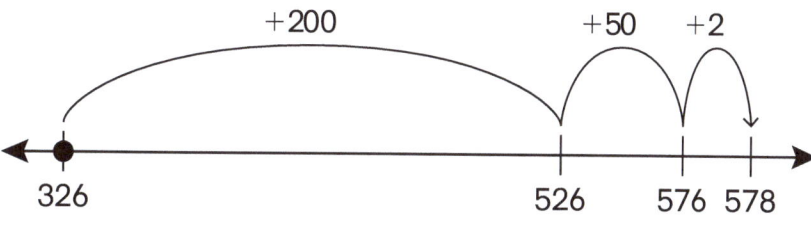

_____ + _____ = _____

Chapter 9 | Lesson 3   four hundred thirteen   413

Think and Grow: Modeling Real Life

There are 289 boys and 323 girls running in a race. How many runners are there in all?

Addition equation:

Model:

_____ runners

Show and Grow — I can think deeper!

7. A textbook has 478 pages in Volume 1 and 443 pages in Volume 2. How many pages are there in all?

_____ pages

8. **DIG DEEPER!** The pictures show your fitness tracker before and after you take a walk. How many steps did you take on your walk?

Before

132

After

895

_____ steps

Name _____

Practice 9.3

Learning Target: Use an open number line to add.

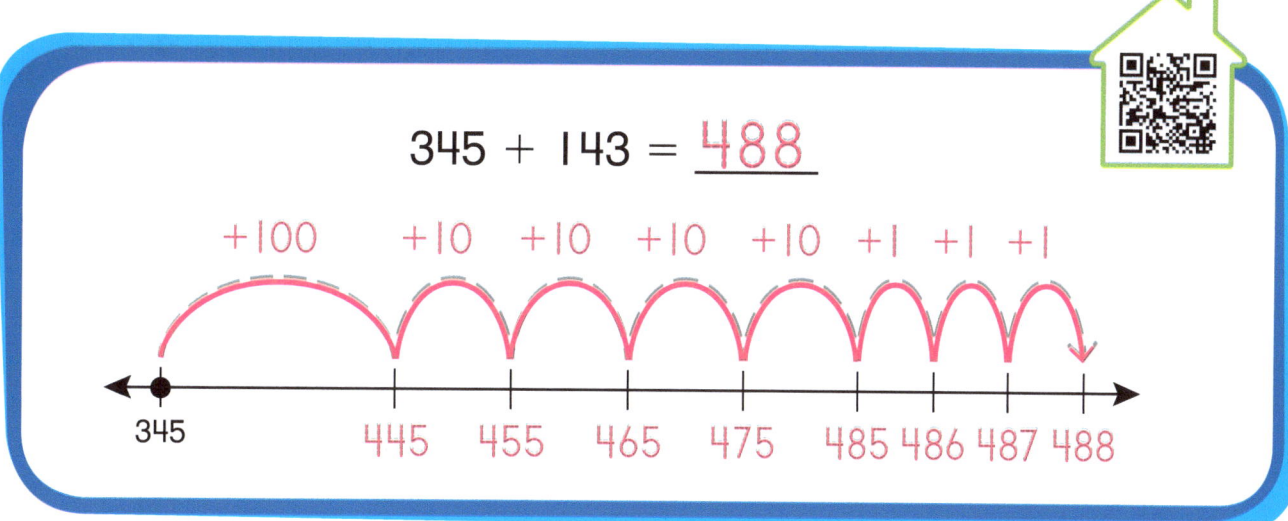

1. 291 + 407 = _____

2. 752 + 138 = _____

3. 372 + 319 = _____

4. **Structure** Use the number lines to show 257 + 321 two ways.

257 + 321 = _____

5. **Modeling Real Life** A florist has 416 daisies and 152 roses. How many flowers are there in all?

_____ flowers

6. **DIG DEEPER!** A school has 872 students. 139 students are in the second grade. How many students are *not* in second grade?

_____ students

Review & Refresh

Draw more lines to show fourths.

7.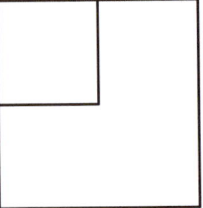

8.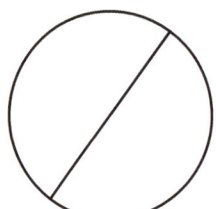

416 four hundred sixteen

Name _____

Learning Target: Use compensation to add.

Use Compensation to Add Three-Digit Numbers

9.4

Explore and Grow

Add to the model to make 300. Make a quick sketch of your work.

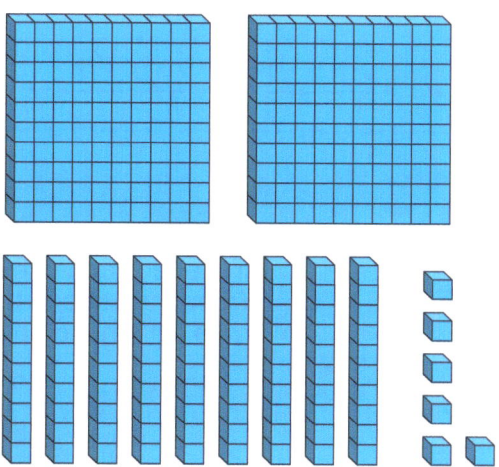

What number did you add to make 300? _____
How can this help you find 296 + 124?

_____

_____

_____

Chapter 9 | Lesson 4

four hundred seventeen   417

Think and Grow

Take ones from one addend to make the other addend a hundred.

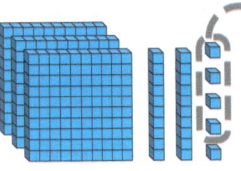
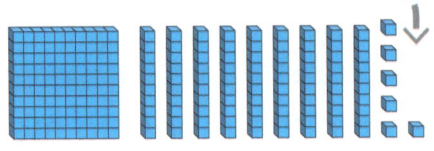

325 + 196 = ?

⊖ 4   ⊕ 4

321 + 200 = 521

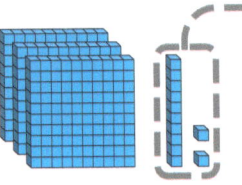

312 + 367 = ?

⊖ 12   ⊕ 12

300 + 379 = 679

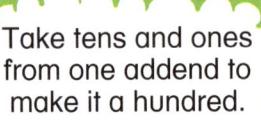

Take tens and ones from one addend to make it a hundred.

Show and Grow — I can do it!

1. Use compensation to add.

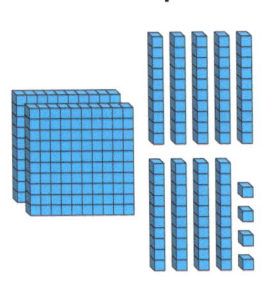
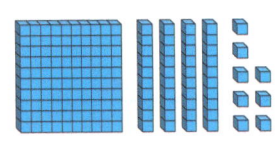

294 + 148 = ?

⊕ ___   ⊖ ___

___ + ___ = ___

418   four hundred eighteen

Name _____

Apply and Grow: Practice

Use compensation to add.

2.

628 + 206 = ?

◯ ___   ◯ ___

___ + ___ = ___

3.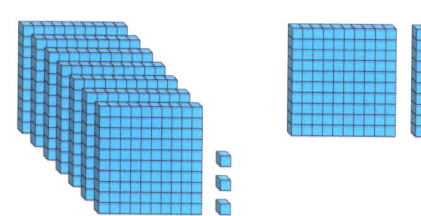

703 + 145 = ?

◯ ___   ◯ ___

___ + ___ = ___

4. 490 + 367 = ?

◯ ___   ◯ ___

___ + ___ = ___

5. 172 + 520 = ?

◯ ___   ◯ ___

___ + ___ = ___

6. 614 + 275 = ___

7. 308 + 549 = ___

8. **Reasoning** Show two different ways to use compensation to find 406 + 113.

406 + 113 = ?

◯ ___   ◯ ___

___ + ___ = ___

406 + 113 = ?

◯ ___   ◯ ___

___ + ___ = ___

Chapter 9 | Lesson 4

four hundred nineteen 419

Think and Grow: Modeling Real Life

You want to raise $500 in 2 days. Do you reach your goal?

Day	Amount Raised
1	$283
2	$205

Addition equation: _____

Compare: _____ ◯ _____

Yes   No

Show and Grow I can think deeper!

9. A museum wants a weekend total of 700 guests. Does the museum reach the goal?

Day	Number of Guests
Saturday	338
Sunday	389

Yes   No

10. **DIG DEEPER!** You want to score 400 in 3 bowling games. What score do you need in the third game to reach your goal?

Game	Score
1	107
2	144

_____

420   four hundred twenty

Name _____

Practice 9.4

Learning Target: Use compensation to add.

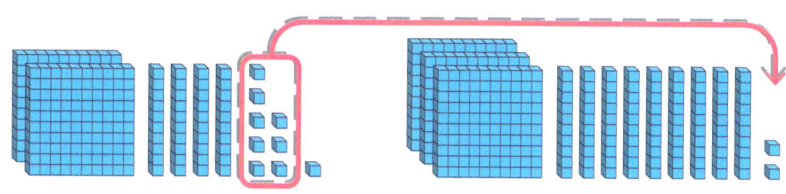

249 + 392 = ?

⊖ __8__   ⊕ __8__

__241__ + __400__ = __641__

Use compensation to add.

1.

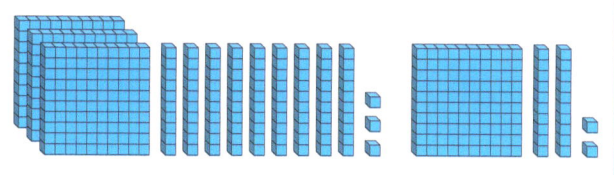

393 + 122 = ?

○ ___   ○ ___

___ + ___ = ___

2.

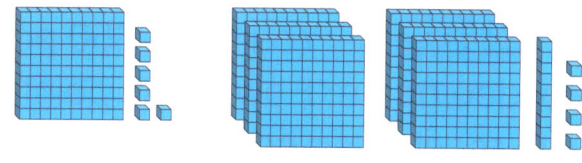

106 + 614 = ?

○ ___   ○ ___

___ + ___ = ___

3. 237 + 315 = ?

○ ___   ○ ___

___ + ___ = ___

4. 285 + 320 = ?

○ ___   ○ ___

___ + ___ = ___

Chapter 9 | Lesson 4   four hundred twenty-one   421

5. **YOU BE THE TEACHER** Your friend uses compensation to find 550 + 298. Is your friend correct? Explain.

$$550 + \quad 298 = ?$$
$$\underline{+2} \quad \underline{+2}$$
$$552 + \quad 300 = 852$$

_____

_____

_____

6. **Modeling Real Life** Newton wants to read 571 pages in two weeks. He reads 321 pages in the first week and 196 pages in the second week. Does he reach his goal?

Yes   No

7. **DIG DEEPER!** You need 850 points to get to level 4 in a video game. How many points do you need in level 3 to reach your goal?

Level	Points
1	348
2	297

_____ points

Review & Refresh

8.   9 5
    − 3 8

9.   8 2
    − 4 0

10.   5 9
    − 2 1

422   four hundred twenty-two

Name _____

Learning Target: Use partial sums to add.

Use Partial Sums to Add Three-Digit Numbers 9.5

Explore and Grow

Model each number. Make quick sketches of your models. Then solve.

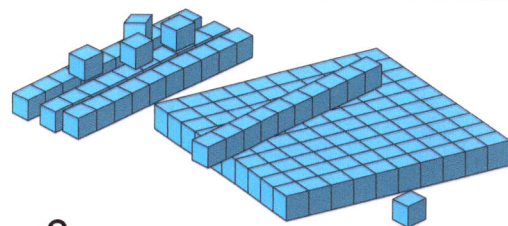

$$324 + 215 = ?$$

	Hundreds	Tens	Ones
324			
215			

____ + ____ + ____

324 + 215 = ____

Chapter 9 | Lesson 5

four hundred twenty-three 423

Think and Grow

First, find the partial sums.

Then add the partial sums to find the whole sum.

	Hundreds	Tens	Ones
	4	2	5
+	2	6	8
Hundreds:	6	0	0	= 400 + 200
Tens:		8	0	= 20 + 60
Ones:		1	3	= 5 + 8
Sum	6	9	3

Show and Grow   I can do it!

1.

	Hundreds	Tens	Ones
	2	3	6
+	3	5	9
Hundreds:			
Tens:			
Ones:			
Sum			

2.

	Hundreds	Tens	Ones
	5	8	2
+	1	7	3
Hundreds:			
Tens:			
Ones:			
Sum			

3.
```
  3 6 4
+ 4 3 2
```

4.
```
  4 5 4
+ 4 8 8
```

5.
```
  1 4 5
+ 3 4 1
```

6.
```
  5 7 6
+ 2 4 8
```

Name _____

 **Apply and Grow: Practice**

7.
```
   2 1 7
 + 4 3 5
```

8.
```
   5 3 2
 + 1 2 9
```

9.
```
   6 5 1
 + 2 3 7
```

10.
```
   7 7 9
 + 1 3 0
```

11.
```
   3 6 2
 + 2 1 7
```

12.
```
   8 0 6
 + 1 1 5
```

13.
```
   4 4 8
 + 3 1 2
```

14.
```
   5 8 1
 + 2 4 3
```

15. **Which One Doesn't Belong?** Which expression does *not* belong with the other three?

200 + 300 + 50 + 20 + 5 + 6

581

500 + 70 + 11

500 + 80 + 5 + 6

Use Math Tools
How can you use base ten blocks to help?

Chapter 9 | Lesson 5   four hundred twenty-five   425

Think and Grow: Modeling Real Life

A video rental store has 348 fewer video games than movies. There are 116 video games. How many movies are there?

Model:

	Hundreds	Tens	Ones
+			
Hundreds:			
Tens:			
Ones:			
Sum			

_____ movies

Show and Grow   I can think deeper!

16. A library has 477 fewer magazines than books. There are 243 magazines. How many books are there?

_____ books

17. **DIG DEEPER!** A clothing store has some shirts on hangers. There are 214 shirts on shelves. The store has 356 shirts in all. How many shirts are on hangers?

_____ shirts

Name _____

Practice 9.5

Learning Target: Use partial sums to add.

	Hundreds	Tens	Ones
	3	6	2
+	4	5	3
Hundreds:	7	0	0	= 300 + 400
Tens:	1	1	0	= 60 + 50
Ones:			5	= 2 + 3
Sum	8	1	5

1.

	Hundreds	Tens	Ones
	4	4	2
+	2	1	5
Hundreds:			
Tens:			
Ones:			
Sum			

2.

	Hundreds	Tens	Ones
	3	3	6
+	4	6	5
Hundreds:			
Tens:			
Ones:			
Sum			

3.
```
  4 5 1
+ 4 0 1
```

4.
```
  3 7 1
+ 2 4 8
```

5.
```
  6 7 2
+ 2 8 3
```

6.
```
  5 2 7
+ 1 0 6
```

Chapter 9 | Lesson 5   four hundred twenty-seven   427

7. **DIG DEEPER!** Find the missing digits. Then find the sum.

	Hundreds	Tens	Ones
	___	4	5
+	3	___	3
Hundreds:	7	0	0	= 400 + 300
Tens:	1	1	0	= ___ + 70
Ones:			8	= 5 + 3
Sum				

8. **Modeling Real Life** There are 180 fewer muffins than rolls. There are 425 muffins. How many rolls are there?

_____ rolls

9. **DIG DEEPER!** A truck driver drives 672 miles on Monday. He drives some more miles on Tuesday. He drives 954 miles in all. How many miles did he drive on Tuesday?

_____ miles

Review & Refresh

10. Circle the closed shapes with only 3 vertices.

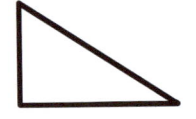  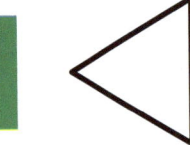  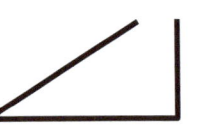  

Name _____

Learning Target: Use models to add.

Use Models to Add Three-Digit Numbers

9.6

 Explore and Grow

Model to solve. Make a quick sketch of your model.

$$\begin{array}{r} 3\ 2\ 7 \\ +\ 4\ 5\ 8 \\ \hline \end{array}$$

Precision
Do you need to regroup? How do you know?

Chapter 9 | Lesson 6

four hundred twenty-nine 429

 **Think and Grow**

272 + 154 = ?

Hundreds	Tens	Ones
1		
2	7	2
+ 1	5	4
	2	6

Hundreds	Tens	Ones
1		
2	7	2
+ 1	5	4
4	2	6

Show and Grow — I can do it!

1. 383 + 255 = ?

Hundreds	Tens	Ones

Hundreds	Tens	Ones
3	8	3
+ 2	5	5

430 four hundred thirty

Name _____

 **Apply and Grow: Practice**

2. 238 + 354 = ?

Hundreds	Tens	Ones

Hundreds	Tens	Ones
☐	☐	
2	3	8
+ 3	5	4

3. 692 + 147 = ?

Hundreds	Tens	Ones

Hundreds	Tens	Ones
☐	☐	
6	9	2
+ 1	4	7

4. 553 + 250 = ?

Hundreds	Tens	Ones

	Hundreds	Tens	Ones
	5	5	3
+	2	5	0

Chapter 9 | Lesson 6   four hundred thirty-one   431

Think and Grow: Modeling Real Life

Your school wants to collect 750 canned goods. Your school collects 432 cans of soup and 386 cans of vegetables. Does your school reach the goal? Explain.

Models:

Hundreds	Tens	Ones

Yes   No

_____

_____

Show and Grow — I can think deeper!

5. A charity needs 600 volunteers. 328 people sign up on Saturday and 219 people sign up on Sunday. Are there enough volunteers? Explain.

Yes   No

_____

_____

432   four hundred thirty-two

Name _____

Practice 9.6

Learning Target: Use models to add 2 three-digit numbers.

327 + 124 = ?

Hundreds	Tens	Ones
☐	1	
3	2	7
+ 1	2	4
		1

Hundreds	Tens	Ones
☐	1	
3	2	7
+ 1	2	4
4	5	1

1. 614 + 250 = ?

Hundreds	Tens	Ones

Hundreds	Tens	Ones
☐	☐	
6	1	4
+ 2	5	0

Chapter 9 | Lesson 6   four hundred thirty-three   433

2. 192 + 717 = ?

Hundreds	Tens	Ones

```
    1  9  2
+   7  1  7
_____
```

3. **Modeling Real Life** The cafeteria needs 700 trays. They have 312 brown trays and 342 orange trays. Does the cafeteria have enough trays? Explain.

    Yes   No

_____

_____

4. **DIG DEEPER!** Organizers place 109 Cuban flags and 28 more Haitian flags than Cuban flags along a parade route. How many Cuban and Haitian flags do organizers place in all?

_____ flags

Review & Refresh

Draw to show the time.

5.

6.

434   four hundred thirty-four

Name _____

Learning Target: Add three-digit numbers.

Add Three-Digit Numbers 9.7

Explore and Grow

Find each sum.

H	T	O
4	4	5
+2	5	4

H	T	O
2	5	3
+3	1	8

H	T	O
6	2	7
+1	9	4

MP Structure Compare the problems. How are they the same? How are they different?

_____

_____

_____

Chapter 9 | Lesson 7   four hundred thirty-five   435

Think and Grow

Add the ones. Regroup 11 ones as 1 ten and 1 one.

```
  1 1
  2 5 9
+ 3 4 2
-------
  6 0 1
```

Add the tens. Regroup 10 tens as 1 hundred and 0 tens. Then add the hundreds.

Show and Grow   I can do it!

1.
```
   1 8 4
 + 4 3 8
```

2.
```
   2 2 7
 + 2 6 7
```

3.
```
   4 2 1
 + 3 5 4
```

4.
```
   2 7 9
 + 5 1 4
```

5.
```
   3 1 3
 + 2 8 8
```

6.
```
   3 9 6
 + 1 5 6
```

7.
```
   6 5 9
 + 2 5 8
```

8.
```
   4 6 3
 + 4 8 5
```

9.
```
   2 9 8
 + 3 7 8
```

Name _____

**Apply and Grow: Practice**

10.
```
   2 4 5
+  6 0 5
---------
```

11.
```
   4 5 0
+  2 9 1
---------
```

12.
```
   1 9 8
+  5 2 7
---------
```

13.
```
   7 4 2
+  1 1 6
---------
```

14.
```
   5 3 7
+  1 7 6
---------
```

15.
```
   3 8 2
+  3 5 1
---------
```

16.
```
   4 6 3
+  1 9 4
---------
```

17.
```
   1 8 6
+  5 6 7
---------
```

18.
```
   6 2 3
+  2 9 8
---------
```

19. **DIG DEEPER!** Find the missing digits.

```
     4 6 2
+  ☐ 4 3
----------
   7 0 5
```

```
   1 ☐ 7
+  1 1 5
----------
   2 5 2
```

```
   3 9 5
+  1 4 ☐
----------
   5 4 0
```

Chapter 9 | Lesson 7   four hundred thirty-seven   437

Think and Grow: Modeling Real Life

A puzzle has 540 pieces. You put 254 pieces together. Your friend puts 286 pieces together. Did you and your friend use all of the pieces?

Addition equation:

Yes   No

Show and Grow   I can think deeper!

20. A sticker book has 800 stickers. You use 413 of them. Your friend uses 377. Did you and your friend use all of the stickers?

Yes   No

21. **DIG DEEPER!** A bus has 850 miles to travel. How many miles does the bus have left to travel?

Day	Number of Miles
1	423
2	417

_____ miles

438   four hundred thirty-eight

Name _____

Practice 9.7

Learning Target: Add three-digit numbers.

Add the ones. Regroup 15 ones as 1 ten and 5 ones.

Add the tens. Regroup 12 tens as 1 hundred and 2 tens. Then add the hundreds.

1.
```
   3 4 1
 + 2 7 8
```

2.
```
   7 0 5
 + 1 2 6
```

3.
```
   5 8 2
 + 2 4 9
```

4.
```
   5 7 3
 + 3 3 8
```

5.
```
   2 6 4
 + 3 1 0
```

6.
```
   5 1 6
 + 1 5 6
```

7.
```
   4 9 0
 + 1 3 7
```

8.
```
   6 2 5
 + 2 9 7
```

9.
```
   3 6 4
 + 3 8 6
```

Chapter 9 | Lesson 7   four hundred thirty-nine   **439**

10. **Open-Ended** Complete the addition problem so that you do *not* need to regroup to add.

	2	5	6
+	3	___	3

11. **Modeling Real Life** The art room has 645 markers. One class is using 312 markers. Another class is using 209. Are both classes using all the markers?

      Yes   No

12. **DIG DEEPER!** 340 water balloons need to be filled. You fill 175 and your friend fills 10 fewer than you. How many more water balloons need to be filled?

_____ water balloons

Review & Refresh

Use place value to find the missing numbers.

13. 324, 325, _____, 327, _____, _____, _____

14. 463, 473, _____, 493, _____, _____, _____

440   four hundred forty

Name _____

Learning Target: Add up to 4 two-digit numbers.

Add Up to 4 Two-Digit Numbers — 9.8

Explore and Grow

Use any strategy to solve.

Newton has 19 red balloons, 23 green balloons, 31 yellow balloons, and 17 blue balloons. How many balloons does he have in all?

_____ balloons

MP Compare Arguments Compare your strategy to your partner's strategy. Which strategy makes the most sense to use with these numbers?

_____

_____

_____

Chapter 9 | Lesson 8

Think and Grow

When adding more than two numbers, look for **compatible numbers** to help you add.

```
  1
  4 2
  2 ③      ┐
  3 5      ├─ 10
+ 2 ⑦     ┘
  ─────
  1 2 7
```

```
  1
  4 ②     ┐
  2 ③     ├─ 5
  3 5
+ 2 7
  ─────
  1 2 7
```

You can make a 10 or use known facts.

Show and Grow   I can do it!

1.
```
    2 6
    8 8
  + 3 2
```

2.
```
    6 0
    1 5
  + 5 5
```

3.
```
    7 7
    9 6
  + 2 4
```

4.
```
    5 7
    1 3
    3 3
  + 4 8
```

5.
```
    8 9
    6 2
    1 0
  + 5 1
```

6.
```
    9 5
    7 1
    4 6
  + 5 3
```

442   four hundred forty-two

Name _____

Apply and Grow: Practice

7.
```
   1 7
   8 4
+  2 3
------
```

8.
```
   2 1
   4 2
+  3 9
------
```

9.
```
   9 2
   5 8
+  1 9
------
```

10.
```
   5 8
   1 2
     6
+  2 4
------
```

11.
```
   4 2
   2 6
   3 3
+  1 4
------
```

12.
```
   1 3
   5 2
   3 7
+  4 8
------
```

13.
```
   6 4
   2 0
   3 5
+  5 6
------
```

14.
```
   3 6
   9 2
   4 0
+  1 5
------
```

15.
```
   1 9
     3
   4 7
+  2 5
------
```

16. **Number Sense** Solve. Which two digits in the ones place did you add first? Explain.

7 + 15 + 36 + 25 = ____

_____

_____

_____

Chapter 9 | Lesson 8   four hundred forty-three   443

Think and Grow: Modeling Real Life

How many seeds does your class plant in all?

Type of Seed	Number Planted
Sunflower	81
Marigold	92
Pumpkin	83
Tomato	78

Addition problem:

_____ seeds

Show and Grow   I can think deeper!

17. How many fish are there in all?

Type of Fish	Number of Fish
Angelfish	43
Rainbow fish	37
Swordtail	29
Tetra	59

_____ fish

18. **DIG DEEPER!** You need 100 craft sticks for a project. You have a 24-pack, a 32-pack, and a 36-pack. How many more craft sticks do you need?

_____ more craft sticks

Name _____

Practice 9.8

Learning Target: Add up to 4 two-digit numbers.

When adding more than two numbers, look for compatible numbers to help you add.

```
   1
  3 ⑦ ⎫
  1 4 ⎬ 10
  2 ③ ⎭
+ 5 4
─────
  1 2 8
```

1.
```
    4 3
    6 2
  + 1 8
  ─────
```

2.
```
    7 4
    3 0
  + 6 9
  ─────
```

3.
```
    3 4
    5 7
  + 2 7
  ─────
```

4.
```
    5 1
    1 6
      6
  + 2 4
  ─────
```

5.
```
    8 4
    6 2
    1 0
  + 3 1
  ─────
```

6.
```
    6 6
    4 9
    3 4
  + 2 1
  ─────
```

7.
```
    5 0
    2 6
    4 5
  + 4 4
  ─────
```

8.
```
    7 3
    1 4
    2 6
  + 2 7
  ─────
```

9.
```
    6 5
      8
    3 2
  + 7 1
  ─────
```

Chapter 9 | Lesson 8   four hundred forty-five

10. **Number Sense** Find the missing number.

    38 + 41 + ☐ + 52 = 159

11. **Modeling Real Life** How many sandwiches are there in all?

Type of Sandwich	Number of Sandwiches
Turkey	59
Ham	23
Cheese	35
Peanut Butter	45

    _____ sandwiches

12. **DIG DEEPER!** You need 210 votes to win a school election. You receive 67 votes from the first grade and 93 votes from the second grade. How many more votes do you need?

    _____ votes

Review & Refresh

Write a number that makes the statement true.

13. 865 < _____

14. _____ > 374

15. 736 = _____

16. 451 > _____

Name _____

Learning Target: Choose and explain a strategy to add.

Explain Addition Strategies 9.9

 **Explore and Grow**

Use two different strategies to find 274 + 519.

Addition Strategies
Add on an Open Number Line
Compensation
Partial Sums
Use Models to Add
Regrouping

Communicate Clearly Explain why you chose one of your strategies.

_____
_____
_____

Chapter 9 | Lesson 9 four hundred forty-seven **447**

Think and Grow

$395 + 128 = ?$

One Way: Use compensation.

$395 +\ \ \ \ \ \ 128\ \ =\ \ ?$

$\oplus\underline{\ \ 5\ \ }\ \ \ \ \ominus\underline{\ \ 5\ \ }$

$\underline{400} + \underline{123} = \underline{523}$

Think: Why do these strategies work?

Another Way: Use a number line.

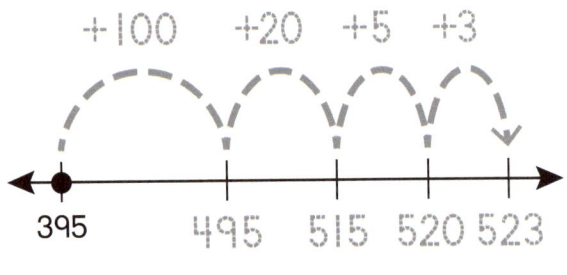

$+100\ \ +20\ \ +5\ \ +3$

395   495   515   520 523

$395 + 128 = \underline{523}$

Think: Are there any other strategies you can use?

Show and Grow — I can do it!

Choose any strategy to solve. Explain how you solved.

1. $379 + 240 =$ _____

Name _____

✓ Apply and Grow: Practice

Choose any strategy to solve. Explain how you solved.

2. 426 + 355 = _____

_____

_____

3. 671 + 219 = _____

_____

_____

4.  **YOU BE THE TEACHER** Your friend uses compensation to solve. Is your friend correct? Explain.

$$182 + 506 = ?$$
$$\oplus \underline{6} \quad \ominus \underline{6}$$
$$188 + 500 = 688$$

_____

_____

Chapter 9 | Lesson 9   four hundred forty-nine   449

Think and Grow: Modeling Real Life

Choose any strategy to solve. Explain how you solved.

You have 567 pennies in a piggy bank and 428 in a jar. How many pennies do you have in all?

Addition equation:

_____ pennies

Show and Grow   I can think deeper!

Choose any strategy to solve. Explain how you solved.

5. A beekeeper has 494 worker bees and 376 drone bees. How many bees does he have in all?

_____ bees

6. There are 365 days in one year. How many days are there in two years?

_____ days

Name _____

Practice 9.9

Learning Target: Choose and explain a strategy to add.

268 + 305 = ?

One Way: Use a number line.

+100 +100 +100 +5

268 368 468 568 573

268 + 305 = __573__

Another Way: Use place value.

```
  1
  2 | 6 | 8
+ 3 | 0 | 5
  5 | 7 | 3
```

Choose any strategy to solve. Explain how you solved.

1. 656 + 181 = _____

   _____

   _____

2. 567 + 348 = _____

   _____

   _____

Chapter 9 | Lesson 9   four hundred fifty-one   451

3. **DIG DEEPER!** Find the missing numbers.

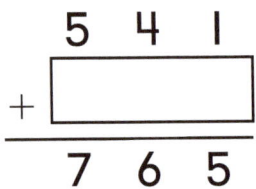   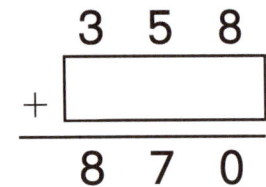
```
  5 4 1        3 5 8        1 0 8
+ [   ]      + [   ]      + [   ]
─────────    ─────────    ─────────
  7 6 5        8 7 0        5 4 2
```

Choose any strategy to solve. Explain how you solved.

4. **Modeling Real Life** A farmer has 415 tomato plants and 250 pepper plants. How many plants does he have in all?

_____ plants

_____

_____

5. **Modeling Real Life** You practice the trumpet for 45 minutes each day. How many minutes do you practice in 4 days?

_____ minutes

_____

_____

Review & Refresh

6. 97 − 71 = _____   7. 56 − 14 = _____

Name _____

Performance Task

A store has four different robot kits.

1. How many parts are there in the green, purple, and orange kits?

   _____ parts

2. **Maintain Accuracy** The orange kit has 183 fewer parts than the yellow kit. How many parts are in the yellow kit?

   _____ parts

3. Your friend wants to buy two kits so that he has 700 parts. Which two kits should he buy?

   _____ and _____

4. a. You have some robot parts at home. You buy two purple kits and one orange kit. Now you have 774 parts. How many parts did you have to start?

   _____ parts

   b. Your cousin has 450 robot parts at home. She buys a kit and now has 36 more parts than you. Which kit did she buy?

   _____ kit

Chapter 9   four hundred fifty-three   453

Three in a Row: Three-Digit Addition

To Play: Players take turns. On your turn, spin both spinners. Add the two numbers and cover the sum. Continue playing until someone gets three in a row.

Name _____

Chapter 9 Practice

9.1 Add 10 and 100

1. 230 + 10 = _____

2. 419 + 10 = _____

3. 623 + 100 = _____

4. 899 + 10 = _____

5. 384 + 100 = _____

6. 167 + 100 = _____

9.2 Use a Number Line to Add Hundreds and Tens

7. 592 + 340 = _____

8. **Modeling Real Life** You have 170 football stickers and some baseball stickers. You have 360 stickers in all. How many baseball stickers do you have?

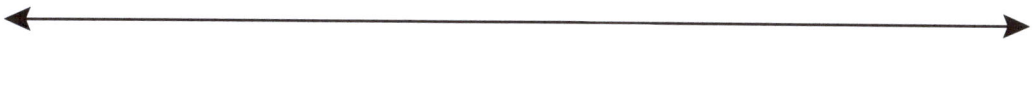

_____ baseball stickers

9.3 Use a Number Line to Add Three-Digit Numbers

9. 365 + 342 = _____

10. 604 + 217 = _____

9.4 Use Compensation to Add Three-Digit Numbers

Use compensation to add.

11. 205 + 631 = ?

○ ___   ○ ___

___ + ___ = ___

12. 452 + 311 = ?

○ ___   ○ ___

___ + ___ = ___

13. **YOU BE THE TEACHER** Newton uses compensation to find 198 + 267. Is he correct? Explain.

198 + 267 = ?
⊕ 2   ⊕ 2
200 + 269 = 469

_____

_____

_____

456   four hundred fifty-six

 **Use Partial Sums to Add Three-Digit Numbers**

14.
```
   2 6 4
 + 4 8 3
```

15.
```
   8 0 7
 + 1 2 6
```

16.
```
   3 2 5
 + 3 2 4
```

17.
```
   6 4 0
 + 2 9 3
```

 **Use Models to Add Three-Digit Numbers**

18. 395 + 410 = ?

Hundreds	Tens	Ones

```
   3 | 9 | 5
 + 4 | 1 | 0
```

Add Three-Digit Numbers

19. **Number Sense** Find the missing digits.

```
    5 6 1
 + ☐ 5 7
   ─────
    9 1 8
```

```
    1 ☐ 5
 +  2 6 4
   ─────
    3 7 9
```

```
    6 4 6
 +  1 4 ☐
   ─────
    7 9 2
```

Chapter 9   four hundred fifty-seven   457

9.8 Add Up to 4 Two-Digit Numbers

20.
```
  5 4
  3 2
+ 2 0
```

21.
```
  4 3
  5 8
+ 1 7
```

22.
```
  1 6
  8 1
+ 7 4
```

23.
```
  9 2
  5 2
  3 8
+ 4 1
```

24.
```
  9 0
    5
  1 3
+ 4 8
```

25.
```
  6 6
  4 4
  3 0
+   9
```

9.9 Explain Addition Strategies

Choose any strategy to solve. Explain how you solved.

26. 538 + 176 = _____

_____

_____

10 Subtract Numbers within 1,000

- Have you ever seen a race car?
- The race car drivers need to complete 500 laps. They have already completed 472 laps. How many laps are left?

Chapter Learning Target:
Understand subtracting numbers.

Chapter Success Criteria:
- I can identify subtraction patterns.
- I can use a number line to count backwards.
- I can explain how to use different subtraction strategies.
- I can model subtraction problems.

Name _____

10 Vocabulary

Organize It

Review Words
compensation
difference
open number line
regroup
sum

Use the review words to complete the graphic organizer.

5 + 3 = 8

8 − 3 = 5

Define It

Match.

1. regroup

2. open number line

3. compensation

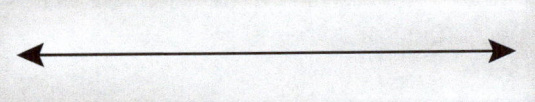

A strategy used to make a ten to help add and subtract numbers

460   four hundred sixty

Name _____

Subtract 10 and 100

Learning Target: Use mental math to subtract 10 and subtract 100.

Model 251. Make a quick sketch of your model.

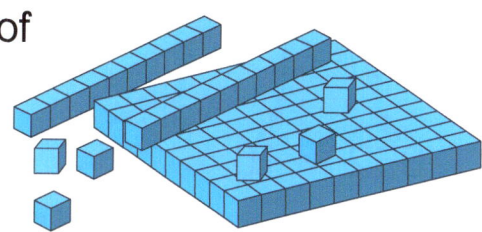

251

Model 10 less than 251. Make a quick sketch of your model.

251 − 10 = _____

Model 100 less than 251. Make a quick sketch of your model.

251 − 100 = _____

Chapter 10 | **Lesson 1**   four hundred sixty-one   **461**

Think and Grow

352:

5 − 1 = 4

352 − 10 = 342

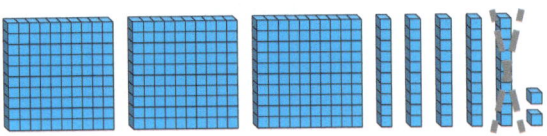

The tens digit decreases by 1.

3 − 1 = 2

352 − 100 = 252

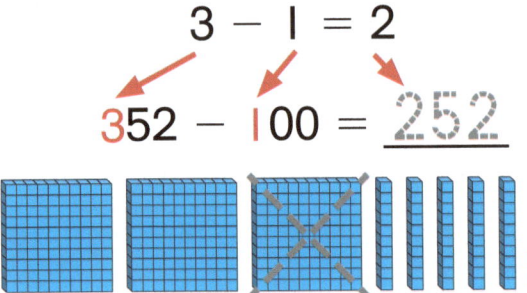

The hundreds digit decreases by 1.

Sometimes when you subtract 10, the tens digit *and* the hundreds digit change.

200 − 10 = ?

20 tens − 1 ten = 19 tens

So, 200 − 10 = 190.

Show and Grow   I can do it!

1. 278 − 10 = ____

   278 − 100 = ____

2. 451 − 10 = ____

   451 − 100 = ____

3. 623 − 10 = ____

   623 − 100 = ____

4. 116 − 10 = ____

   116 − 100 = ____

Name _____

 **Apply and Grow: Practice**

5. 100 − 10 = _____

6. 599 − 100 = _____

7. 614 − 10 = _____

8. 890 − 10 = _____

9. 768 − 100 = _____

10. 523 − 10 = _____

11. 362 − 100 = _____

12. 396 − 10 = _____

13. 604 − 10 = _____

14. 799 − 100 = _____

15. 449 − _____ = 349

16. _____ − 10 = 227

17. Number Sense Use each number once to complete the equations.

470   560   100   460

_____ − 10 = _____   _____ − _____ = 460

Chapter 10 | Lesson 1   four hundred sixty-three 463

Think and Grow: Modeling Real Life

You have $106. You spend $10.
How much money do you have left?

Subtraction equation:

$ _____

Show and Grow I can think deeper!

18. You have 334 tickets. You exchange 100 of them for a prize. How many tickets do you have left?

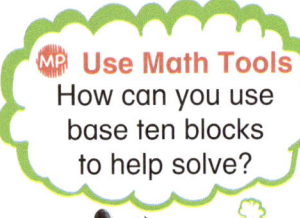

Use Math Tools How can you use base ten blocks to help solve?

_____ tickets

19. **DIG DEEPER!** You score 745 points in a video game. You lose some points. Now you have 645. How many points did you lose?

_____ points

20. **Repeated Reasoning** How can you mentally subtract 10 or 100 from a number?

_____

_____

Name _____

Practice 10.1

Learning Target: Use mental math to subtract 10 and subtract 100.

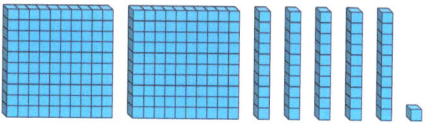

251

251 − 10 = **241**   251 − 100 = **151**

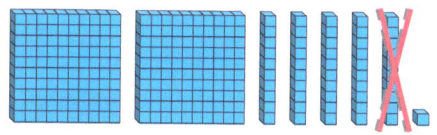   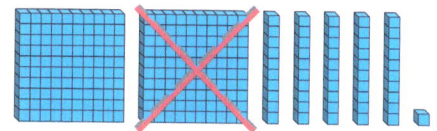

1. 642 − 10 = _____

2. 416 − 100 = _____

3. 890 − 100 = _____

4. 371 − 10 = _____

5. 501 − 100 = _____

6. 955 − 100 = _____

7. 203 − 10 = _____

8. 888 − 100 = _____

9. 690 − 10 = _____

10. 107 − 10 = _____

11. 723 − _____ = 713

12. _____ − 100 = 433

Chapter 10 | Lesson 1   four hundred sixty-five   465

13. **YOU BE THE TEACHER** Your friend says that 678 − 110 = 568. Is your friend correct? Explain.

   _____

   _____

Compare.

14. 582 − 10 ◯ 683 − 100

15. 985 − 100 ◯ 895 − 10

16. **Modeling Real Life** Newton sends out 233 invitations. 100 people respond to the invitation. How many people have *not* responded yet?

   _____ people

17. **DIG DEEPER!** 648 runners sign up for a marathon. 638 runners finish the race. How many runners do *not* finish?

   _____ runners

Review & Refresh

18.

   ____ rows of ____

   ____ + ____ = ____

19.

   ____ rows of ____

   ____ + ____ + ____ = ____

Name _____

Learning Target: Use an open number line to subtract hundreds and tens.

Use a Number Line to Subtract Hundreds and Tens 10.2

Explore and Grow

Skip count back by tens five times on the number line.

555

555 − _____ = _____

Skip count back by hundreds five times on the number line.

555

555 − _____ = _____

Chapter 10 | Lesson 2

four hundred sixty-seven 467

Think and Grow

$621 - 230 = ?$

One Way:

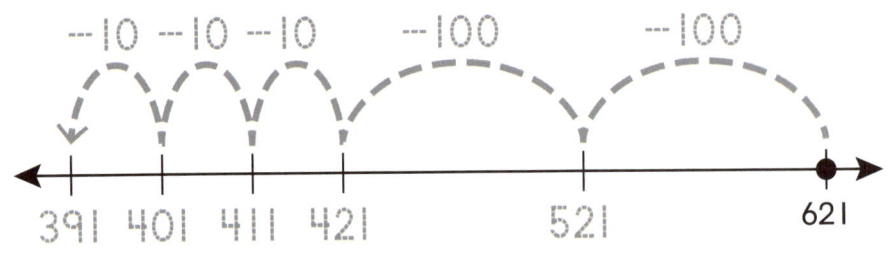

Start at 621. Count back by hundreds, then by tens.

Another Way:

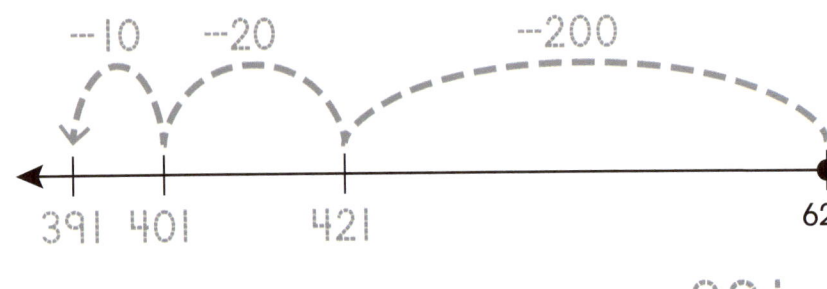

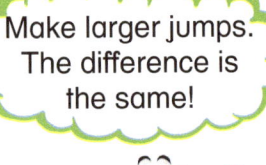

Make larger jumps. The difference is the same!

$621 - 230 = \underline{391}$

Show and Grow — I can do it!

1. $520 - 330 = \underline{}$

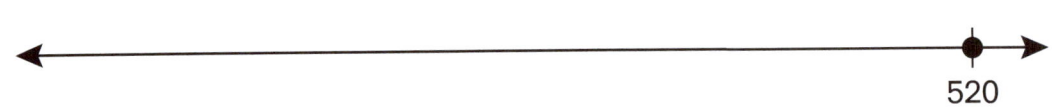

2. $259 - 170 = \underline{}$

Name _____

✓ Apply and Grow: Practice

3. 640 − 150 = _____

4. 453 − 210 = _____

5. 329 − 220 = _____

6. **Reasoning** Complete the number line and the equation.

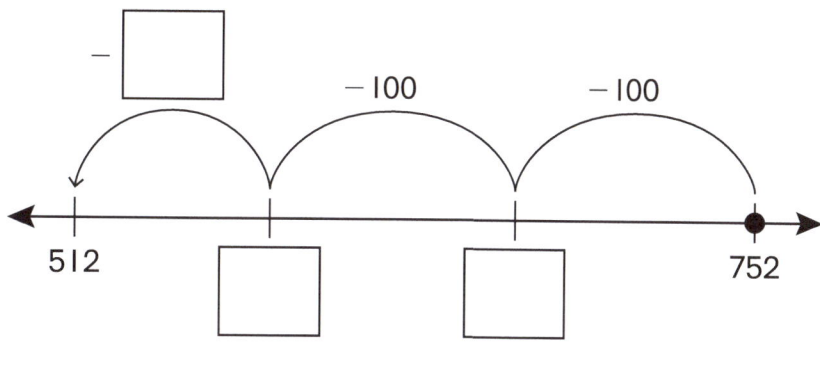

_____ − _____ = _____

Chapter 10 | Lesson 2

Think and Grow: Modeling Real Life

A batting cage has 360 baseballs. There are 130 fewer softballs than baseballs. How many softballs are there?

Subtraction equation:

Model:

⬅————————————➡

_____ softballs

Show and Grow I can think deeper!

7. A crocodile weighs 535 pounds. A kangaroo weighs 340 pounds less than the crocodile. How much does the kangaroo weigh?

_____ pounds

8. **DIG DEEPER!** A train has 850 seats. A plane has 390 fewer seats than the train. A bus has 370 fewer seats than the plane. How many seats does the bus have?

_____ seats

470 four hundred seventy

Name _____

Practice 10.2

Learning Target: Use an open number line to subtract hundreds and tens.

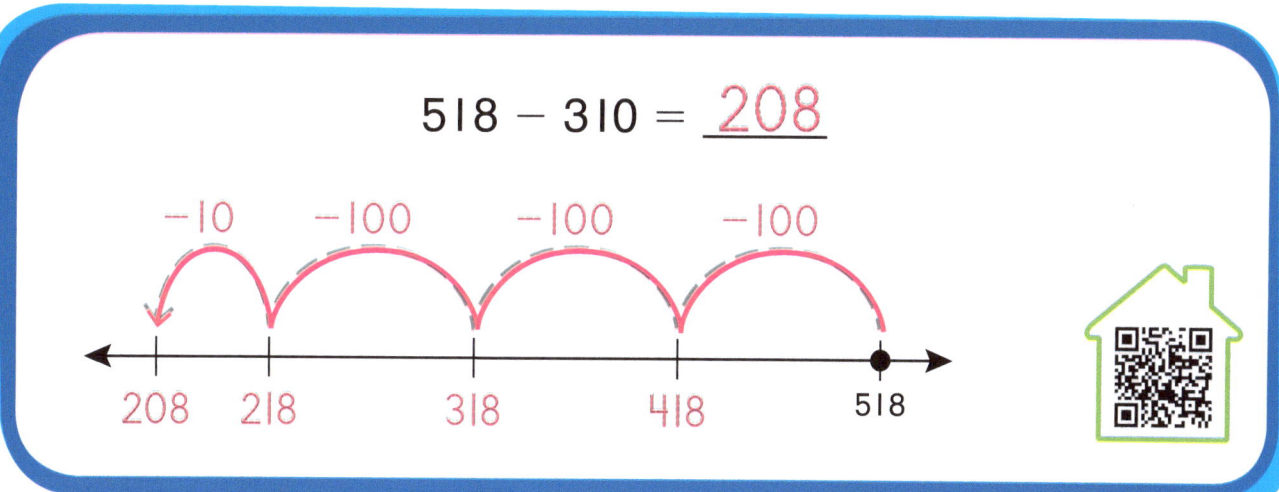

1. 670 − 520 = _____

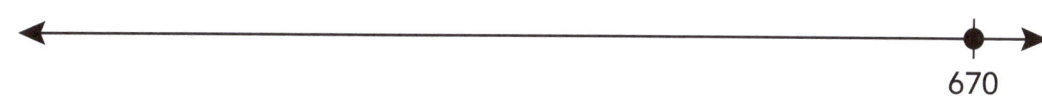

2. 749 − 150 = _____

3. 583 − 320 = _____

Chapter 10 | Lesson 2   four hundred seventy-one   471

4. **Structure** Write the equation shown by the number line.

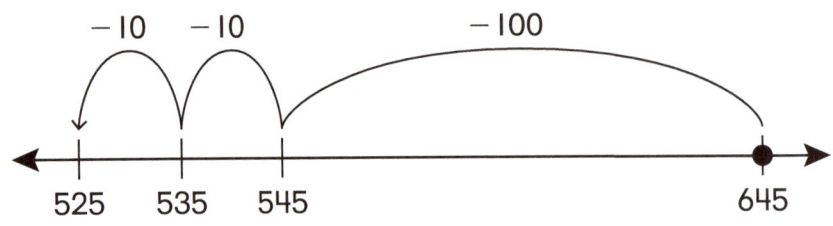

_____ − _____ = _____

5. **Modeling Real Life** A bee pollinates 955 flowers in a day. A second bee pollinates 150 fewer flowers. How many flowers does the second bee pollinate?

_____ flowers

6. **DIG DEEPER!** A library has 990 books. It has 250 fewer movies than books. It has 410 fewer magazines than movies. How many magazines does the library have?

_____ magazines

Review & Refresh

7.

Favorite Activity

Activity	Number of students
Reading	1
Computer	3
Kickball	4

How many students chose computer?

_____ students

Name _____

Use a Number Line to Subtract Three-Digit Numbers

10.3

Learning Target: Use a number line to subtract.

Explore and Grow

Use each difference as the starting number in the next equation.

$$425 - 200 = \underline{}$$

$$\underline{} - 20 = \underline{}$$

$$\underline{} - 2 = \underline{}$$

Use a Similar Problem How does this help you find $425 - 222$?

_____

_____

Chapter 10 | Lesson 3   four hundred seventy-three   473

Think and Grow

$739 - 143 = ?$

One Way:

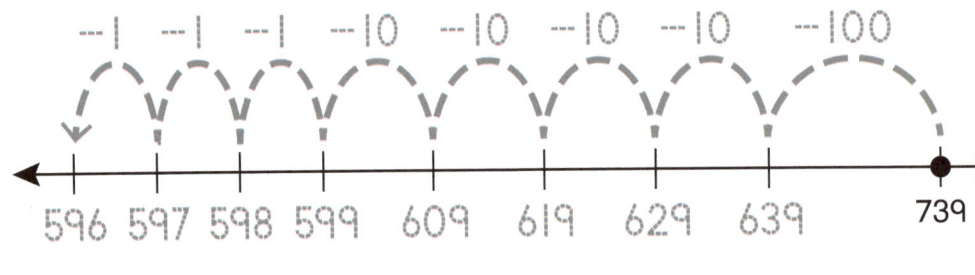

> Start at 739. Count back by hundreds, then by tens, then by ones.

Another Way:

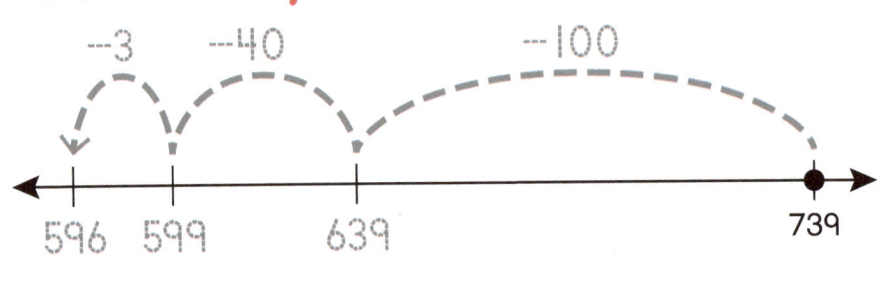

> Make larger jumps.

$739 - 143 = \underline{596}$

Show and Grow *I can do it!*

1. $674 - 236 = \underline{}$

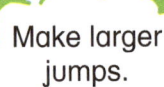

2. $438 - 162 = \underline{}$

Name _____

 **Apply and Grow: Practice**

3. 534 − 311 = _____

4. 745 − 109 = _____

5. 436 − 84 = _____

6. **Structure** Write the equation shown by the number line.

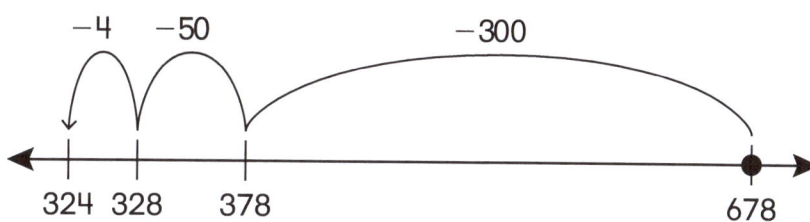

_____ − _____ = _____

Chapter 10 | Lesson 3   four hundred seventy-five   **475**

Think and Grow: Modeling Real Life

Your school recycles 762 bottles. 245 are glass. The rest are plastic. How many bottles are plastic?

Subtraction equation:

Model:

⟵——————————————⟶

_____ bottles

Show and Grow I can think deeper!

7. A squirrel collects 619 nuts for the winter. 421 are acorns. The rest are walnuts. How many walnuts are there?

_____ walnuts

8. **DIG DEEPER!** You have 384 photos. You put your photos into two photo albums. Each album can hold up to 208 photos. How many photos can you put in each album? Explain.

_____ photos in Album 1   _____ photos in Album 2

_____

_____

Name _____

Practice

Learning Target: Use a number line to subtract.

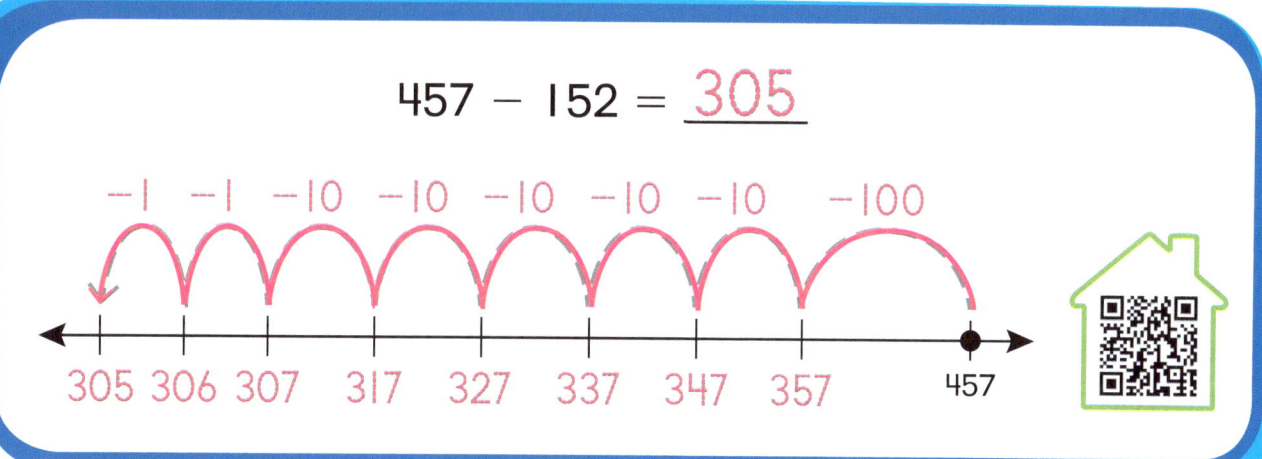

1. 953 − 328 = _____

2. 674 − 218 = _____

3. 594 − 107 = _____

4. **Structure** Use the number lines to show 531 − 396 two ways.

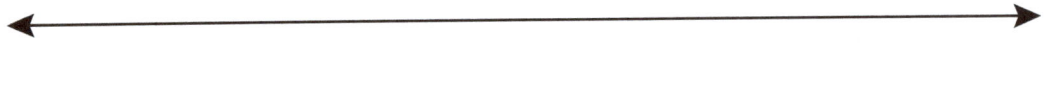

531 − 396 = _____

5. **Modeling Real Life** You earn 631 points in a video game. You trade in 475 points for a special power. How many points do you have left?

_____ points

6. **DIG DEEPER!** You have 137 books. You put your books on two bookshelves. Each shelf can hold up to 72 books. How many books can you put on each shelf? Explain.

_____ books on Shelf 1   _____ books on Shelf 2

_____

_____

Review & Refresh

7.

Hundreds	Tens	Ones
_____	_____	_____

_____ hundreds, _____ tens, and _____ ones is _____.

478   four hundred seventy-eight

Name _____

Use Compensation to Subtract Three-Digit Numbers — 10.4

Learning Target: Use compensation to subtract.

 Explore and Grow

Find 315 − 196.

Find 319 − 200.

MP Structure How are the problems the same? How are they different? Which problem can you solve using mental math?

_____

_____

_____

_____

Chapter 10 | Lesson 4 — four hundred seventy-nine — 479

Think and Grow

> It is easier to subtract 400 than to subtract 389. You subtract 11 more than 389, so you must add 11 to 323 to find the answer.

$$723 - 389 = \ ?$$
$$\downarrow +11$$
$$723 - \underline{400} = 323$$
$$\downarrow +11$$
$$723 - 389 = \underline{334}$$

> You subtract 4 less than 204, so you must subtract 4 from 362 to find the answer.

$$562 - 204 = \ ?$$
$$\downarrow -4$$
$$562 - \underline{200} = 362$$
$$\downarrow -4$$
$$562 - 204 = \underline{358}$$

Show and Grow   I can do it!

Use compensation to subtract.

1. $654 - 197 = \ ?$
   $\downarrow +3$
   $654 - \underline{} = \underline{}$
   $654 - 197 = \underline{}$ $\downarrow +3$

2. $835 - 309 = \ ?$
   $\downarrow -9$
   $835 - \underline{} = \underline{}$
   $835 - 309 = \underline{}$ $\downarrow -9$

3. $571 - 212 = \ ?$
   $\downarrow \square$
   $571 - \underline{} = \underline{}$
   $571 - 212 = \underline{}$ $\downarrow \square$

4. $611 - 392 = \ ?$
   $\downarrow \square$
   $611 - \underline{} = \underline{}$
   $611 - 392 = \underline{}$ $\downarrow \square$

Name _____

Apply and Grow: Practice

Use compensation to subtract.

5. 428 − 212 = ?
   ↓ ☐
   428 − ___ = ___
   428 − 212 = ___ ↓ ☐

6. 943 − 295 = ?
   ↓ ☐
   943 − ___ = ___
   943 − 295 = ___ ↓ ☐

7. 489 − 196 = ?
   ↓ ☐
   489 − ___ = ___
   489 − 196 = ___ ↓ ☐

8. 709 − 503 = ?
   ↓ ☐
   709 − ___ = ___
   709 − 503 = ___ ↓ ☐

9. 613 − 307 = _____

10. 861 − 499 = _____

11. **Maintain Accuracy** Should you add to or subtract from 194 to find the difference? Explain.

    387 − 194 = ?
    ↓ ☐
    387 − ___ = ___
    387 − 194 = ___ ↓ ☐

    _____
    _____
    _____

Chapter 10 | Lesson 4

Think and Grow: Modeling Real Life

A fish lays 861 eggs. A turtle lays 198 eggs. How many fewer eggs does the turtle lay than the fish?

Subtraction equation:

_____ fewer eggs

Show and Grow   I can think deeper!

12. A print shop has 650 sheets of white paper and 295 sheets of colored paper. How many fewer sheets of colored paper are there than white paper?

_____ fewer sheets of colored paper

13. A party store has 725 different cards and 506 different balloons. How many more cards are there than balloons?

_____ more cards

14. **Analyze a Problem** How are Exercises 12 and 13 similar? How are they different?

_____

_____

Name _____

Practice 10.4

Learning Target: Use compensation to subtract.

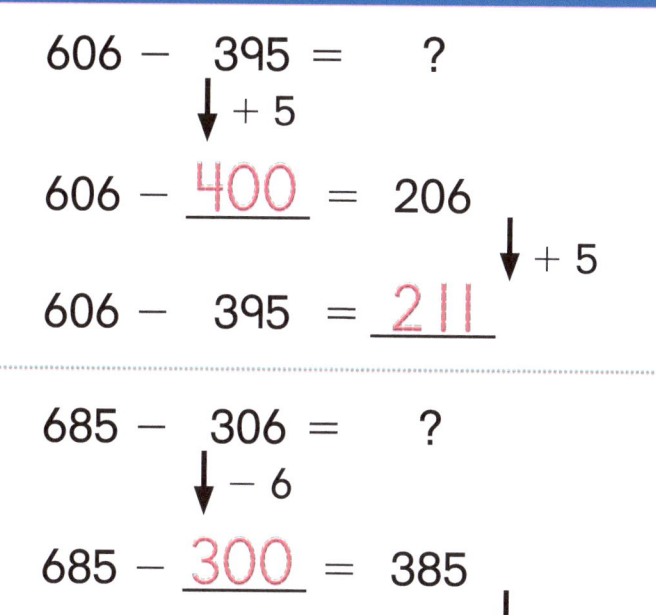

606 − 395 = ?
          ↓ + 5
606 − __400__ = 206
                  ↓ + 5
606 − 395 = __211__

685 − 306 = ?
          ↓ − 6
685 − __300__ = 385
                  ↓ − 6
685 − 306 = __379__

Add or subtract to make the number being subtracted a hundred.

Use compensation to subtract.

1. 972 − 415 = ?
             ↓ − 15
   972 − ___ = ___
                  ↓ − 15
   972 − 415 = ___

2. 328 − 186 = ?
             ↓ + 14
   328 − ___ = ___
                  ↓ + 14
   328 − 186 = ___

3. 703 − 598 = ?
             ↓ □
   703 − ___ = ___
                  ↓ □
   703 − 598 = ___

4. 841 − 603 = ?
             ↓ □
   841 − ___ = ___
                  ↓ □
   841 − 603 = ___

5. 439 − 210 = _____

6. 719 − 302 = _____

Chapter 10 | Lesson 4   four hundred eighty-three 483

7. **DIG DEEPER!** Write a subtraction equation that has the same difference as 796 − 304. The first two numbers each have 3 digits.

____ − ____ = ____

8. **Modeling Real Life** You write a 225-word essay. Your friend writes a 598-word essay. How many fewer words do you write?

_____ fewer words

9. **Modeling Real Life** How many more students like math than science?

Favorite Subject

Math	348
Language Arts	256
Science	197

_____ more students

Review & Refresh

Find the missing digits.

10.
```
   ☐ 5
 + 4 ☐
 -----
   8 1
```

11.
```
   ☐ 1
 + 3 ☐
 -----
   9 8
```

12.
```
   ☐ 7
 + 1 ☐
 -----
   4 4
```

484   four hundred eighty-four

Name _____

Use Models to Subtract Three-Digit Numbers 10.5

Learning Target: Use models to subtract.

 Explore and Grow

Model to solve. Make a quick sketch of your model.

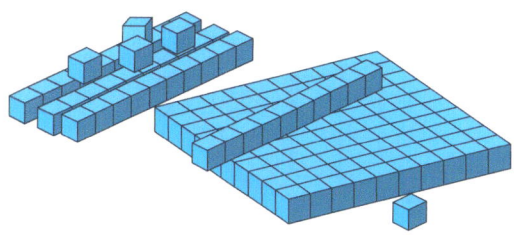

$$323 - 219 = ?$$

Hundreds	Tens	Ones

$323 - 219 = $ _____

Chapter 10 | Lesson 5

four hundred eighty-five 485

# Think and Grow

318 − 121 = ?

Hundreds	Tens	Ones
2	11	
3	1	8
1	2	1
		7

Hundreds	Tens	Ones
2	11	
3	1	8
1	2	1
1	9	7

Show and Grow — I can do it!

1. 429 − 165 = ?

Hundreds	Tens	Ones

Hundreds	Tens	Ones
4	2	9
1	6	5

486 four hundred eighty-six

Apply and Grow: Practice

2. 359 − 167 = ?

Hundreds	Tens	Ones

Hundreds	Tens	Ones
☐	☐	☐
3	5	9
− 1	6	7

3. 527 − 384 = ?

Hundreds	Tens	Ones

Hundreds	Tens	Ones
☐	☐	☐
5	2	7
− 3	8	4

4. 673 − 245 = ?

Hundreds	Tens	Ones

6	7	3
− 2	4	5

5. **Patterns** Write and solve the next problem in the pattern.

4	2	9		5	2	9				
− 3	4	1		− 2	4	1		−		

Chapter 10 | Lesson 5

four hundred eighty-seven 487

Think and Grow: Modeling Real Life

There are 549 people in a parade. 158 of them are in the marching band. How many people are *not* in the marching band?

Models:

Hundreds	Tens	Ones

_____ people

Show and Grow   I can think deeper!

6. A school library has 784 books. 256 of them are checked out. How many books are *not* checked out?

_____ books

7. A horse weighs 371 pounds more than a pig. The horse weighs 914 pounds. How much does the pig weigh?

_____ pounds

488   four hundred eighty-eight

Name _____

Practice 10.5

Learning Target: Use models to subtract.

326 − 154 = ?

Hundreds	Tens	Ones
2	12	
~~3~~	~~2~~	6
− 1	5	4
		2

Hundreds	Tens	Ones
2	12	
~~3~~	~~2~~	6
− 1	5	4
1	7	2

1. 738 − 544 = ?

Hundreds	Tens	Ones

Hundreds	Tens	Ones
7	3	8
− 5	4	4

Chapter 10 | Lesson 5

four hundred eighty-nine 489

2. 519 − 248 = ?

Hundreds	Tens	Ones

```
   5 | 1 | 9
 − 2 | 4 | 8
```

3. **DIG DEEPER!** Complete the subtraction problem so that you need to regroup to subtract.

```
   7 | ___ | 9
 − 3 |  4  | 5
```

4. **Modeling Real Life** A clown makes 315 balloon animals. 156 are giraffes. How many balloon animals are *not* giraffes?

_____ balloon animals

5. **Modeling Real Life** Your friend has 102 more downloaded songs than you. Your friend has 213 downloaded songs. How many downloaded songs do you have?

_____ downloaded songs

Review & Refresh

6.
```
    4 6 3
  + 1 9 4
```

7.
```
    1 8 6
  + 5 6 7
```

8.
```
    6 2 3
  + 2 9 8
```

Name _____

Learning Target: Subtract three-digit numbers.

Explore and Grow

Find each difference.

H	T	O
5	2	9
− 2	1	8

H	T	O
5	5	3
− 3	1	6

H	T	O
3	2	3
− 1	9	4

MP Structure Compare the problems. How are they the same? How are they different?

_____

_____

_____

Chapter 10 | Lesson 6

four hundred ninety-one 491

Think and Grow

There are not enough ones to subtract 7. So, regroup 3 tens and 5 ones as 2 tens and 15 ones.

$635 - 287 = ?$

There are not enough tens to subtract 8. So, regroup 6 hundreds and 2 tens as 5 hundreds and 12 tens.

Show and Grow — I can do it!

1. 423 − 174

2. 542 − 367

3. 315 − 151

4. 568 − 276

5. 821 − 346

6. 727 − 289

7. 434 − 188

8. 963 − 335

9. 741 − 254

492 four hundred ninety-two

Name _____

✓ Apply and Grow: Practice

10.
```
   3 4 5
 - 1 8 5
 _____
```

11.
```
   6 2 7
 - 4 1 8
 _____
```

12.
```
   9 1 6
 - 7 2 3
 _____
```

13.
```
   8 2 9
 - 3 6 7
 _____
```

14.
```
   5 4 1
 - 2 9 1
 _____
```

15.
```
   3 5 1
 - 1 8 2
 _____
```

16.
```
   4 6 5
 - 1 9 7
 _____
```

17.
```
   6 4 3
 - 2 8 9
 _____
```

18.
```
   6 7 3
 - 4 9 8
 _____
```

19. DIG DEEPER! Find the missing digits.

```
   4 5 1              9 5 7              6 □ 2
 - □ 0 7            - 6 7 □            - 1 5 8
 _____            _____            _____
   1 4 4              2 7 9              4 8 4
```

Chapter 10 | Lesson 6   four hundred ninety-three   **493**

Think and Grow: Modeling Real Life

A jeweler has 616 bracelets and 668 necklaces. He sells 269 bracelets. How many bracelets are left?

Subtraction equation:

_____ bracelets

Show and Grow   I can think deeper!

20. A vendor has 354 hats and 294 pairs of sunglasses. She sells 186 hats. How many hats are left?

_____ hats

21. There are 449 watercolor paintings and 373 oil paintings in a school art show. 238 paintings win a ribbon. How many do *not* win a ribbon?

_____ paintings

22. **Analyze a Problem** Explain how Exercises 20 and 21 are different.

_____

Name _____

Practice 10.6

Learning Target: Subtract three-digit numbers.

There are not enough ones to subtract 8. So, regroup 6 tens and 4 ones as 5 tens and 14 ones.

There are not enough tens to subtract 7. So, regroup 9 hundreds and 5 tens as 8 hundreds and 15 tens.

964 − 578 = ?

```
      5  14
   9  6́  4́
 −  5  7  8
 ─────────
            6
```

```
    15
   8  5́  14
   9́  6́  4́
 − 5  7  8
 ──────────
   3  8  6
```

1.
```
    8  7  3
  − 4  3  8
```

2.
```
    3  4  1
  − 2  7  8
```

3.
```
    9  1  3
  − 1  5  6
```

4.
```
    4  5  6
  − 1  8  7
```

5.
```
    6  2  5
  − 2  9  7
```

6.
```
    9  5  1
  − 6  8  2
```

7.
```
    4  5  2
  − 3  7  4
```

8.
```
    9  6  1
  − 5  9  3
```

9.
```
    7  4  6
  − 2  8  9
```

Chapter 10 | Lesson 6   four hundred ninety-five   495

10. **Open-Ended** Complete the subtraction problem so that you do *not* need to regroup to subtract.

```
   4 | 5 | 3
 - 2 | __ | 1
```

11. **YOU BE THE TEACHER** Descartes finds 731 − 246. Is he correct? Explain.

```
   6  13
   7̸  8̸  1
 - 2  4  6
   4  9  5
```

_____

_____

_____

12. **Modeling Real Life** 453 bananas and 456 apples are shipped to a store. When they arrive, 268 of the bananas are rotten. How many bananas are *not* rotten?

_____ bananas

13. **DIG DEEPER!** There are 432 red shirts and 293 blue shirts in stock. 516 shirts are sold. How many shirts are left?

_____ shirts

Review & Refresh

14. Count by fives.

680, 685, _____, _____, _____, _____, _____

Name _____

Learning Target: Subtract from three-digit numbers with zeros.

Subtract from Numbers That Contain Zeros 10.7

Explore and Grow

Find each difference.

```
  4 0 0        3 9 9
– 1 7 8      – 1 7 7
```

Structure How are the problems the same? How are they different? Which problem can you solve without regrouping?

_____
_____
_____
_____

Think and Grow

First, regroup 5 hundreds and 0 tens as 4 hundreds and 10 tens.

Next, regroup 10 tens and 0 ones as 9 tens and 10 ones. Then subtract.

500 − 283 = ?

One Way: Regroup.

$$\begin{array}{r} \overset{4\ 10}{\cancel{5}\ \cancel{0}\ 0} \\ -\ 2\ 8\ 3 \\ \hline \end{array} \rightarrow \begin{array}{r} \overset{\ \ \ \ 9}{\overset{4\ \cancel{10}\ 10}{\cancel{5}\ \cancel{0}\ \cancel{0}}} \\ -\ 2\ 8\ 3 \\ \hline \end{array} \rightarrow \begin{array}{r} \overset{\ \ \ \ 9}{\overset{4\ \cancel{10}\ 10}{\cancel{5}\ \cancel{0}\ \cancel{0}}} \\ -\ 2\ 8\ 3 \\ \hline 2\ 1\ 7 \end{array}$$

Another Way: Use compensation.

500 − 283 = ?

⊖ __1__   ⊖ __1__

__499__ − __282__ = ?

$$\begin{array}{r} 4\ 9\ 9 \\ -\ 2\ 8\ 2 \\ \hline 2\ 1\ 7 \end{array}$$

Show and Grow — I can do it!

Use regrouping or compensation to subtract.

1. 300 − 139 = ____

2. 402 − 265 = ____

3. 800 − 547 = ____

4. 910 − 252 = ____

498   four hundred ninety-eight

Name _____

Apply and Grow: Practice

Use regrouping or compensation to subtract.

5. 310 − 186 = ____

6. 620 − 458 = ____

7. 906 − 729 = ____

8. 807 − 389 = ____

9. 503 − 296 = ____

10. 301 − 282 = ____

11. 400 − 197 = ____

12. 600 − 289 = ____

13. **Structure** Show two ways to find 500 − 314.

Think and Grow: Modeling Real Life

There are 400 paper lanterns. 279 of them are let go. How many paper lanterns are left?

Subtraction equation:

_____ paper lanterns

Show and Grow — I can think deeper!

14. There are 803 fans at a stadium. 226 of them leave. How many fans are left?

_____ fans

15. **DIG DEEPER!** A florist plants 600 flowers. The table shows how many have bloomed. How many flowers have *not* bloomed yet?

Month	Number of Blooms
May	296
June	232

_____ flowers

Name _____

Practice 10.7

Learning Target: Subtract from three-digit numbers with zeros.

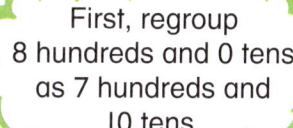
First, regroup 8 hundreds and 0 tens as 7 hundreds and 10 tens.

Next, regroup 10 tens and 0 ones as 9 tens and 10 ones. Then subtract.

$800 - 517 = ?$

One Way: Regroup.

```
  7 10            9            9
  8 0 0    →    7 10 10   →   7 10 10
            →    8 0 0    →   8 0 0
- 5 1 7       - 5 1 7       - 5 1 7
                              2 8 3
```

Another Way: Use compensation.

$800 \quad - \quad 517 \quad = ?$

⊖ __1__   ⊖ __1__   →   7 9 9
                           − 5 1 6
__799__ − __516__ = ?   2 8 3

Use regrouping or compensation to subtract.

1. $700 - 465 =$ ____

2. $302 - 176 =$ ____

3. $910 - 186 =$ ____

4. $800 - 691 =$ ____

5. **Communicate Clearly** Explain why you might want to use compensation to subtract. Give an example.

   _____

   _____

6. **Modeling Real Life** There are 300 coins on a desk. 178 fall off. How many coins are left on the desk?

   _____ coins

7. **DIG DEEPER!** There are 500 students in a school. How many students are absent?

School Attendance	
Boys	234
Girls	178

   _____ students

   Review & Refresh

   8. 29 + 34 = _____
   9. 46 + 13 = _____

Name _____

Use Addition to Subtract 10.8

Learning Target: Use addition to subtract on an open number line.

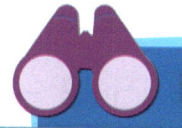 **Explore and Grow**

Use the number lines to solve.

445 − 220 = _____

⟵——————————————⟶

220 + _____ = 445

⟵——————————————⟶

MP Use a Similar Problem How are the equations the same? How are they different?

_____

_____

_____

Chapter 10 | Lesson 8   five hundred three 503

Think and Grow

Start at 375. Add 100 to get to 475. Continue adding until you reach 513.

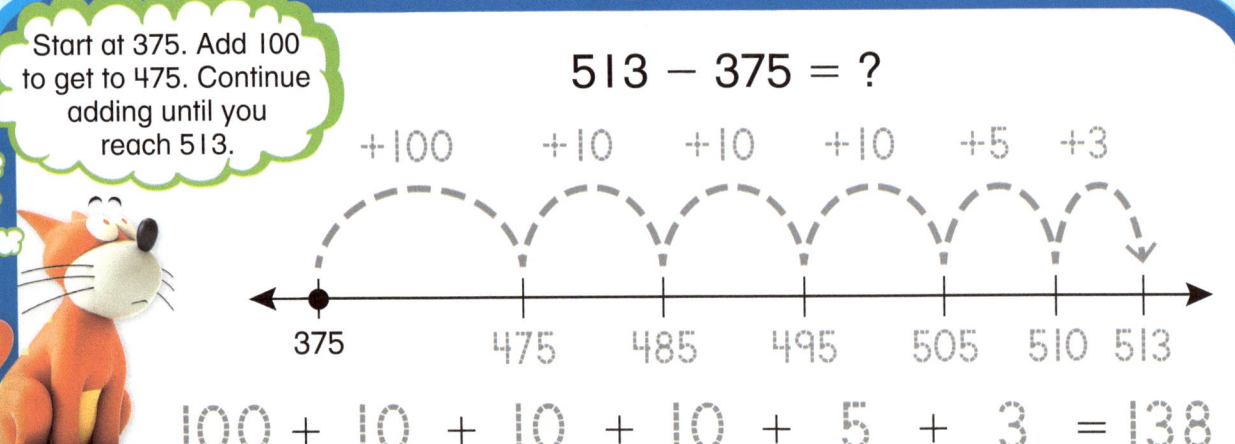

513 − 375 = ?

_100_ + _10_ + _10_ + _10_ + _5_ + _3_ = _138_

513 − 375 = _138_   Check:

```
  1 1
  3 7 5
+ 1 3 8
-------
  5 1 3  ✓
```

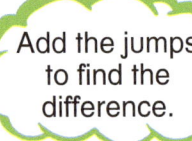

Add the jumps to find the difference.

Show and Grow — I can do it!

Add to find the difference. Check your answer.

1. 488 − 137 = _____

137

+ _____

2. 792 − 446 = _____

+ _____

Name _____

 **Apply and Grow: Practice**

Add to find the difference. Check your answer.

3. 521 − 364 = _____

   + _____

4. 856 − 213 = _____

   + _____

5. 492 − 137 = _____

   + _____

6. **Structure** Write the equation shown by the number line.

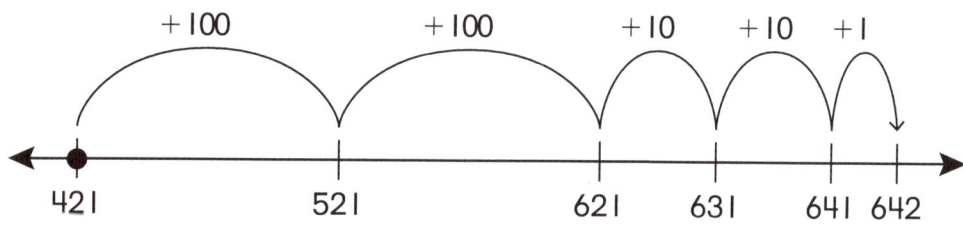

_____ − _____ = _____

Chapter 10 | Lesson 8   five hundred five   505

Think and Grow: Modeling Real Life

A machine has some bouncy balls. 115 are sold. There are 227 left. How many bouncy balls were there to start?

Equation:

Model:

Check:

_____

_____ bouncy balls

Show and Grow   I can think deeper!

7. There are some fans at a baseball game. 148 leave early. There are 182 left. How many fans were at the baseball game?

_____ fans

8. **DIG DEEPER!** Your school collects 518 cans for a food drive. Your class collects 142 cans. Another class collects 204. How many cans did the rest of the classes collect?

_____ cans

506   five hundred six

Name _____

Practice 10.8

Learning Target: Use addition to subtract on an open number line.

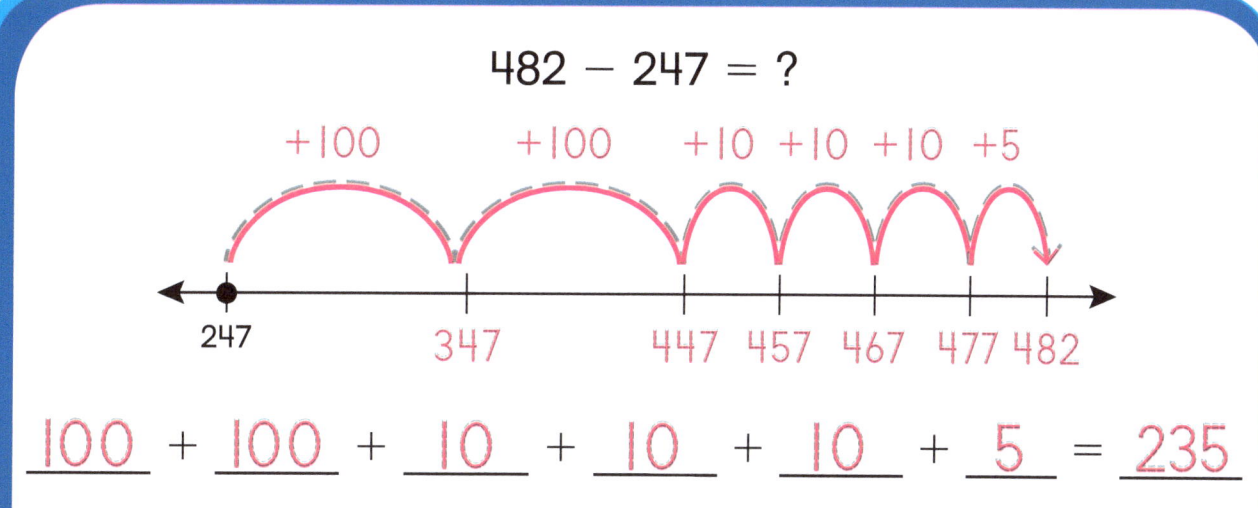

$482 - 247 = ?$

$\underline{100} + \underline{100} + \underline{10} + \underline{10} + \underline{10} + \underline{5} = \underline{235}$

$482 - 247 = \underline{235}$

Check:

Add to find the difference. Check your answer.

1. $721 - 314 = \underline{}$

2. $654 - 334 = \underline{}$

Chapter 10 | Lesson 8   five hundred seven   507

3. **YOU BE THE TEACHER** Descartes adds to find 400 − 279. Is he correct? Explain.

   400 − 279 = 121

   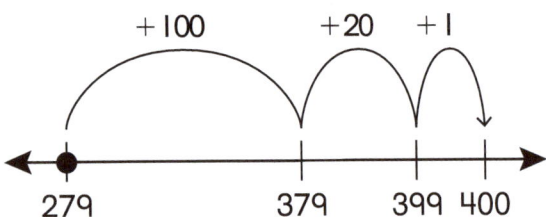

   _____

   _____

   _____

4. **Modeling Real Life** There are some people in a national park. 124 of them leave. There are 535 people left. How many people were in the park to start?

   _____ people

5. **DIG DEEPER!** You are making a costume. You have 514 silver and gold jewels in all. You sew 220 silver jewels and 156 gold jewels on your costume. How many jewels do you have left?

   _____ jewels

Review & Refresh

6.

   _____ flat surfaces

   _____ vertices

   _____ edges

7.

   _____ flat surfaces

   _____ vertices

   _____ edges

Name _____

Learning Target: Choose and explain a strategy to subtract.

Explain Subtraction Strategies

 **Explore and Grow**

Use two different strategies to find 474 − 119.

Subtraction Strategies
Subtract on an Open Number Line
Compensation
Use Models to Subtract
Regrouping

Communicate Clearly Explain why you chose one of your strategies.

_____

_____

_____

Chapter 10 | Lesson 9   five hundred nine   509

Think and Grow

Think: Why do these strategies work?

453 − 134 = ?

Think: Are there any other strategies you can use?

One Way: Use a number line.

Another Way: Use place value.

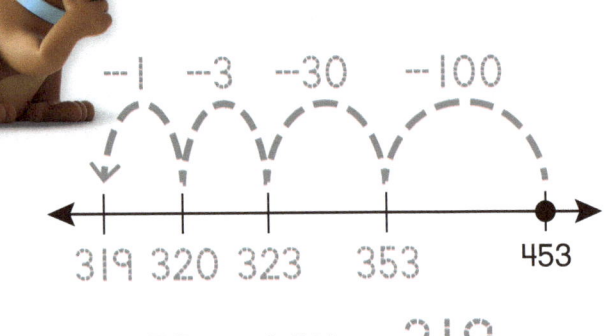

453 − 134 = 319

Show and Grow   I can do it!

Choose any strategy to solve. Explain how you solved.

1. 477 − 224 = _____

   _____

   _____

2. 686 − 397 = _____

   _____

   _____

510   five hundred ten

Name _____

 **Apply and Grow: Practice**

Choose any strategy to solve. Explain how you solved.

3. 502 − 321 = _____

_____

_____

4. 900 − 756 = _____

_____

_____

5. **Reasoning** Your friend solves a subtraction problem. Write the problem your friend solves. Explain what strategy was used to solve.

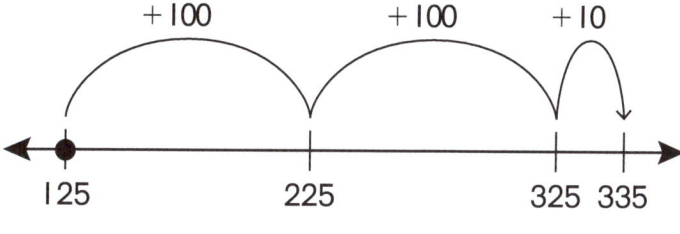

_____ − _____ = _____

_____

_____

Chapter 10 | Lesson 9   five hundred eleven   511

Think and Grow: Modeling Real Life

Choose any strategy to solve. Explain how you solved.

There are 941 songs in a music library. 365 of them are pop songs. 189 are rock songs. How many songs are *not* pop songs?

Subtraction equation:

_____ songs

_____

_____

Show and Grow   I can think deeper!

Choose any strategy to solve. Explain how you solved.

6. There are 743 penguins in a colony. 235 are in the water. 159 are in caves. How many penguins are *not* in the water?

_____ penguins

_____

_____

Name _____

Practice 10.9

Learning Target: Choose and explain a strategy to subtract.

$628 - 307 = ?$

One Way: Use compensation.

$628 - 307 = ?$
         ↓ -7
$628 - 300 = 328$
$628 - 307 = 321$ ↓ -7

Another Way: Use place value.

```
  6 | 2 | 8
- 3 | 0 | 7
  3 | 2 | 1
```

Choose any strategy to solve. Explain how you solved.

1. $408 - 196 =$ _____

   _____

   _____

2. $723 - 515 =$ _____

   _____

   _____

Chapter 10 | Lesson 9   five hundred thirteen   513

3. **DIG DEEPER!** Newton wants to use mental math to find 452 − 239. Is this a good strategy for him to use? Explain.

   _____

   _____

4. **Modeling Real Life** 767 people work at a store. 205 are cashiers. 314 stock shelves. How many people are *not* cashiers? Explain.

   _____ people

   _____

   _____

5. **Modeling Real Life** You have a pack of 900 craft sticks. You use 638 for a project. Your friend uses 127. How many craft sticks were *not* used? Explain.

   _____ craft sticks

   _____

   _____

Review & Refresh

6. Circle the longer object.

Name _____

Performance Task 10

The table shows the number of laps that four cars complete in a racing season.

Car	Laps
Red	300
Yellow	274
Green	234
Blue	217

1. How many fewer laps does the blue car complete than the yellow car?

    _____ laps

2. How many more laps does the red car complete than the green car?

    _____ laps

3. The purple car completes 500 laps and the orange car completes 250 laps. Order the cars from the greatest number of laps to the least number of laps.

    _____, _____, _____, _____, _____, _____

4. How many cars complete an even number of laps?

    _____ cars

5. The red and yellow cars are on Team Go Fast. The green and blue cars are on Team Speed. Which team completes more laps? How many more laps?

    Team Go Fast   Team Speed

    _____ more laps

Chapter 10   five hundred fifteen   515

Greatest and Least

To Play: Roll a die 3 times and record each number. Use the numbers to write the greatest and the least three-digit numbers. Find the difference and record your answer.

1st Roll	2nd Roll	3rd Roll	Greatest Number	Least Number	Difference

Name _____

Chapter Practice 10

10.1 Subtract 10 and 100

1. 230 − 10 = _____

2. 956 − 10 = _____

3. 597 − 100 = _____

4. 384 − 100 = _____

5. 705 − 10 = _____

6. 157 − 100 = _____

10.2 Use a Number Line to Subtract Hundreds and Tens

7. 481 − 250 = _____

8. **Modeling Real Life** 325 crackers come in a box. You set out 160 for a party. How many crackers are left in the box?

_____ crackers

Use a Number Line to Subtract Three-Digit Numbers

9. 604 − 97 = _____

10. **MP Structure** Write the equation shown by the number line.

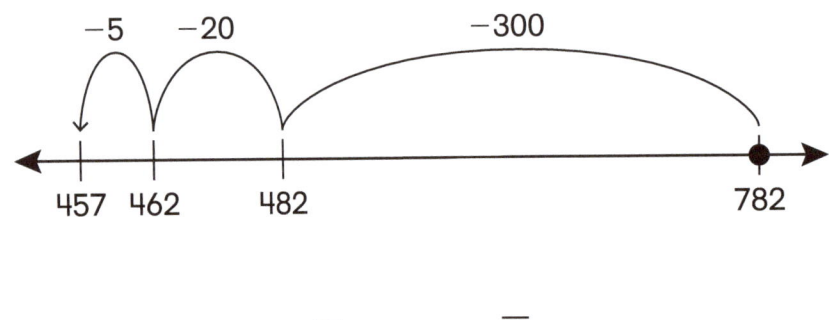

_____ − _____ = _____

Use Compensation to Subtract Three-Digit Numbers

Use compensation to subtract.

11. 603 − 497 = ?
    ↓ ☐

    603 − ___ = ___
                  ↓ ☐
    603 − 497 = ___

12. 852 − 115 = ?
    ↓ ☐

    852 − ___ = ___
                  ↓ ☐
    852 − 115 = ___

518   five hundred eighteen

10.5 Use Models to Subtract Three-Digit Numbers

13. 992 − 645 = ?

Hundreds	Tens	Ones
9	9	2
− 6	4	5

10.6 Subtract Three-Digit Numbers

14.
```
  2 4 0
−   1 6 3
```

15.
```
  9 5 7
−   4 8 9
```

16.
```
  5 1 6
−   1 4 5
```

17. **Modeling Real Life** There are 420 T-shirts and 120 pairs of shorts at a store. 135 T-shirts are sold. How many T-shirts are left?

_____ T-shirts

10.7 Subtract from Numbers that Contain Zeros

18. 600 − 365 = _____

19. 402 − 195 = _____

10.8 Use Addition to Subtract

Add to find the difference. Check your answer.

20. 213 − 102 = _____

+ _____
_____

21. 564 − 317 = _____

+ _____
_____

10.9 Explain Subtraction Strategies

Choose any strategy to solve. Explain how you solved.

22. 573 − 309 = _____

_____

_____

_____

11 Measure and Estimate Lengths

- What kind of seeds do people plant?
- Is the garden sign 2 inches long or 2 feet long? How do you know?

Chapter Learning Target:
Understand measurement.

Chapter Success Criteria:
- I can define length.
- I can explain how to use a ruler to measure objects.
- I can compare the measurements of different objects.
- I can measure objects.

Name _____

11 Vocabulary

Review Words
height
length

Organize It

Use the review words to complete the graphic organizer.

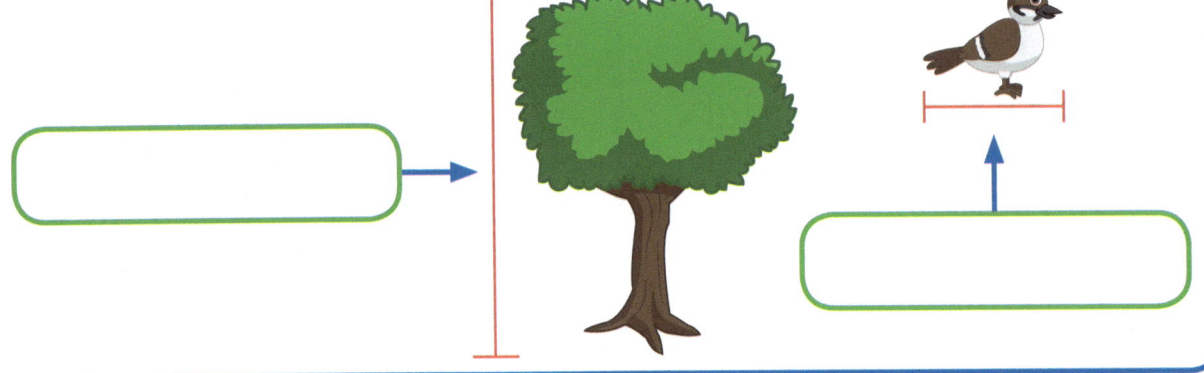

Define It

Use your vocabulary cards to match.

1. centimeter

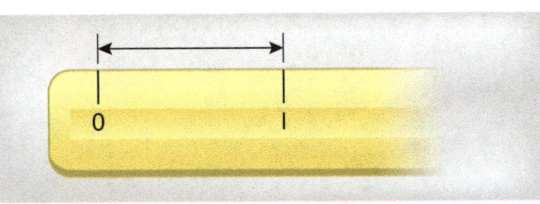

2. inch

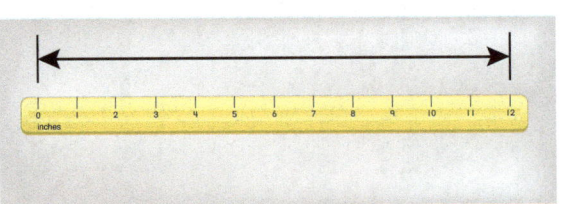

3. foot

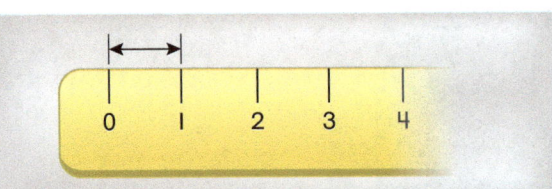

Chapter 11 Vocabulary Cards

centimeter	estimate
foot	inch
meter	yard

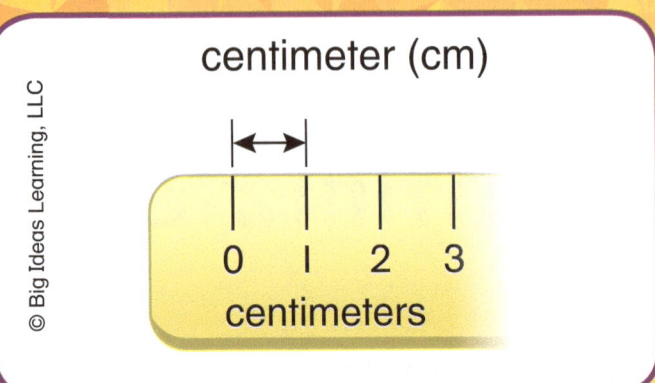
centimeter (cm)

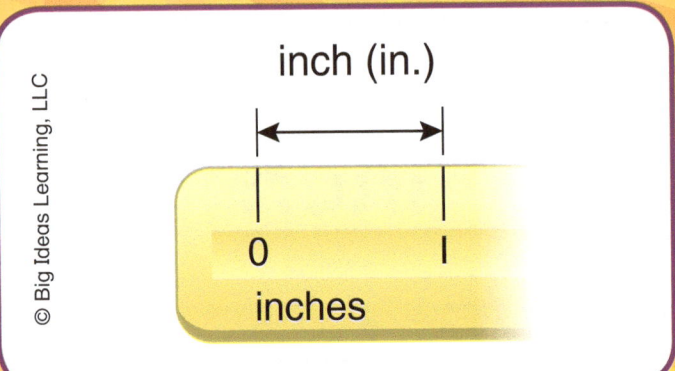
inch (in.)

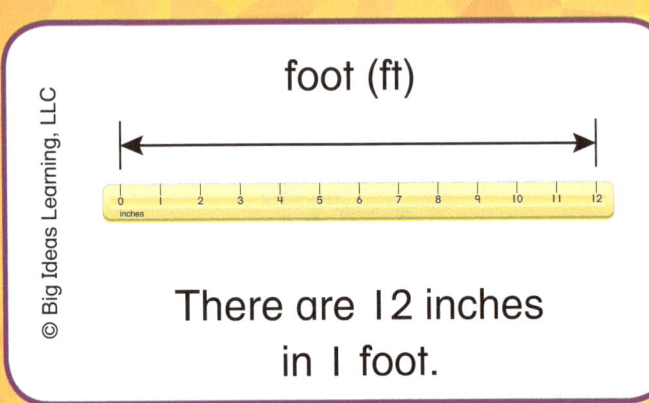
foot (ft)

There are 12 inches in 1 foot.

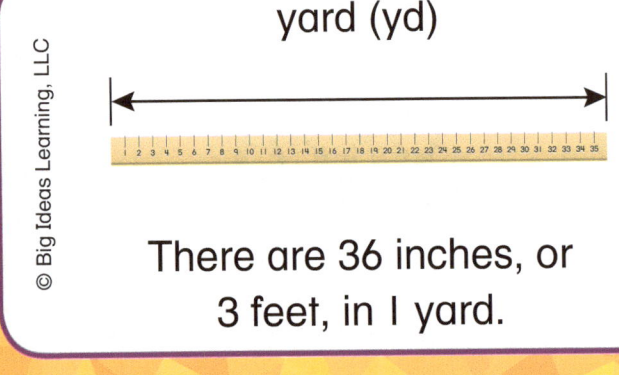
yard (yd)

There are 36 inches, or 3 feet, in 1 yard.

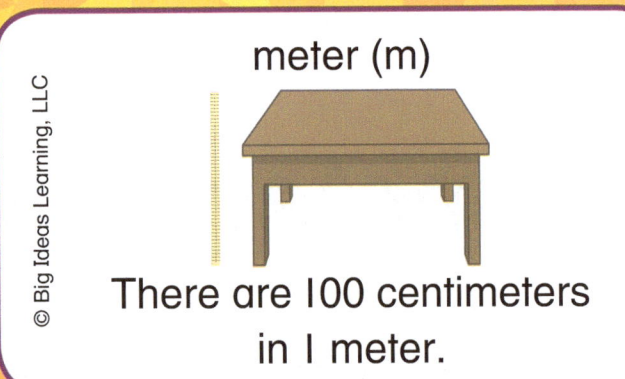
meter (m)

There are 100 centimeters in 1 meter.

Name _____

Learning Target: Measure the length of an object in centimeters.

Measure Lengths in Centimeters 11.1

Explore and Grow

Use a centimeter cube to find the length of each string.

_____ centimeters

_____ centimeters

_____ centimeters

Communicate Clearly Explain how you measured.

_____

_____

_____

Chapter 11 | Lesson 1   five hundred twenty-three   523

Think and Grow

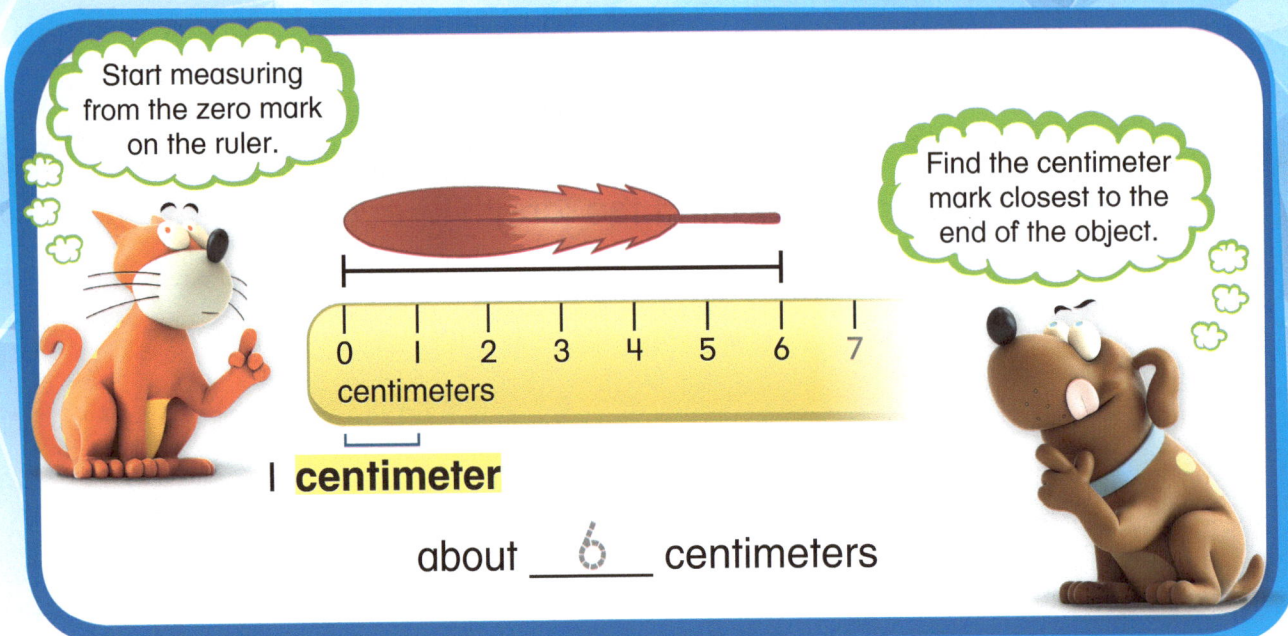

about __6__ centimeters

Show and Grow I can do it!

Measure.

1.  about _____ centimeters

2.  about _____ centimeters

3. 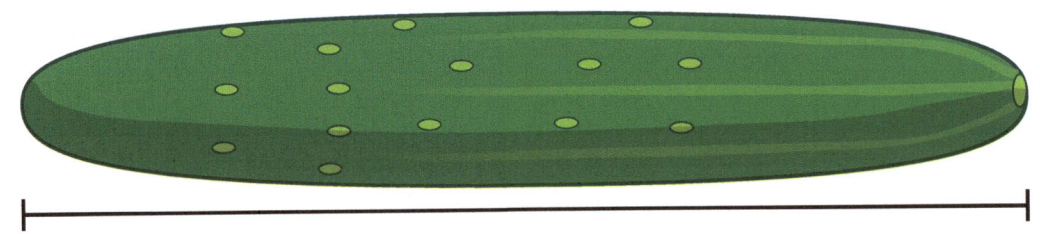 about _____ centimeters

Name _____

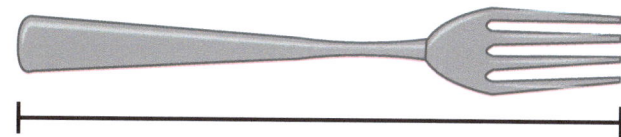

Measure.

4. ![fork with measurement bar]

about _____ centimeters

5. ![screw with measurement bar]

about _____ centimeters

6. Draw a pencil that is about 9 centimeters long.

7. **YOU BE THE TEACHER** Newton says the ribbon is about 14 centimeters long. Is he correct? Explain.

_____

_____

Chapter 11 | Lesson 1

Think and Grow: Modeling Real Life

Will the hammer fit inside a toolbox that is 40 centimeters long? Explain.

Circle: Yes   No

_____

_____

Show and Grow   I can think deeper!

8. Will the sunglasses fit inside a case that is 10 centimeters long? Explain.

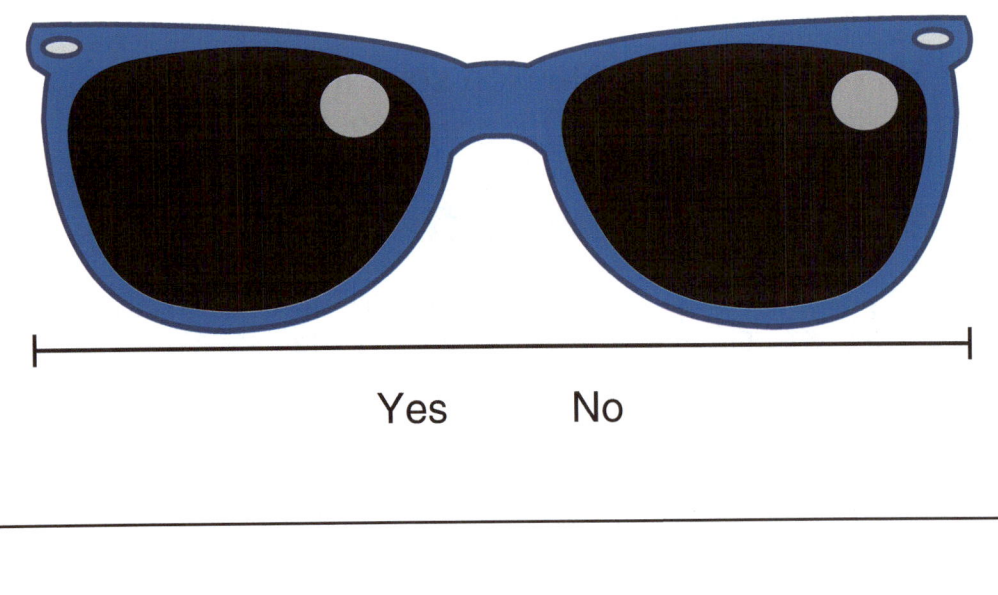

Yes   No

_____

_____

Name _____

Practice

Learning Target: Measure the length of an object in centimeters.

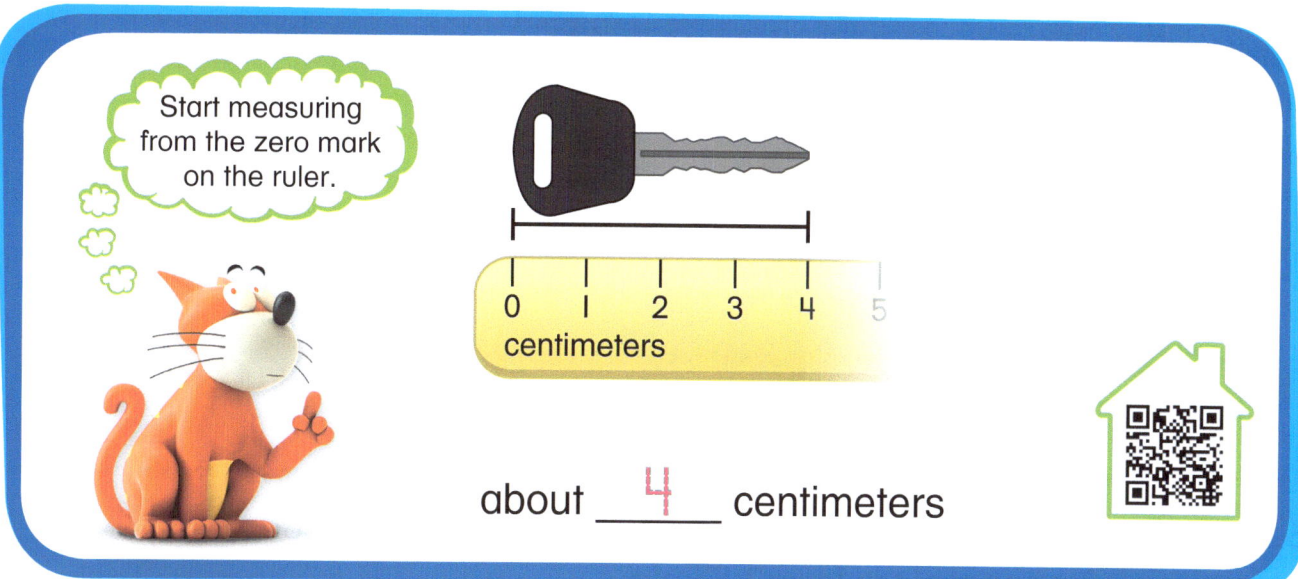

about __4__ centimeters

Measure.

1.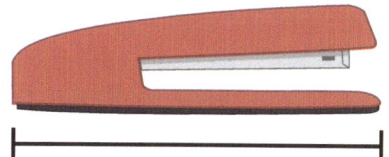

about _____ centimeters

2.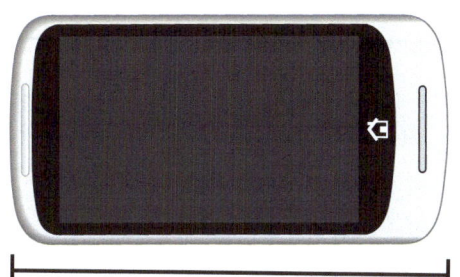

about _____ centimeters

3.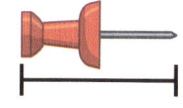

about _____ centimeters

4.

about _____ centimeters

Chapter 11 | Lesson 1

five hundred twenty-seven 527

5. **Precision** Which crayon is shorter than 8 centimeters?

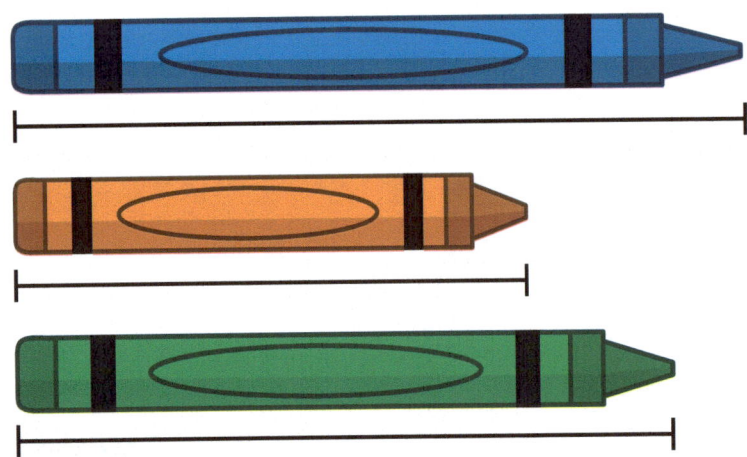

6. **Modeling Real Life** Will the pen fit inside a pouch that is 18 centimeters long? Explain.

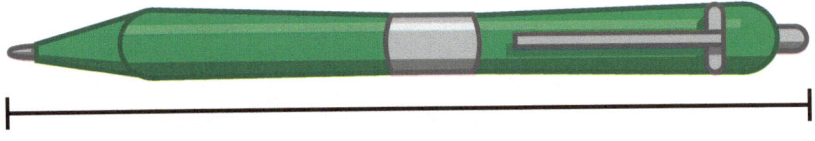

Yes   No   _____

7. **DIG DEEPER!** Draw a pencil that is 2 centimeters longer than the pen in Exercise 6. Will it fit inside the pouch?

Yes   No

Review & Refresh

8.
```
  1 7
+ 3 8
-----
```

9.
```
  6 3
+ 2 7
-----
```

10.
```
  4 2
+ 5 9
-----
```

Name _____

Learning Target: Measure the length of an object in centimeters or meters.

Measure Objects Using Metric Length Units 11.2

Explore and Grow

Which real-life objects are shorter than a centimeter ruler?

Chapter 11 | Lesson 2

five hundred twenty-nine 529

Think and Grow

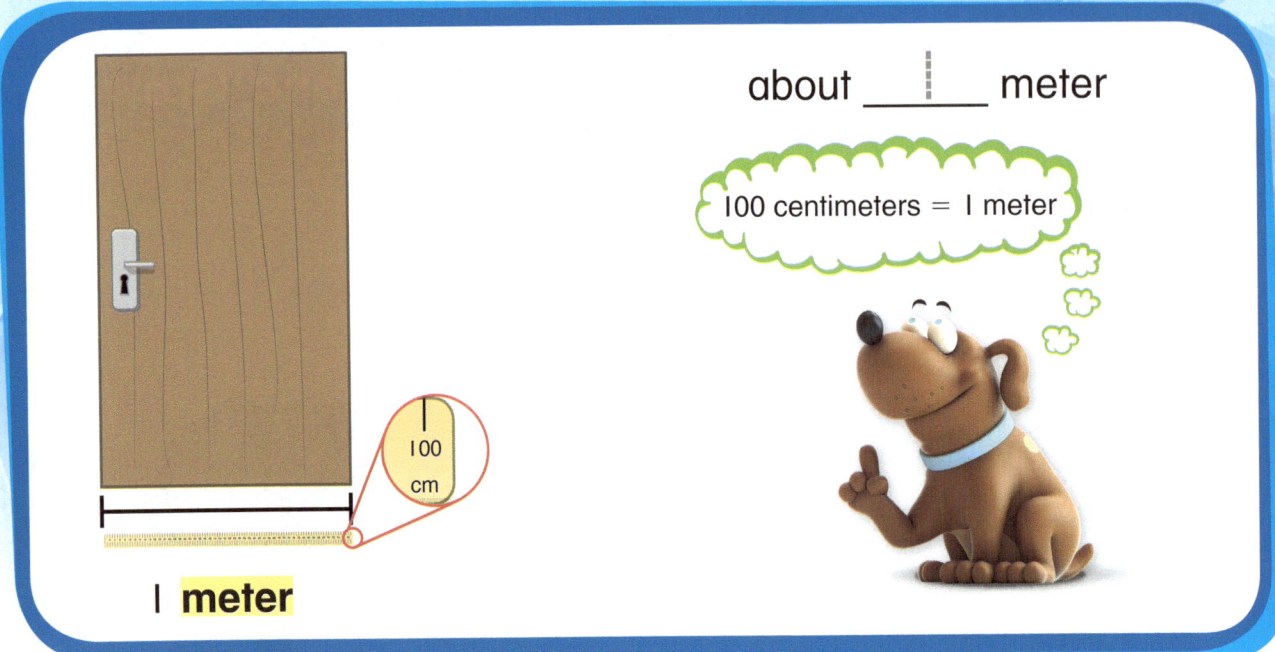

about _____ meter

100 centimeters = 1 meter

1 **meter**

Show and Grow   I can do it!

Find and measure the object shown in your classroom.

1.

   about _____ meters

2.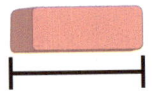

   about _____ centimeters

3.

   about _____ meters

Name _____

✓ Apply and Grow: Practice

Find and measure the object shown in your classroom.

4.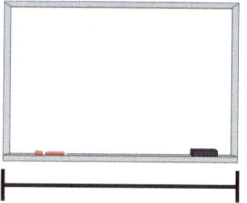

   about _____ meters

5.

   about _____ centimeters

6.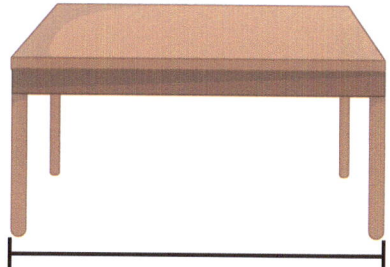

   about _____ meters

7.

   about _____ centimeters

8. **Choose Tools** Would you measure the length of a bus with a centimeter ruler or a meter stick? Why?

   _____

   _____

Chapter 11 | Lesson 2   five hundred thirty-one   531

Think and Grow: Modeling Real Life

Your friend says a car has a length of about 4. Is the car about 4 meters long or about 4 centimeters long? Explain.

The car is about 4 _____ long.

Show and Grow   I can think deeper!

9. Your friend says a shoe has a length of about 12. Is the shoe about 12 centimeters long or about 12 meters long? Explain.

The shoe is about 12 _____ long.

10. **DIG DEEPER!** Your friend places 2 of the same real objects end to end. Together, they have a length of about 18 centimeters. Which object did your friend use? Explain.

  MATHEMATICS

Name _____

Practice

Learning Target: Measure the length of an object in centimeters or meters.

about __1__ meter

Find and measure the object.

1.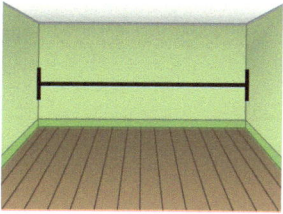

about _____ meters

2.

about _____ centimeters

3.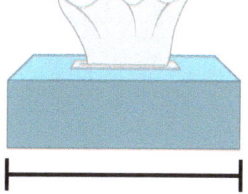

about _____ centimeters

4.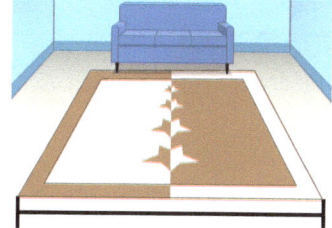

about _____ meters

Chapter 11 | Lesson 2

five hundred thirty-three 533

5. **Precision** Complete the sentences using *centimeters* or *meters*.

A window is about 2 _____ long.

A finger is about 8 _____ long.

A zucchini is about 12 _____ long.

An airplane is about 20 _____ long.

6. **Modeling Real Life** Your friend says that the length of a soccer field is about 91. Is the soccer field about 91 centimeters long or about 91 meters long? Explain.

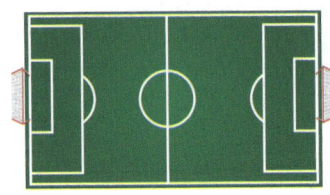

The soccer field is about 91 _____ long.

_____

_____

7. **DIG DEEPER!** Order the lengths from shortest to longest.

| 200 centimeters | 3 centimeters | 1 meter |

_____ , _____ , _____

Review & Refresh

8. $3 + 7 = \underline{} + 3$

9. $5 + 4 = 4 + \underline{}$

10. $6 + 0 = \underline{} + 6$

11. $1 + 2 = 2 + \underline{}$

Name _____

Estimate Lengths in Metric Units 11.3

Learning Target: Estimate the length of an object in centimeters or meters.

Find an object that is shorter than the string.

———————————————

13 centimeters

Without using a ruler, tell how long you think the object is.

_____ centimeters

Explain.

_____
_____
_____
_____
_____

Chapter 11 | Lesson 3 five hundred thirty-five **535**

Think and Grow

The yarn is about 11 centimeters long. What is the best estimate of the length of the push pin?

7 centimeters

(2 centimeters)

13 centimeters

Use the length of the object you know to **estimate** the length of the other object.

The push pin is much shorter than the yarn. So, 7 centimeters is not a good estimate.

Show and Grow — I can do it!

1. The chalk is about 8 centimeters long. What is the best estimate of the length of the toothpick?

6 centimeters

4 centimeters

9 centimeters

2. The fishing pole is about 1 meter long. What is the best estimate of the length of the alligator?

3 meters

1 meter

2 meters

Name _____

Apply and Grow: Practice

3. The hover board is about 1 meter long. What is the best estimate of the length of the surfboard?

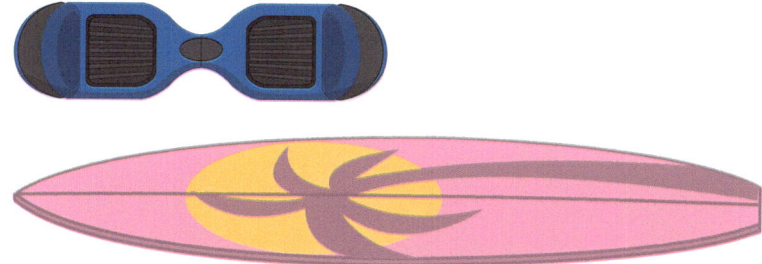

4 meters

2 meters

10 meters

4. The pineapple is about 25 centimeters long. What is the best estimate of the length of the asparagus?

3 centimeters

20 centimeters

10 centimeters

5. What is the best estimate of the length of a piece of notebook paper?

21 centimeters   1 meter

5 centimeters

6. What is the best estimate of the height of a traffic light?

1 meter   5 meters

30 centimeters

7. Precision Match.

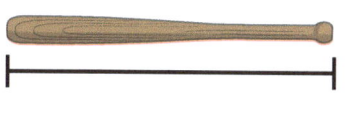  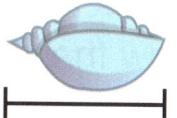 

about
1 meter

about
5 centimeters

about
10 meters

about
50 centimeters

Chapter 11 | Lesson 3   five hundred thirty-seven   537

Think and Grow: Modeling Real Life

The leaf is about 8 centimeters long. Draw a tree branch that is about 16 centimeters long.

Show and Grow   I can think deeper!

8. The piece of celery is about 10 centimeters long. Draw a carrot that is about 5 centimeters long.

9. **DIG DEEPER!** Each bead is about 2 centimeters long. Draw a rectangular bead that is about 3 centimeters long.

Justify a Result How did you use the length of the given beads to draw the rectangular bead?

_____

_____

Name _____

Practice 11.3

Learning Target: Estimate the length of an object in centimeters or meters.

The key is about 5 centimeters long. What is the best estimate of the length of the bracelet?

(15 centimeters)

30 centimeters

3 centimeters

1. The swimming pool is about 12 meters long. What is the best estimate of the length of the raft?

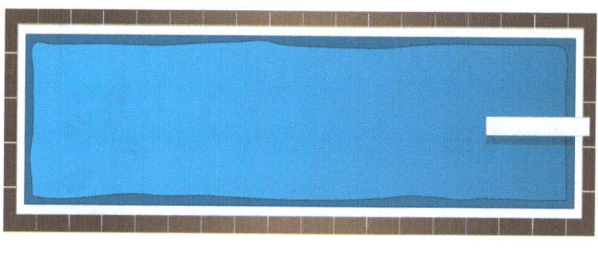

14 meters

2 meters

8 meters

2. What is the best estimate of the height of a tulip?

14 centimeters

4 meters

3 centimeters

3. What is the best estimate of the height of a giraffe?

50 meters

6 meters

10 centimeters

Chapter 11 | Lesson 3

4. **Does It Make Sense?** Newton says the best estimate for the height of a skyscraper is 4 meters. Do you agree? Explain.

_____

_____

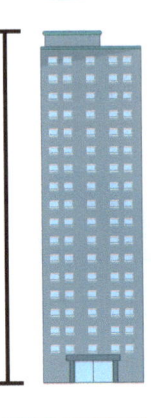

5. **Modeling Real Life** A granola bar is about 9 centimeters long. Draw its wrapper that is about 12 cm long.

6. **DIG DEEPER!** About how much taller is the tomato plant than the student?

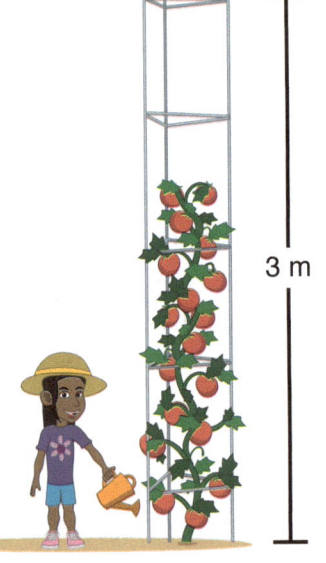

3 m

Review & Refresh

Is the equation true or false?

7. $13 - 5 \stackrel{?}{=} 15 - 7$

   ___ $\stackrel{?}{=}$ ___

   True   False

8. $3 + 6 \stackrel{?}{=} 11 - 3$

   ___ $\stackrel{?}{=}$ ___

   True   False

Name _____

Learning Target: Measure the length of an object in inches.

Measure Lengths in Inches 11.4

Use an inch tile to find the length of each string.

_____ inches

_____ inches

_____ inches

Communicate Clearly Explain how you measured.

_____

_____

Chapter 11 | Lesson 4

Think and Grow

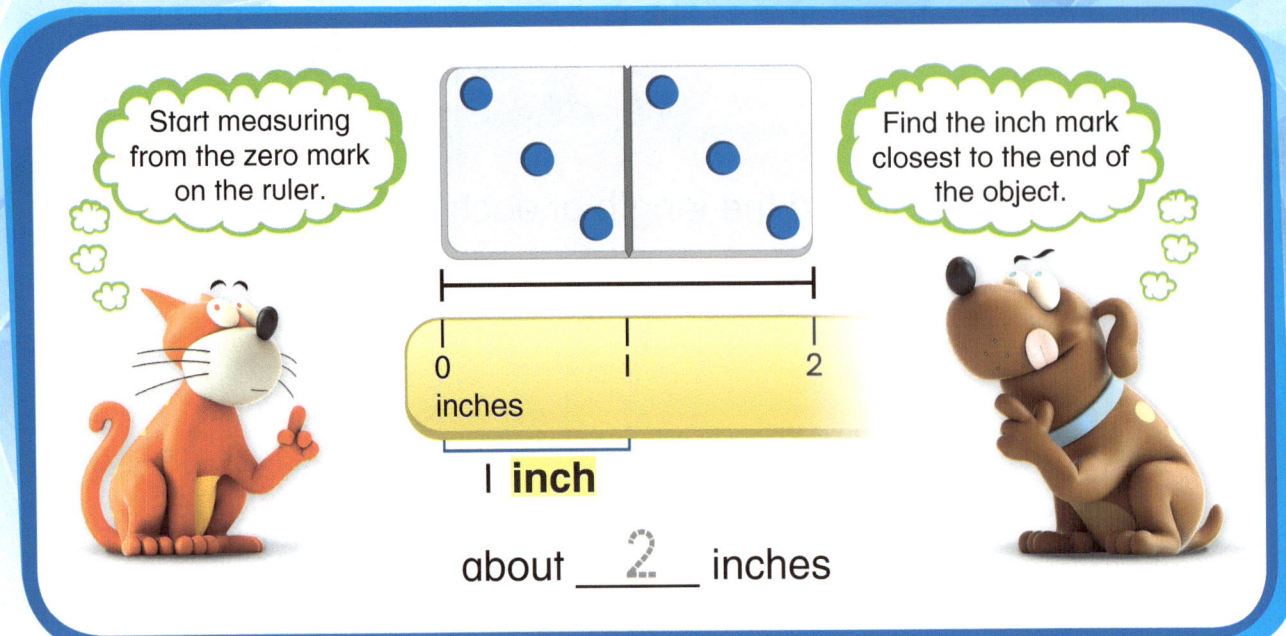

about __2__ inches

Show and Grow   I can do it!

Measure.

1.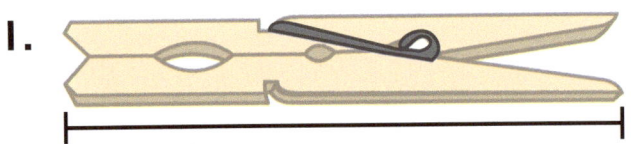

   about _____ inches

2.

   about _____ inch

3.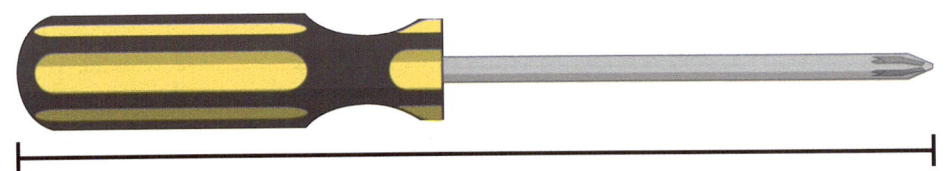

   about _____ inches

Name _____

✓ Apply and Grow: Practice

Measure.

4.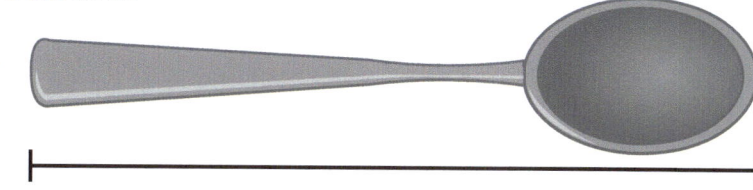

about _____ inches

5.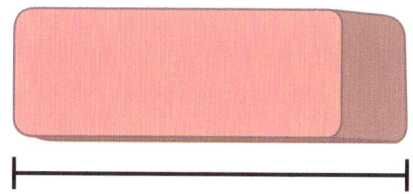

about _____ inches

6. Draw a crayon that is about 4 inches long.

7. **YOU BE THE TEACHER** Your friend says the watch is about 6 inches long. Is your friend correct? Explain.

_____

_____

Chapter 11 | Lesson 4   five hundred forty-three   543

Think and Grow: Modeling Real Life

Will the toothbrush fit inside a case that is 4 inches long? Explain.

Circle: Yes   No

_____

_____

Show and Grow   I can think deeper!

8. Will the colored pencil fit inside a pencil box that is 8 inches long? Explain.

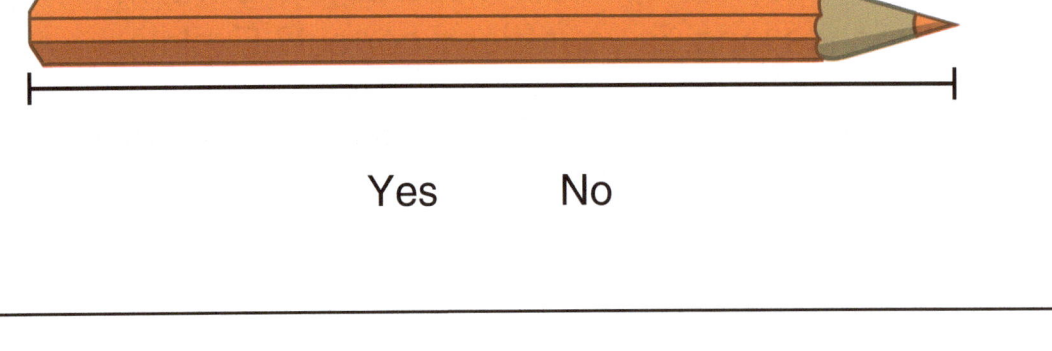

Yes   No

_____

_____

Name _____

Practice

Learning Target: Measure the length of an object in inches.

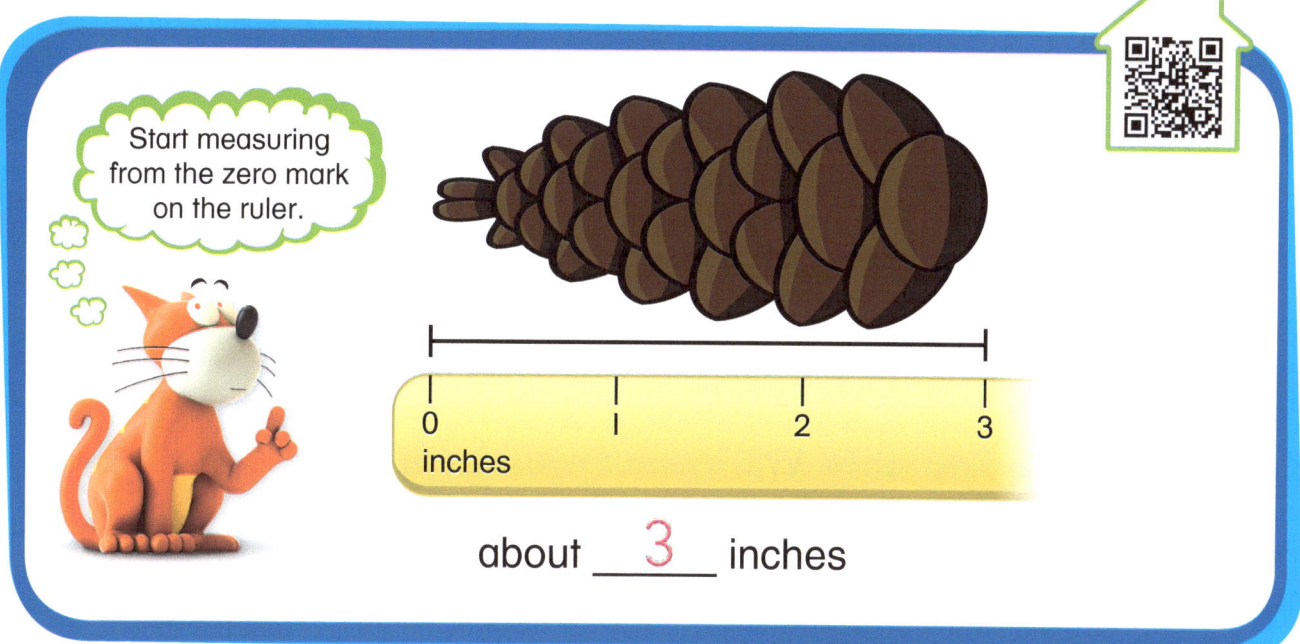

about __3__ inches

Measure.

1.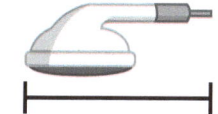

    about _____ inch

2.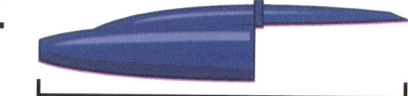

    about _____ inches

3.

    about _____ inches

Chapter 11 | Lesson 4

4. **DIG DEEPER!** A foam dart is longer than 4 inches, but shorter than 6 inches. Draw the foam dart.

5. **Modeling Real Life** Will the screwdriver fit inside a case that is 5 inches long? Explain.

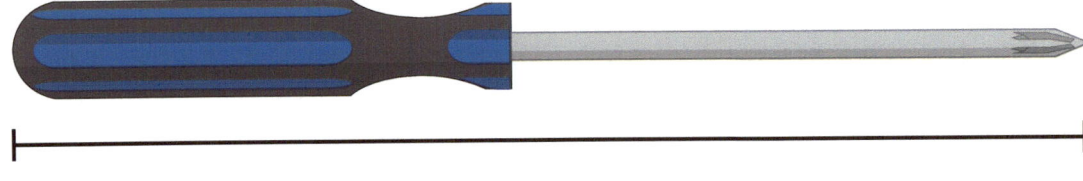

Yes   No

_____

_____

Review & Refresh

6. Write how many tens. Circle groups of 10 tens. Write how many hundreds. Then write the number.

   _____ tens   _____ hundreds   _____

Name _____

Learning Target: Use an inch ruler, yard stick, or measuring tape to measure an object in inches, feet, or yards.

Measure Objects Using Customary Length Units 11.5

Explore and Grow

Which real-life objects are longer than an inch ruler?

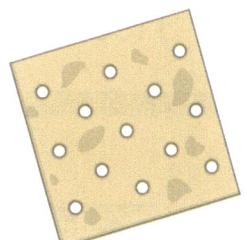

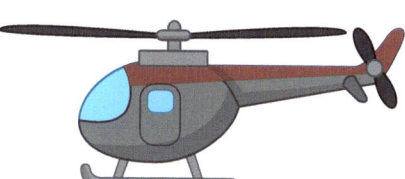

Chapter 11 | Lesson 5

Think and Grow

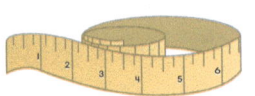

Use an inch ruler to measure shorter lengths. There are 12 inches in 1 **foot**.

Use a yardstick to measure greater lengths. There are 36 inches, or 3 feet, in 1 **yard**.

Use a measuring tape to measure lengths that are not straight or flat.

Show and Grow   I can do it!

Find the object shown in your classroom. Choose an inch ruler, a yardstick, or a measuring tape to measure the object. Then measure.

1.

   Tool: _____

   Length: about _____

2.

   Tool: _____

   Length: about _____

3.

   Tool: _____

   Length: about _____

Name _____

✓ Apply and Grow: Practice

Find the object shown in your classroom. Choose an inch ruler, a yardstick, or a measuring tape to measure the object. Then measure.

4.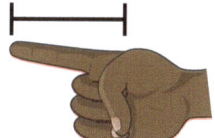

   Tool: _____

   Length: about _____

5.

   Tool: _____

   Length: about _____

6. Find and measure an object using a measuring tape.

   Object: _____

   Length: about _____

7. Find and measure an object using an inch ruler.

   Object: _____

   Length: about _____

8. **Choose Tools** Would you measure the length of the playground with an inch ruler or a yardstick? Explain.

   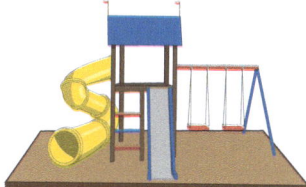

   _____

   _____

Chapter 11 | Lesson 5   five hundred forty-nine   549

Think and Grow: Modeling Real Life

Your friend says her height is about 4. Is she about 4 inches tall, about 4 feet tall, or about 4 yards tall? Explain.

She is about 4 _____ tall.

_____

_____

Show and Grow   I can think deeper!

9. Your friend says the length of a baseball bat is about 1. Is the bat about 1 inch long, about 1 foot long, or about 1 yard long? Explain.

    The bat is about 1 _____ long.

    _____

    _____

10. Your friend says the length around an orange is about 9. Is the length about 9 inches long, about 9 feet long, or about 9 yards long? Explain.

    The length is about 9 _____ long.

    _____

    _____

550   five hundred fifty

Name _____

Practice 11.5

Learning Target: Use an inch ruler, yard stick, or measuring tape to measure object in inches, feet, or yards.

 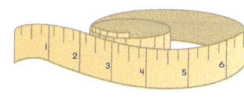

Use an inch ruler to measure shorter lengths. There are 12 inches in 1 foot.

Use a yardstick to measure greater lengths. There are 36 inches, or 3 feet, in 1 yard.

Use a measuring tape to measure lengths that are not straight or flat.

Find the object shown. Choose an inch ruler, a yardstick, or a measuring tape to measure the object. Then measure.

1.

   Tool: _____

   Length: about _____

2.

   Tool: _____

   Length: about _____

3. Find and measure an object using an inch ruler.

   Object: _____

   Length: about _____

4. Find and measure an object using a yard stick.

   Object: _____

   Length: about _____

Chapter 11 | Lesson 5   five hundred fifty-one   551

5. **YOU BE THE TEACHER** Descartes says the best tool to measure the length around a basketball is an inch ruler. Is he correct? Explain.

   _____

   _____

6. **Modeling Real Life** Your friend says that the length of a toothbrush is about 8. Is the toothbrush about 8 inches, about 8 feet, or about 8 yards long? Explain.

   The toothbrush is about 8 _____ long.

   _____

   _____

7. **DIG DEEPER!** Order the lengths from shortest to longest.

   | 1 yard | 39 inches | 2 feet |

   _____ , _____ , _____

Review & Refresh

8. You read for 55 minutes. Your friend reads 28 fewer minutes. How many minutes does your friend read?

   _____ minutes

9. You score 23 points. Your two friends score 56 and 18 points. How many points do you and your friends score in all?

   _____ points

Name _____

Learning Target: Estimate the length of an object in inches, feet, or yards.

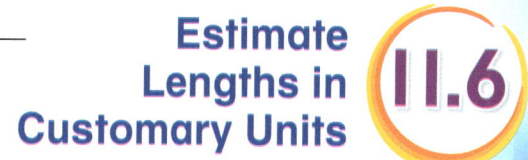

Estimate Lengths in Customary Units 11.6

Explore and Grow

Find an object that is shorter than the string. Draw the object.

———————————————————
5 inches

Without using a ruler, tell how long you think the object is.

_____ inches

Explain.

_____
_____
_____
_____

Chapter 11 | Lesson 6

five hundred fifty-three 553

Think and Grow

The rope is about 5 inches long. What is the best estimate of the length of the battery?

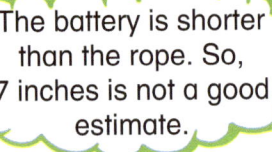

7 inches

4 inches

2 inches

The battery is shorter than the rope. So, 7 inches is not a good estimate.

The battery is much shorter than the rope. So, 4 inches is not a good estimate.

Show and Grow — I can do it!

1. The pipe cleaner is about 3 inches long. What is the best estimate of the length of the craft stick?

   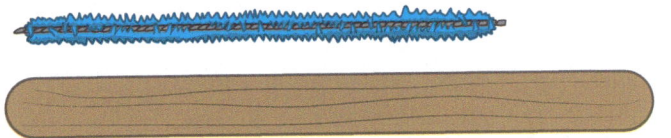

   4 inches

   8 inches

   1 inch

2. The dog leash is about 5 feet long. What is the best estimate of the length of the dog collar?

   3 feet

   1 foot

   5 feet

554   five hundred fifty-four

Name _____

 Apply and Grow: Practice

3. The poster is about 18 inches long. What is the best estimate for the length of the bed?

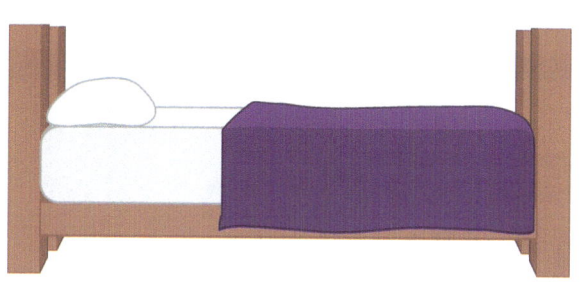

30 inches

75 inches

4 inches

4. The jump rope is about 6 feet long. What is the best estimate of the length of the dog?

10 feet

2 feet

4 feet

5. What is the best estimate of the length of a garage?

8 inches   8 feet   8 yards

6. What is the best estimate of the height of a flag pole?

20 inches   20 feet   20 yards

7. Precision Match.

5 inches   5 feet   5 yards

Chapter 11 | Lesson 6

 Think and Grow: Modeling Real Life

The sticker is about 1 inch long. Draw another sticker that is about 2 inches long.

Show and Grow I can think deeper!

8. The worm is about 4 inches long. Draw a caterpillar that is about 2 inches long.

9. **DIG DEEPER!** Each toy truck is about 2 inches long. Draw a building block that is about 3 inches long.

Justify a Result How did you use the length of the toy trucks to draw the building block?

_____

_____

Name _____

Practice 11.6

Learning Target: Estimate the length of an object in inches, feet, or yards.

The clock is 1 foot long. What is the best estimate of the length of the white board?

(7 feet)

15 feet

3 feet

1. The driveway is about 20 yards long. What is the best estimate of the length of the truck?

3 yards

6 yards

15 yards

2. What is the best estimate of the height of a basketball hoop?

3 inches

3 feet

3 yards

3. What is the best estimate of the length of a hair brush?

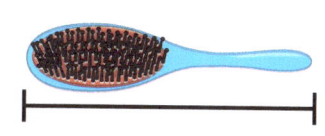

8 inches

8 feet

8 yards

Chapter 11 | Lesson 6

five hundred fifty-seven 557

4. **Does It Make Sense?** Descartes says the best estimate for the height of the Statue of Liberty is 5 yards. Do you agree? Explain.

_____

_____

5. **Modeling Real Life** The bug is about 4 inches long. Draw a bug that is about 2 inches long.

6. **DIG DEEPER!** Each paperclip is about 2 inches long. Draw a pen that is about 5 inches long.

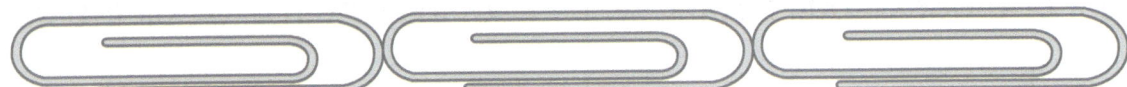

Review & Refresh

7. 12 − 4 = _____

8. 15 − 6 = _____

Name _____

Learning Target: Measure the same object using two different measurement units.

Measure the length of the string in inches then in centimeters.

_____ inches   _____ centimeters

Analyze a Problem Are there more inches or centimeters? Why?

_____
_____
_____
_____

Chapter 11 | Lesson 7   five hundred fifty-nine **559**

Think and Grow

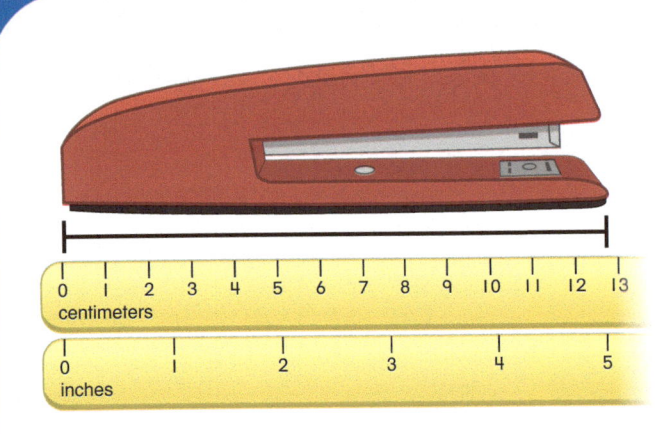

about __13__ centimeters

about __5__ inches

Did you use more centimeters or more inches to measure?

(centimeters)   inches

Show and Grow — I can do it!

Find and measure the object shown in your classroom two ways.

1.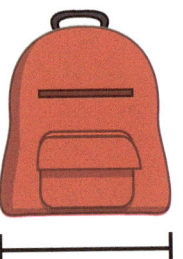

about _____ centimeters

about _____ inches

Did you use fewer centimeters or fewer inches to measure?

centimeters   inches

2.

about _____ meters

about _____ feet

Did you use fewer meters or fewer feet to measure?

meters   feet

Name _____

✓ Apply and Grow: Practice

Find and measure the object shown in your classroom two ways.

3.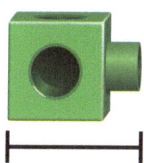

about _____ centimeters

about _____ inch

Did you use fewer centimeters or fewer inches to measure?

centimeters   inches

4.

about _____ meters

about _____ feet

Did you use more meters or more feet to measure?

meters   feet

5. Would you use more centimeters, inches, or feet to measure the length of a calculator?

centimeters

inches

feet

6. **Repeated Reasoning** What do you notice about the relationship between inches and centimeters? feet and meters?

_____

_____

Chapter 11 | Lesson 7

five hundred sixty-one   561

Think and Grow: Modeling Real Life

Do you use fewer centimeters or fewer meters to measure the length of your house? Explain.

centimeters   meters

_____

_____

Show and Grow   I can think deeper!

7. Do you use fewer feet or fewer yards to measure the length of a football field? Explain.

feet   yards

_____

_____

8. Do you use more meters or more feet to measure the length of your school? Explain.

meters   feet

_____

_____

562   five hundred sixty-two

Name _____

Practice 11.7

Learning Target: Measure the same object using two different measurement units.

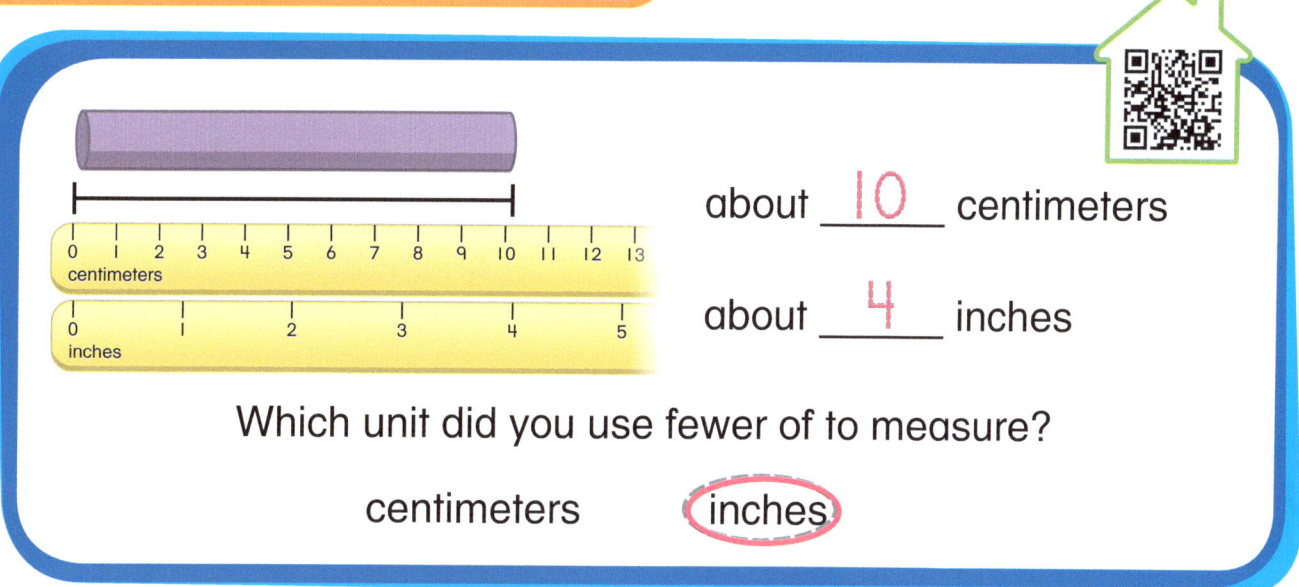

about __10__ centimeters

about __4__ inches

Which unit did you use fewer of to measure?

centimeters   (inches)

Find and measure the object shown in two ways.

1.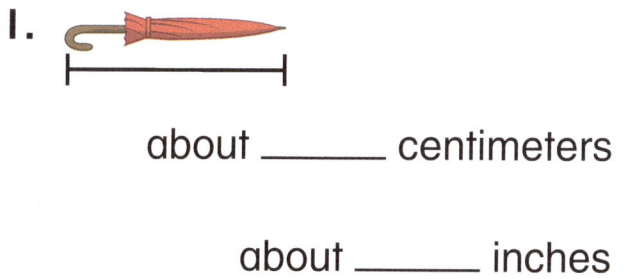

    about _____ centimeters

    about _____ inches

    Did you use more centimeters or more inches to measure the length of the umbrella?

    centimeters   inches

2.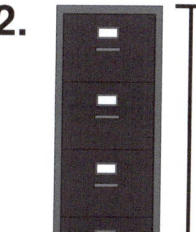

    about _____ meters

    about _____ feet

    Did you use fewer meters or fewer feet to measure the height of the cabinet?

    meters   feet

3. Would you use more centimeters, inches, or feet to measure the height of a lamp?

    centimeters   inches   feet

4. Would you use fewer inches, meters, or feet to measure the length of a sink?

    inches   meters   feet

Chapter 11 | Lesson 7

five hundred sixty-three 563

Reasoning Order the lengths from shortest to longest.

5. 12 centimeters   12 feet   12 inches

   _____ , _____ , _____

6. 2 feet   2 meters   2 centimeters

   _____ , _____ , _____

7. **Precision** What is the best estimate of the height of a maraca?

   9 inches   10 centimeters   3 centimeters

8. **Modeling Real Life** Do you use fewer feet or fewer yards to measure the length of a hallway? Explain.

   _____

   _____

Review & Refresh

Circle the values of the underlined digit.

9.	63<u>4</u>	4	4 ones	4 hundreds
10.	<u>9</u>18	900	9 hundreds	100
11.	2<u>5</u>7	0	5 tens	50

564   five hundred sixty-four

Name _____

Measure and Compare Lengths

Learning Target: Compare the lengths of two objects.

Explore and Grow

Measure the fish. Circle the longer fish.

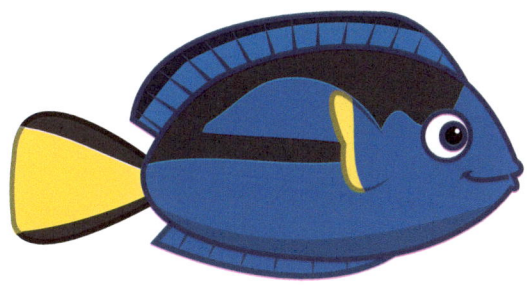

_____ centimeters

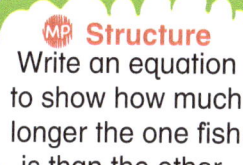

Structure
Write an equation to show how much longer the one fish is than the other.

_____ centimeters

Chapter 11 | Lesson 8

five hundred sixty-five

Think and Grow

How many inches longer is the ribbon than the bow?

____4____ inches

____2____ inches

____4____ − ____2____ = ____2____   ____2____ inches

Show and Grow   I can do it!

1. How many centimeters longer is the marker than the paper clip?

_____ centimeters

_____ centimeters

_____ − _____ = _____   _____ centimeters

Name _____

**Apply and Grow: Practice**

2. How many centimeters shorter is the binder clip than the stick of gum?

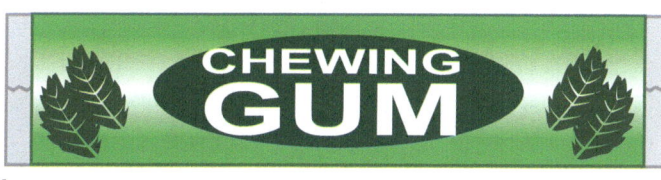

_____ centimeters

_____ centimeters

_____ − _____ = _____   _____ centimeters

3. A finger is 4 centimeters longer than the fingernail. How long is the finger?

_____ centimeters

4. Writing Explain how you found the length of the finger in Exercise 3.

_____

_____

Chapter 11 | Lesson 8

Think and Grow: Modeling Real Life

Whose path to school is longer? How much longer is it?

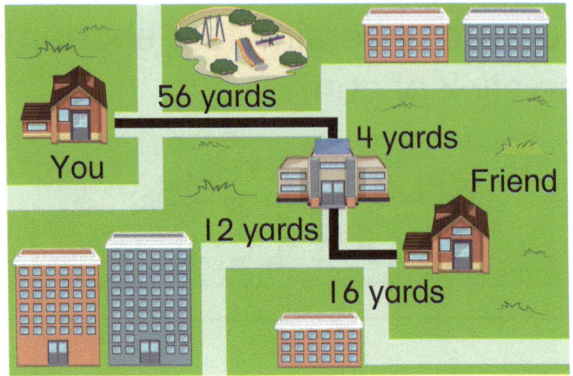

Addition equations:

Whose path is longer: Your path   Friend's path

Subtraction equation:

_____ yards

Show and Grow — I can think deeper!

5. Whose path to the pond is shorter? How much shorter is it?

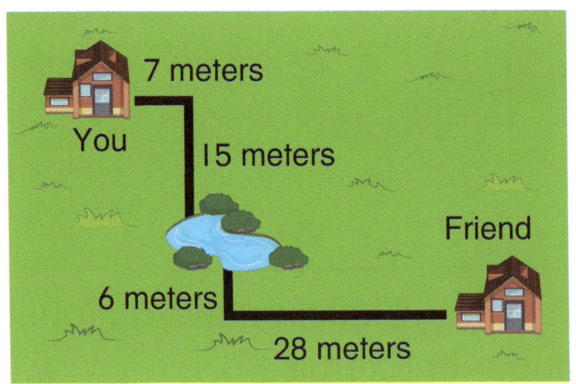

Your path   Friend's path

_____ meters

Name _____

Practice 11.8

Learning Target: Compare the lengths of two objects.

How many centimeters shorter is the football charm than the shark tooth?

__3__ centimeters

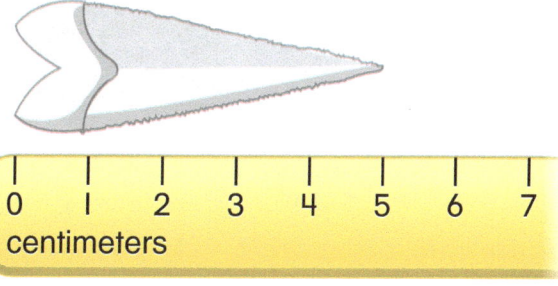

__5__ centimeters

__5__ − __3__ = __2__

__2__ centimeters

1. How many inches longer is the branch than the worm?

_____ inches

_____ inches

_____ − _____ = _____   _____ inches

Chapter 11 | Lesson 8

five hundred sixty-nine 569

2. **DIG DEEPER!** The length of a piece of string is 8 inches long. You cut off 5 inches. Draw the length of the string that is left.

3. **Modeling Real Life** Whose path to the playground is longer? How much longer is it?

Your path   Friend's path

_____ yards

Review & Refresh

4. Count by ones.

   ____, ____, 71, ____, 73, ____, ____, 76

5. Count by fives.

   85, 90, ____, ____, ____, ____, ____, ____

6. Count by tens.

   ____, 43, 53, ____, ____, ____, 93, ____

Name _____

Performance Task 11

You are planting a rooftop garden. You want to build a fence around the garden. You have a piece of wood that is 16 feet long.

1. a. Which designs can you make?

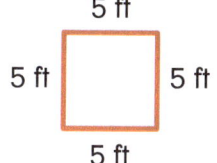 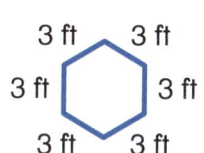 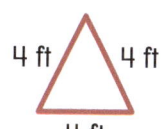

b. You choose the rectangular design. Use repeated addition to find the length of each side in inches.

5 ft = _____ + _____ + _____ + _____ + _____ = _____ in.

2 ft = _____ + _____ = _____ in.

2. Each seed you plant must be 6 inches apart and 6 inches away from the sides. Draw to find the number of seeds you can plant in your garden.

_____ in.

_____ in.

Make a Plan
What is the first step to solve?

_____ seeds

Spin and Cover

To Play: Players take turns. On your turn, spin one spinner. Then cover the item you would measure using that unit. Continue playing until all objects are covered.

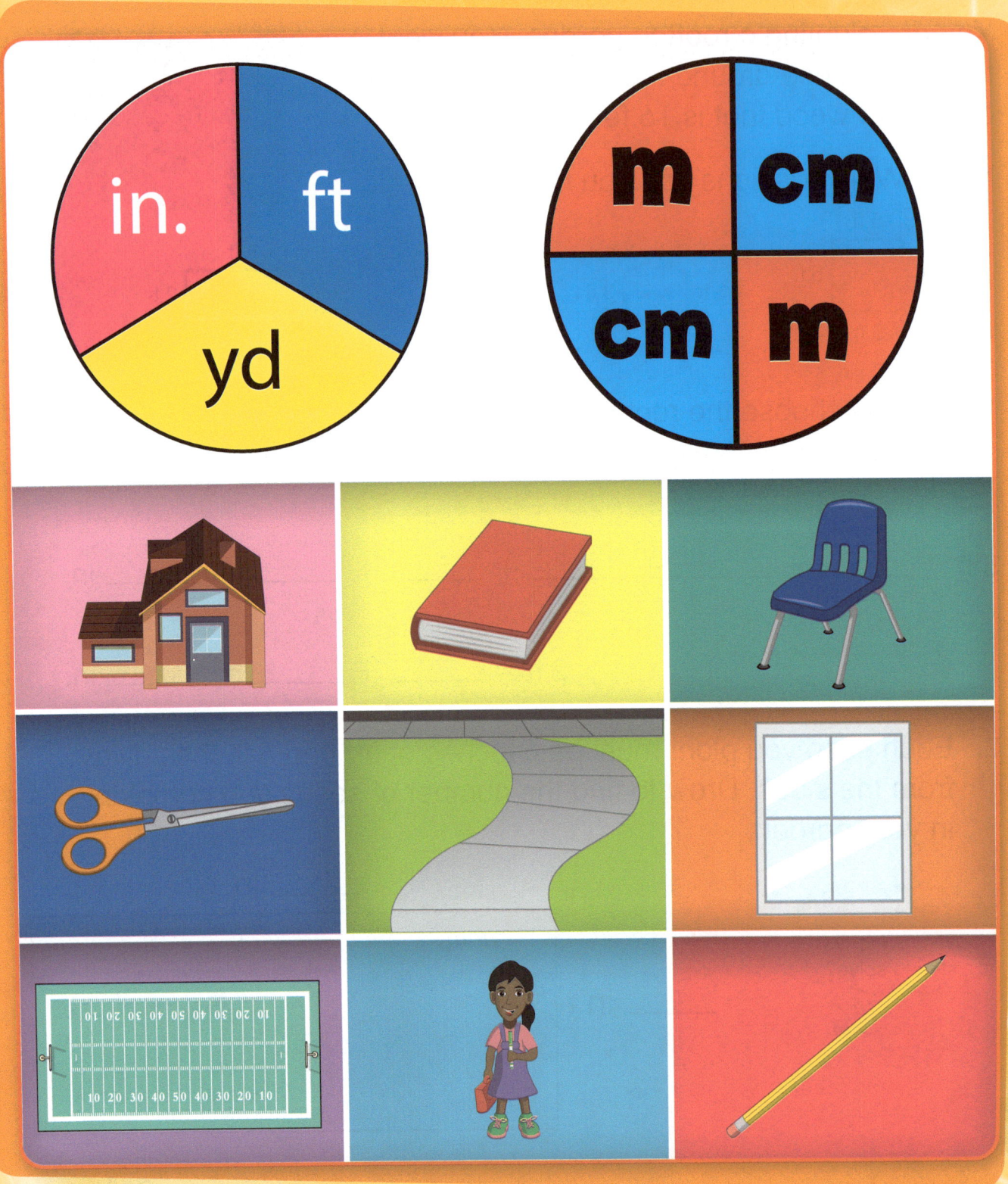

Name _____

Chapter 11 Practice

 **11.1 Measure Lengths in Centimeters**

Measure.

1.
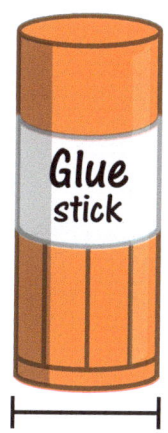

about _____ centimeters

2.
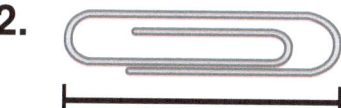

about _____ centimeters

 **11.2 Measure Objects Using Metric Lengths**

Find and measure the object.

3.
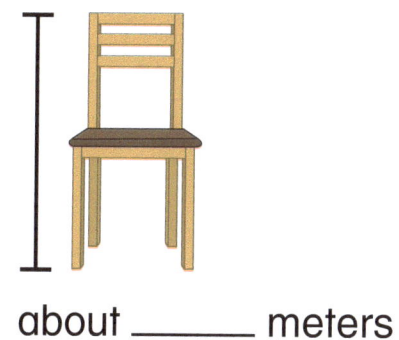

about _____ meters

4.
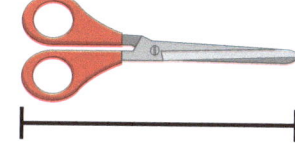

about _____ centimeters

Chapter 11   five hundred seventy-three   573

11.3 Estimate Lengths in Metric Units

5. The book is about 20 centimeters long. What is the best estimate of the length of the bookmark?

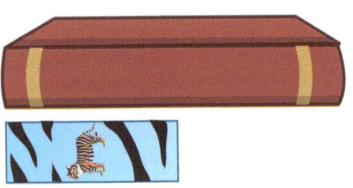

          25 centimeters

          5 centimeters

          10 centimeters

6. What is the best estimate of the length of a paintbrush?

          22 centimeters

          1 meter

          7 centimeters

11.4 Measure Lengths in Inches

Measure.

7.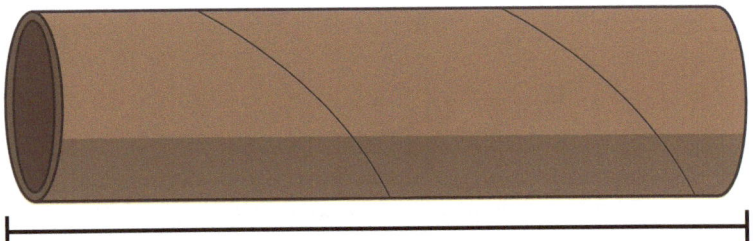

about _____ inches

8.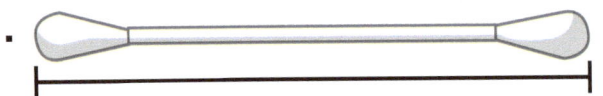

about _____ inches

574   five hundred seventy-four

11.5 Measure Objects Using Customary Length Units

Find the object shown. Choose an inch ruler, a yardstick, or a measuring tape to measure the object. Then measure.

9.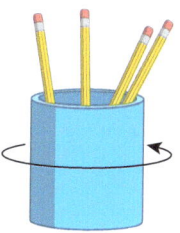

Tool: _____

Length: about _____

10.

Tool: _____

Length: about _____

11.6 Estimate Lengths in Customary Units

11. The couch is about 8 feet long. What is best estimate of the length of the end table?

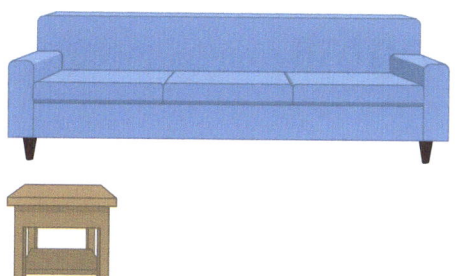

2 feet

5 feet

10 feet

12. What is the best estimate of the length of a pond?

30 inches

30 feet

30 yards

11.7 Measure Objects Using Different Length Units

13. Would you use more centimeters, meters, or inches to measure the length of a pencil?

centimeters   meters   inches

14. Would you use fewer centimeters, meters, or feet to measure the length of the teacher's desk?

centimeters   meters   feet

15. **YOU BE THE TEACHER** Newton says he uses more feet than meters to measure the length of a bicycle. Is he correct? Explain.

_____

_____

11.8 Measure and Compare Lengths

16. A guinea pig cage is 51 centimeters longer than the guinea pig. How long is the cage?

_____ centimeters

576 five hundred seventy-six

12 Solve Length Problems

- Do you play any musical instruments?
- A guitar is 41 inches long. A ukulele is 18 inches shorter than the guitar. How long is the ukulele?

Chapter Learning Target:
Understand length problems.

Chapter Success Criteria:
- I can define length.
- I can explain how different measurement tools are used.
- I can compare measurement tools to solve problems.
- I can reflect on the measurement strategy I used.

12 Vocabulary

Review Words
bar model
length unit
measure

Organize It

Use the review words to complete the graphic organizer.

You: | 5 |
Friend: | 2 | 3 |

Define It

Match the review word to its model.

1. length unit

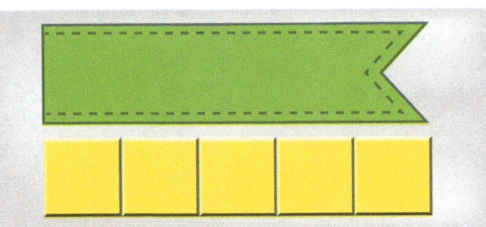

2. measure

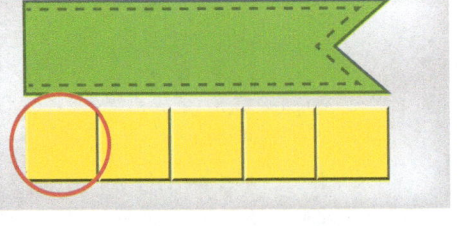

Name _____

Learning Target: Use a number line to solve length word problems.

Use a Number Line to Add and Subtract Lengths

Explore and Grow

Your goldfish is 4 centimeters long. It grows 6 more centimeters. Use the number line and your ruler to show how long the goldfish is now.

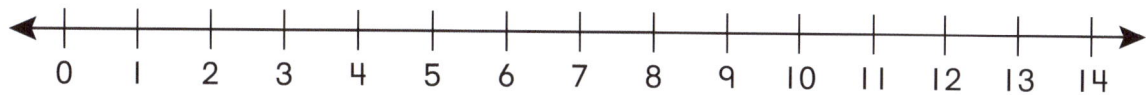

_____ centimeters

Repeated Reasoning What is the same about your ruler and the number line? What is different?

_____

_____

_____

_____

Chapter 12 | **Lesson 1** five hundred seventy-nine **579**

Think and Grow

An ant walks 5 centimeters and stops. Then it walks 4 centimeters. How far does the ant walk in all?

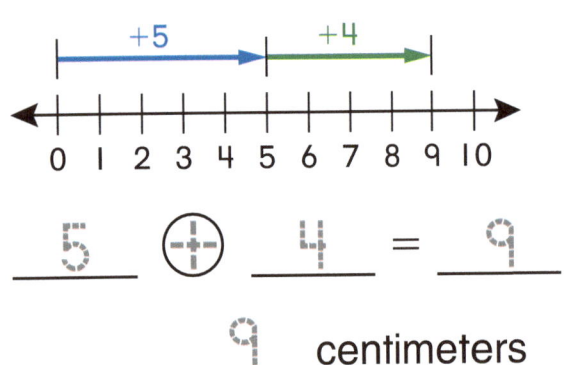

__5__ ⊕ __4__ = __9__

__9__ centimeters

A paper is 11 inches long. You cut off 3 inches. How long is the paper now?

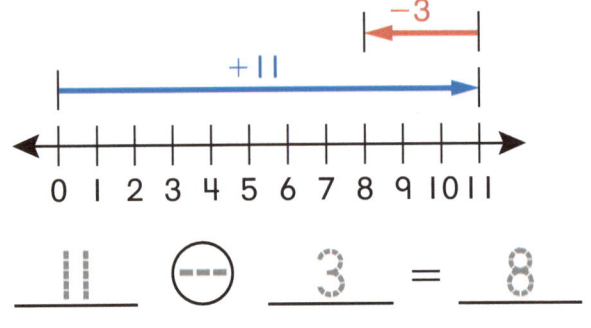

__11__ ⊖ __3__ = __8__

__8__ inches

Show and Grow I can do it!

1. You swim 15 meters and take a break. Then you swim 10 meters. How many meters do you swim?

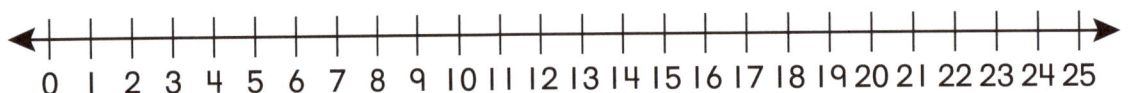

____ ◯ ____ = ____   ____ meters

2. A ribbon is 16 yards long. You cut off 7 yards. How long is the ribbon now?

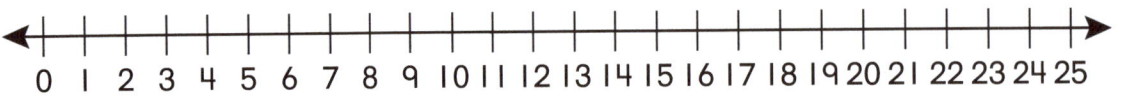

____ ◯ ____ = ____   ____ yards

Name _____

 **Apply and Grow: Practice**

3. A snake is 24 inches long. It sheds 14 inches of its skin. How much skin does it *not* shed?

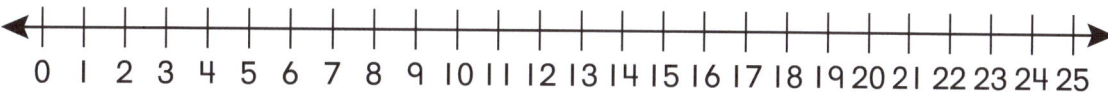

_____ ◯ _____ = _____   _____ inches

4. A photo is 15 centimeters long. You cut off 3 centimeters from the left and 3 centimeters from the right. How long is the photo now?

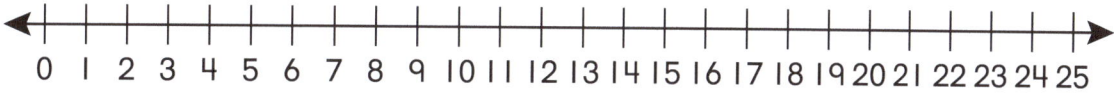

_____ ◯ _____ ◯ _____ = _____   _____ centimeters

5. **Structure** Write an equation that matches the number line.

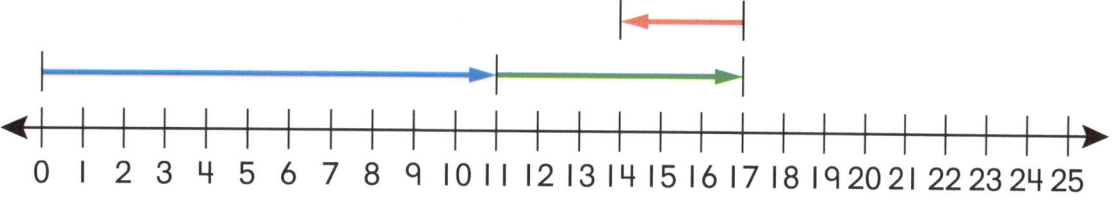

_____ ◯ _____ ◯ _____ = _____

Chapter 12 | Lesson 1   five hundred eighty-one   581

Think and Grow: Modeling Real Life

You want to make a bracelet that is 6 inches long. You make 4 inches before lunch. You make 2 inches after lunch. Did you finish the bracelet?

Model:

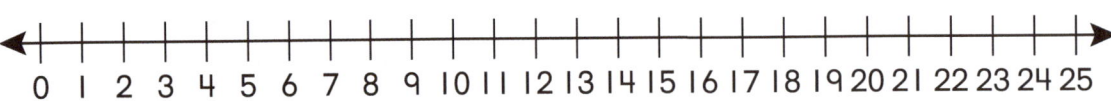

Did you finish?   Yes   No

Show and Grow   I can think deeper!

6. You are painting a fence that is 24 feet long. You paint 10 feet on Saturday. You paint 13 feet on Sunday. Did you finish painting the fence?

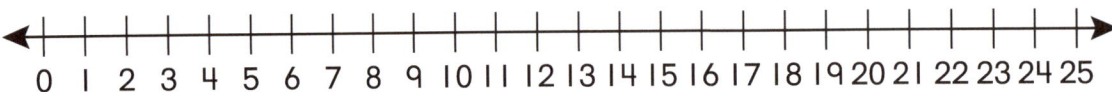

Yes   No

7. **DIG DEEPER!** You throw a disc 9 meters. On your second throw, the disc travels 3 meters more than your first throw. How many meters did the disc travel in all?

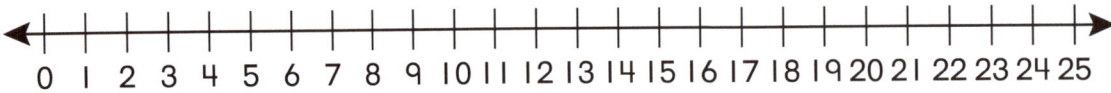

_____ meters

582   five hundred eighty-two

Name _____

Practice 12.1

Learning Target: Use a number line to solve length word problems.

Your hair is 10 centimeters long. You cut off 2 centimeters. How long is your hair now?

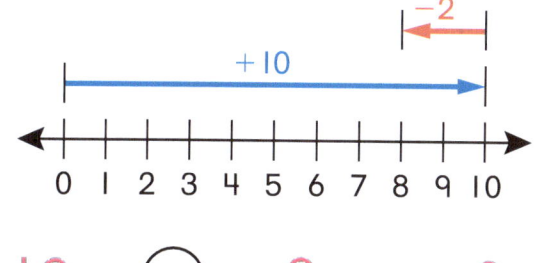

__10__ ⊖ __2__ = __8__

__8__ centimeters

Your paper airplane flies 4 meters. Your friend's airplane flies 3 meters farther. How far did his airplane fly?

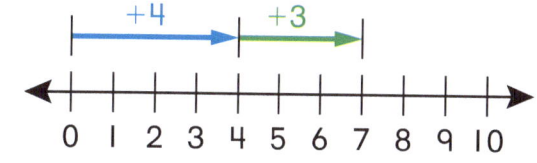

__4__ ⊕ __3__ = __7__

__7__ meters

1. You kick a ball 13 yards. Your friend kicks it back 9 yards. How far is the ball from you now?

____ ◯ ____ = ____

____ yards

2. Your shoelace is 20 inches long. Your friend's is 4 inches longer than yours. How long is your friend's shoelace?

____ ◯ ____ = ____

____ inches

Chapter 12 | Lesson 1

3. **Structure** One power cord is 7 feet long. Another power cord is 5 feet long. Use the number line to find the combined length of the power cords.

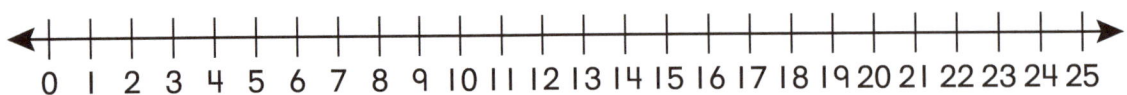

4. **Modeling Real Life** A worker needs to pave a bike path that is 25 feet long. He completes 13 feet on Monday and 11 feet on Tuesday. Did he complete the paving?

Yes   No

5. **DIG DEEPER!** You throw a baseball 5 yards. On your second throw, the baseball travels 2 yards more than your first throw. How many yards did the baseball travel in all?

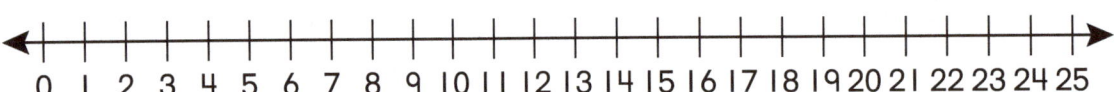

_____ yards

Review & Refresh

Compare.

6. 210 ◯ 200 + 10

7. 532 ◯ 500 + 20 + 3

584   five hundred eighty-four

Name _____

Problem Solving: Length 12.2

Learning Target: Solve *compare* length word problems.

 Explore and Grow

How much longer is the red ribbon than the blue ribbon?

 **Make a Plan** Should you add or subtract to solve? How do you know?

____ ◯ ____ = ____

____ inches

Chapter 12 | Lesson 2

Think and Grow

A blue boat is 28 feet long. A red boat is 20 feet long. A white boat is 16 feet long. How much shorter is the white boat than the blue boat?

Think: What do you know? What do you need to find?

Blue boat: | 28 |

White boat: | 16 | ? |

__16__ + __?__ = __28__   __28__ − __16__ = __?__

So, ? = __12__.

__12__ feet

Show and Grow   I can do it!

1. An orange fish is 10 centimeters long. A yellow fish is 35 centimeters long. A red fish is 19 centimeters long. How much longer is the yellow fish than the red fish?

Yellow fish:

Red fish:

____ ◯ ____ = ____

So, ? = ____.

____ centimeters

Name _____

✓ Apply and Grow: Practice

2. A green scarf is 60 inches long. An orange scarf is 45 inches long. A red scarf is 36 inches long. How much longer is the green scarf than the red scarf?

_____ inches

3. **DIG DEEPER!** A pink ribbon is 90 centimeters long. A purple ribbon is 35 centimeters long. A blue ribbon is 46 centimeters long. How much longer is the pink ribbon than the total length of the purple and blue ribbons?

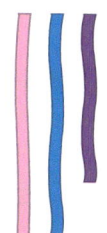

_____ centimeters

4. **Maintain Accuracy** How much taller is Student 3 than the shortest student?

Height (inches)	
Student 1	49
Student 2	48
Student 3	53
Student 4	52

_____ inches

Chapter 12 | Lesson 2   five hundred eighty-seven   587

Think and Grow: Modeling Real Life

You hop 27 inches and then 24 inches. Your friend hops 3 inches less than you. How far does your friend hop?

Think: What do you know? What do you need to find?

Model:

_____ inches

Show and Grow   I can think deeper!

5. You throw a ball 36 feet and then 41 feet. Your friend throws a ball 5 feet farther than you. How far does your friend throw the ball?

_____ feet

6. **DIG DEEPER!** A black horse runs 53 meters and then 45 meters. A brown horse runs 62 meters and then 31 meters. Which horse ran the longer distance in all? How many more meters did the horse run?

Black horse   Brown horse

_____ more meters

Name _____

Practice 12.2

Learning Target: Solve *compare* length word problems.

You are 43 inches tall. Your friend is 45 inches tall. Your cousin is 61 inches tall. How much taller is your cousin than you?

Think: What do you know? What do you need to find?

Cousin: | 61 |
You: | 43 | ? |

__43__ + __?__ = __61__   __61__ − __43__ = __?__

So, ? = __18__.

__18__ inches

1. The distance to the principal's office is 24 yards. The distance to the bathroom is 15 yards. The distance to your teacher's desk is 2 yards. How much farther away is the principal's office than the bathroom?

Principal's office: [ ]

Bathroom: [ ]

____ ◯ ____ = ____

So, ? = ____.

____ yards

Chapter 12 | Lesson 2   five hundred eighty-nine   589

2. **YOU BE THE TEACHER** You launch a rocket 63 meters. Your friend launches it 28 meters, and your cousin launches it 86 meters. Your cousin says that he launches the rocket 58 meters farther than you. Is he correct? Explain.

_____

_____

3. **Modeling Real Life** You create a drawing that is 15 centimeters long and then add on 7 more centimeters. Your friend creates a drawing that is 3 centimeters longer than yours. How long is your friend's drawing?

_____ centimeters

4. **DIG DEEPER!** A frog hops 36 inches and then 22 inches. A toad hops 14 inches and then 43 inches. Which animal hopped the longer distance in all? How many more inches did the animal hop?

        Frog   Toad

_____ more inches

Review & Refresh

5. 635 + 10 = _____

   635 + 100 = _____

6. 824 + _____ = 924

   824 + _____ = 834

7. 309 + _____ = 409

   309 + _____ = 319

Name _____

Learning Target: Solve length word problems to find missing measurements.

Problem Solving: Missing Measurement

Explore and Grow

You and your friend each have a piece of yarn. The total length of both pieces is 16 centimeters. Use a ruler to measure your yarn. Then draw your friend's yarn.

Choose Tools Can you use inch tiles to help solve? Why or why not?

Communicate Clearly Explain how you found the length of your friend's yarn.

_____

_____

_____

Chapter 12 | Lesson 3

Think and Grow

A tree is 43 inches tall. After 1 year, the tree is 67 inches tall. How many inches did the tree grow?

Think: What do you know? What do you need to find?

67 − 40 = 27
27 − 3 = 24

__43__ + __?__ = __67__

Think of 67 − 43 = ?.

40 3

So, ? = __24__.

__24__ inches

Show and Grow — I can do it!

1. A rope is 31 meters long. You cut a piece off. Now the rope is 14 meters long. How much rope did you cut off?

____ ◯ ____ = ____

So, ? = ____.

____ meters

Name _____

✓ Apply and Grow: Practice

2. A celery stalk is 20 centimeters long. You cut off the leaves. Now it is 13 centimeters long. How much did you cut off?

_____ centimeters

3. Descartes walked some and then ran 39 yards. He went a total of 75 yards. How far did he walk?

_____ yards

4. Your coat zipper is 18 inches long. The zipper gets stuck at 11 inches. How much of the zipper will *not* zip?

_____ inches

5. **Number Sense** The path to school is 181 meters long in all. How long is the missing part of the path?

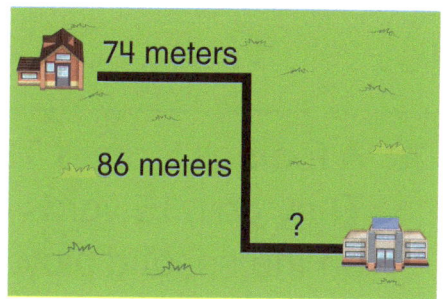

_____ meters

Chapter 12 | Lesson 3

Think and Grow: Modeling Real Life

You make a paper chain that is 8 feet long. You add 7 feet of chain to the end. Then 6 feet of the chain breaks off. How long is the chain now?

Think: What do you know? What do you need to find?

_____ feet

Show and Grow — I can think deeper!

6. You build a tower that is 48 centimeters tall. You add 34 centimeters to the tower height. Your tower breaks and 29 centimeters fall off. How tall is your tower now?

_____ centimeters

7. A football team is 78 yards away from scoring. They gain 15 yards on the first play and 21 yards on the second play. How far is the team from scoring now?

_____ yards

Name _____

Practice 12.3

Learning Target: Solve length word problems to find missing measurements.

Last year your turtle was 14 centimeters long. Now it is 22 centimeters long. How much did it grow?

Think: What do you know? What do you need to find?

22 − 10 = 12
12 − 4 = 8

__14__ + __?__ = __22__

Think of 22 − 14 = ?.

10   4

So, ? = __8__.

__8__ centimeters

1. A piece of fabric is 36 inches long. Another piece is 18 inches long. What is the total length of both pieces of fabric?

_____ inches

2. A rose is 61 centimeters long. You cut off some of the stem. Now it is 48 centimeters long. How much did you cut off?

_____ centimeters

Chapter 12 | Lesson 3   five hundred ninety-five   595

3. **Maintain Accuracy** Newton's balloon is 18 inches long. Descartes's balloon is 23 inches long. Your friend's balloon is 12 inches long. Which sentences are true?

Newton's balloon is 6 inches longer than your friend's.

Your friend's balloon is 11 inches longer than Descartes's.

Descartes's balloon is 5 inches longer than Newton's.

4. **DIG DEEPER!** A branch is ♥ feet long. You cut ♦ feet off. The branch is now ● feet long.

Which equation models the problem?

♥ + ♦ = ●   ● − ♦ = ♥

♥ − ♦ = ●   ● + ♥ = ♦

5. **Modeling Real Life** A piece of wood is 16 feet long. You cut off 6 feet, but it is still too long. You cut off 2 more feet. How long is the piece of wood now?

_____ feet

Review & Refresh

6.
```
   3 7 1
 + 1 5 8
```

7.
```
   6 7 2
 + 2 8 7
```

8.
```
   5 2 0
 + 3 8 6
```

Name _____

Learning Target: Solve length word problems.

Practice Measurement Problems 12.4

Explore and Grow

Newton's piece of string is 24 centimeters long. He gives Descartes 12 centimeters of the string. How long is the string that Newton has left? Draw a picture and write an equation to solve.

____ ◯ ____ = ____

____ cm

Maintain Accuracy Compare the lengths of string. Is one longer, or are they the same length? Explain.

_____

_____

_____

_____

_____

Chapter 12 | Lesson 4

five hundred nintey-seven 597

Think and Grow

Your dog is 51 centimeters tall. Your friend's dog is 18 centimeters shorter than your dog. How tall is your friend's dog?

One Way:

Your dog: 51
Your friend's dog: ? 18

? + 18 = 51
51 − 18 = ?

So, ? = 33.

Another Way:

51 − 18 = ?

51 − 18 = ?
   / \
  10   8
       / \
      1   7

So, ? = 33.

33 centimeters

Show and Grow — I can do it!

1. Your blanket is 66 inches long. Your friend's blanket is 9 inches longer than yours. How long is your friend's blanket?

___ ◯ ___ = ___

So, ? = ___.

___ inches

Name _____

 **Apply and Grow: Practice**

2. A blue whale is 31 meters long. A humpback whale is 16 meters long. How much longer is the blue whale than the humpback whale?

_____ meters

3. Newton runs 450 meters. Descartes runs 25 meters less than Newton. How far do they run in all?

_____ meters

4. **Reasoning** Solve the problem below two different ways.

You want to read 100 books during the school year. You read 25 books in the fall and 54 books in the winter. How many books do you still need to read?

_____ books

Chapter 12 | Lesson 4

Think and Grow: Modeling Real Life

A yellow subway train is 18 meters longer than a blue subway train. The yellow subway train is 92 meters long. How long is the blue subway train?

Equation:

_____ meters

Show and Grow   I can think deeper!

5. A brown rabbit hops 24 inches less than a white rabbit. The brown rabbit hops 48 inches. How many inches does the white rabbit hop?

_____ inches

6. Your kite string is 47 yards long. You tie 6 yards of string to the end. Now your kite string is 21 yards longer than your friend's kite string. How long is your friend's kite string?

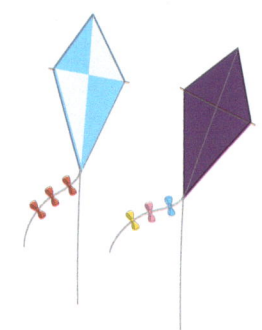

_____ yards

Name _____

Practice 12.4

Learning Target: Solve length word problems.

You need 56 centimeters of wire for a science project. You have 73 centimeters of wire. How much do you need to cut off?

One Way:

Wire you have: 73
Wire you need: 56 ?

56 + ? = 73
73 − 56 = ?
So, ? = 17.

Another Way:

73 − 56 = ?

73 − 56 = ?
     / \
    50   6

So, ? = 17.

____17____ centimeters

1. A swimming pool is 28 feet long. The pool cover is 32 feet long. How much longer is the pool cover?

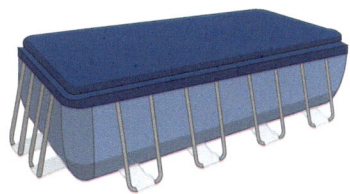

____ ◯ ____ = ____

So, ? = ____.

____ feet

Chapter 12 | Lesson 4

2. **Writing** Write and solve a word problem about the colored pencils.

   _____

   _____

   _____

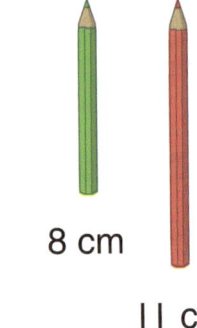

8 cm

11 cm

15 cm

3. **Modeling Real Life** You cast out your fishing line 14 yards less than your friend. Your friend casts out her line 33 yards. How many yards do you cast out your fishing line?

_____ yards

4. **Modeling Real Life** Your nightstand is 24 inches tall. You put a 20-inch lamp on it. Now your nightstand and lamp are 19 inches taller than your bed. How tall is your bed?

_____ inches

Review & Refresh

5. Write the number in expanded form and word form.

   645

   _____ + _____ + _____   _____

6. Write the number in standard form and word form.

   800 + 60 + 2

   _____   _____

Name _____

Performance Task 12

1. A recorder is 1 foot long. A clarinet is 24 inches long. Which instrument is longer? How much longer is the instrument?

      Recorder   Clarinet

   _____ inches

2. A piano has 27 more keys than a keyboard. There are 52 white keys and 36 black keys on a piano.
   a. How many keys are on the keyboard?

   _____ keys

   b. The number of black keys on the piano is equal to the number of white keys on the keyboard. How many black keys are on the keyboard?

   _____ black keys

3. A drum set has drums and cymbals on stands.
   a. The cymbals are 77 centimeters from the ground. You raise the stand 18 centimeters. The cymbals are now 23 centimeters higher than one of the drums. What is the height of the drum?

   _____ centimeters

   b. Another drum is 60 centimeters from the ground. You raise it 12 centimeters. Are both drums the same height?

   Yes   No

Draw and Cover

To Play: Players take turns. On your turn, pick a Draw and Cover Card and solve. Then cover the sea turtle that has the answer. Continue playing until all sea turtles are covered.

Name _____

Chapter Practice 12

12.1 Use a Number Line to Add and Subtract Lengths

1. You throw a ball 12 yards. Your friend throws it back 8 yards. How far is the ball from you now?

_____ ◯ _____ = _____   _____ yards

12.2 Problem Solving: Length

2. Your cat's first collar was 6 inches long. Now your cat has a collar that is 13 inches long. Your puppy's collar is 11 inches long. How much longer is your cat's collar now?

_____ ◯ _____ = _____

So, ? = _____ .

_____ inches

12.3 Problem Solving: Missing Measurement

3. You must be 54 inches tall to ride a rollercoaster. At 8 years old, you were 48 inches tall. You grow 3 inches the next year. How much more do you still need to grow to be able to ride the roller coaster?

_____ inches

4. **Maintain Accuracy** A car tire is 61 centimeters tall. A truck tire is 84 centimeters tall. A monster truck tire is 167 centimeters tall. Which sentences are true?

The car tire is 23 centimeters taller than the truck tire.

The truck tire is 83 centimeters shorter than the monster truck tire.

The monster truck tire is 106 centimeters taller than the car tire.

12.4 Practice Measurement Problems

5. A kangaroo jumps 24 feet. A frog jumps 19 feet less than the kangaroo. How far does the frog jump?

_____ feet

6. A store owner wants to add on to the parking lot to make it 38 meters long. It is currently 21 meters long. How many meters does the store owner want to add?

_____ meters

606 six hundred six

Cumulative Practice 1–12

1. Which expressions have a sum less than 12?

   ○ 5 + 3   ○ 4 + 6

   ○ 1 + 0   ○ 7 + 8

2. Find each difference.

   ```
     8 0 0         5 0 2         3 5 0
   − 4 9 5       − 1 7 8       − 1 7 6
   ```

3. A blue sailboat is 44 feet long. A white sailboat is 36 feet long. A green sailboat is 22 feet long. Which sentences are true?

   ○ The blue sailboat is 8 feet longer than the green sailboat.

   ○ The green sailboat is 14 feet shorter than the white sailboat.

   ○ The green sailboat is 22 feet shorter than the blue sailboat.

   ○ The blue sailboat is 12 feet longer than the white sailboat.

4. What is the value of the underlined digit?

 739

 ○ 3 ones   ○ 3 hundreds

 ○ 3 tens   ○ 300

5. Use mental math to solve.

 403 − 10 = _____   898 − 100 = _____

 640 − 10 = _____   204 − 10 = _____

 843 − _____ = 833   _____ − 100 = 731

6. The cracker is about 2 inches long. What is the best estimate of the length of the cracker box?

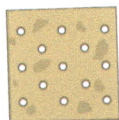

 ○ 3 inches   ○ 10 inches

 ○ 16 inches   ○ 5 inches

608   six hundred eight

7. You take 14 pictures on Friday. You take 20 more on Saturday. Your friend takes 34 pictures in all on Friday and Saturday. How many pictures did you and your friend take in all?

   ○ 34 pictures   ○ 58 pictures

   ○ 24 pictures   ○ 68 pictures

8. Which expressions are equal to 245 + 386?

   ○ 631   ○ 500 + 130 + 11

   ○ 200 + 300 + 40 + 80 + 5 + 6   ○ 500 + 120 + 5

9. Newton runs 7 yards, takes a break, and runs 3 more yards. Which number line shows how many yards Newton runs?

○ 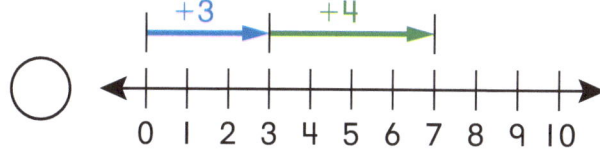   ○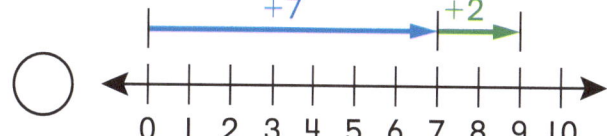

○ 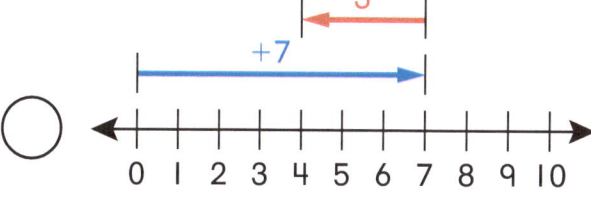   ○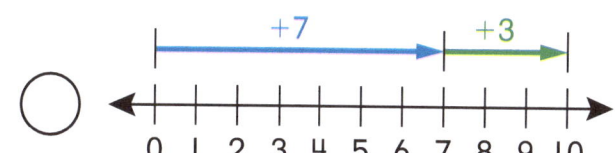

Chapter 12   six hundred nine   609

10. Find the sum.

$$\begin{array}{r} 5\,4 \\ 6\,3 \\ 1\,0 \\ +\,2\,7 \\ \hline \end{array}$$

○ 154   ○ 164

○ 144   ○ 155

---

11. Find each difference.

    80 − 53 = ?

    79 − 13 = ?

    90 − 32 = ?

    64 − 40 = ?

---

12. Complete the sentences using *centimeters* or *meters*.

    A teacher's desk is about 2 _____ long.

    A paper clip is about 8 _____ long.

    A carrot is about 12 _____ long.

    A boat is about 20 _____ long.

13 Represent and Interpret Data

- What types of writing tools do you use? What tool is your favorite?
- You measure the lengths of 20 pencils. How can you organize the data?

Chapter Learning Target:
Understand data.

Chapter Success Criteria:
- I can identify a tool to collect data.
- I can create a tally chart to make a graph.
- I can represent data in different ways.
- I can interpret data in different ways.

13 Vocabulary

Review Words
tally chart
tally mark

Organize It

Use the review words to complete the graphic organizer.

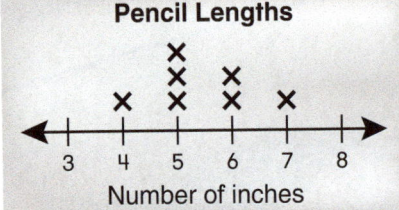

Favorite Class	
Math	卌	
Science	卌

Define It

Use your vocabulary cards to identify the word.

1.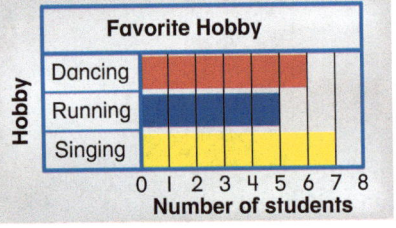

2.

Chapter 13 Vocabulary Cards

bar graph	data
key	line plot
picture graph	survey

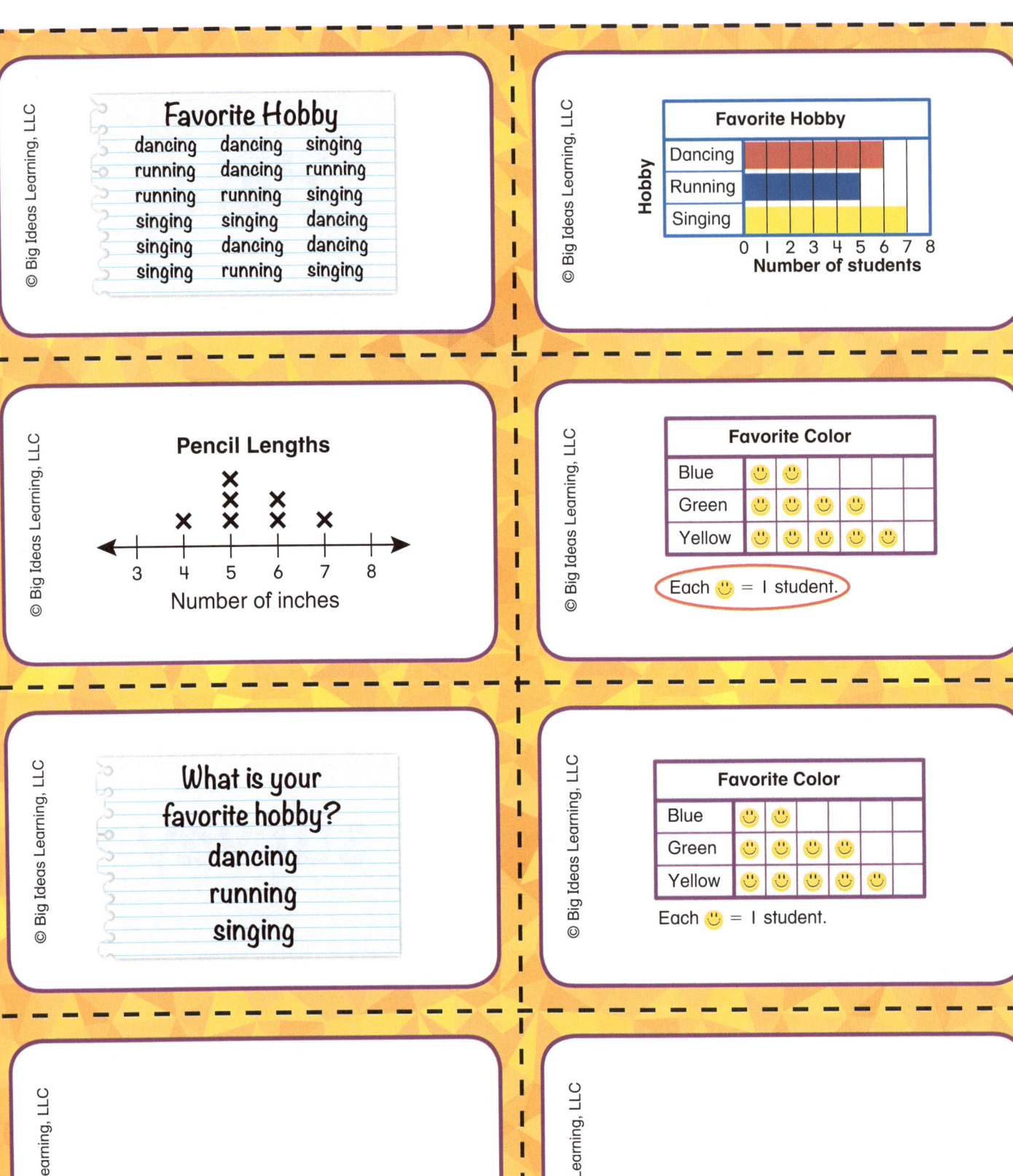

Name _____

Learning Target: Use a tally chart to organize and understand data.

Sort and Organize Data 13.1

Explore and Grow

Look at your color tiles. Complete the tally chart.

Tile Colors	
Blue	
Green	
Red	
Yellow	

Write and answer a question about your tally chart.

_____

_____

Chapter 13 | Lesson 1

six hundred thirteen 613

Think and Grow

Newton conducts a **survey**. He asks 10 students about their favorite outside activity. He records the **data**. Use the data to complete the tally chart.

basketball	riding a bike
riding a bike	riding a bike
jump rope	jump rope
running	riding a bike
riding a bike	basketball

Favorite Outside Activity	
Basketball	||
Jump rope	||
Riding a bike	|||||
Running	|

How many students chose basketball? __2__

Which activity is the most favorite? __riding a bike__

Show and Grow — I can do it!

1. Use the data to complete the tally chart.

math	science
social studies	language arts
science	social studies
math	math
language arts	math
math	science
science	language arts
math	math

Favorite Subject	
Math	
Science	
Social studies	
Language arts	

How many students chose math? _____

Which subject is the most favorite? _____

Name _____

 **Apply and Grow: Practice**

2. Use the data to complete the tally chart.

owl	reindeer
polar bear	fox
reindeer	owl
fox	polar bear
polar bear	reindeer
fox	owl
fox	polar bear
fox	reindeer
reindeer	fox

Favorite Arctic Animal	
Fox	
Reindeer	
Polar bear	
Owl	

Which animal is the least favorite? _____

How many students did *not* choose fox? How do you know?

_____

Did more students choose fox or owl?	Did fewer students choose reindeer or polar bear?
_____	_____
How many more? ____ more	How many fewer? ____ fewer

3. **Reasoning** Which sentences are correct?

You survey 30 students.

11 students chose whale.

4 more students chose seal than penguin.

20 students did *not* choose seal.

Favorite Antarctic Animal	
Penguin	𝍢𝍢 IIII
Whale	𝍢 I
Seal	𝍢 𝍢

Chapter 13 | Lesson 1

six hundred fifteen 615

Think and Grow: Modeling Real Life

Newton wants to survey 25 students. How many more students does he need to survey?

Favorite Field Trip	
Library	|||
Zoo	||||| ||
Museum	||||
Play	|||||

Addition equation:

_____ students

Show and Grow — I can think deeper!

4. Descartes wants to survey 20 students. How many more students does he need to survey?

Favorite Shoes	
Sandals	|||||	
Sneakers	||||
Slippers	||||| ||
Dress shoes		

_____ students

How many more students need to choose sneakers so that the numbers of students who choose sneakers and sandals are equal?

_____ students

616   six hundred sixteen

Name _____

Practice 13.1

Learning Target: Use a tally chart to organize and understand data.

Use the data to complete the tally chart.

board game
computer
computer
puzzle
charades
board game
charades
computer
charades
charades

Favorite Indoor Activity	
Computer	|||
Charades	||||
Board game	||
Puzzle		

How many students chose charades?

___4___

Which activity is the least favorite?

___puzzle___

1. Use the data to complete the tally chart.

sidewalk chalk   tag
tag   catch
tag   bubbles
catch   sidewalk chalk
tag   catch
catch   tag
tag   tag

Favorite Outdoor Activity	
Tag	
Catch	
Bubbles	
Sidewalk chalk	

Which activity is the most favorite? _____

Did more students choose catch or sidewalk chalk? _____

How many more? _____ more

Chapter 13 | Lesson 1

2. **Modeling Real Life** Newton wants to survey 15 friends. How many more friends does he need to survey?

Fur Color	
Brown	|||||
Orange	||
White		
Black	|||

_____ friends

3. **Writing** In Exercise 2, what question did Newton ask?

_____

_____

4. **Modeling Real Life** You want to survey 30 students. How many more students do you need to survey?

_____ students

Favorite Playtime Activity	
Blocks		
Puppets	||||| ||||
Cars	||||| ||
Coloring	|||

How many more students need to choose coloring so that the numbers of students who choose coloring and puppets are equal?

_____ students

Review & Refresh

5. 153 − 10 = _____

6. 978 − 10 = _____

7. 642 − 100 = _____

8. 1,000 − 100 = _____

Name _____

Learning Target: Understand the data shown by a picture graph.

Read and Interpret Picture Graphs 13.2

 **Explore and Grow**

How are the tally chart and the picture graph the same? How are they different?

Favorite Pet	
Bird	||
Cat	||||
Dog	𝍢 ||

Favorite Pet							
Bird	🙂	🙂					
Cat	🙂	🙂	🙂	🙂			
Dog	🙂	🙂	🙂	🙂	🙂	🙂	🙂

Each 🙂 = 1 student.

_____

_____

Chapter 13 | Lesson 2

six hundred nineteen 619

Think and Grow

picture graph

Favorite Season

Spring	🙂	🙂	🙂	🙂	🙂			
Summer	🙂	🙂	🙂	🙂	🙂	🙂	🙂	🙂
Fall	🙂	🙂	🙂	🙂	🙂	🙂		
Winter	🙂	🙂	🙂					

Each 🙂 = 1 student. ← key

How many students chose fall? __6__

Which season is the least favorite? __winter__

Show and Grow — I can do it!

1.

Favorite Insect

Bumblebee	🙂	🙂						
Ladybug	🙂	🙂	🙂	🙂	🙂	🙂	🙂	🙂
Grasshopper	🙂	🙂	🙂	🙂	🙂			
Butterfly	🙂	🙂	🙂	🙂	🙂	🙂	🙂	

Each 🙂 = 1 student.

How many students chose butterfly? _____

Which insect is the most favorite? _____

Which insect is the least favorite? _____

Name _____

 Apply and Grow: Practice

2.

Favorite School Trip								
Science center	😊	😊	😊	😊	😊			
Park	😊	😊						
Sporting event	😊	😊	😊	😊	😊	😊	😊	😊
Museum	😊	😊	😊					

Each 😊 = 1 student.

How many students chose sporting event? _____

Which school trip is the least favorite? _____

How many more students chose science center than the park? _____

3. **Maintain Accuracy** Use the numbers to complete the sentences.

   1   2   3   4

Number of Siblings				
Your cousin	○			
Your friend	○	○	○	○
Newton	○	○		
Descartes	○	○	○	

Each ○ = 1 sibling.

Newton has _____ siblings.

Your friend has _____ siblings.

Your friend has _____ more siblings than your cousin.

Chapter 13 | Lesson 2   six hundred twenty-one   621

Think and Grow: Modeling Real Life

Favorite Ocean Animal

Crab	🙂	🙂	🙂	🙂	🙂	🙂				
Octopus	🙂	🙂	🙂	🙂	🙂	🙂	🙂	🙂			
Jellyfish	🙂	🙂	🙂							
Sea turtle	🙂	🙂	🙂	🙂	🙂	🙂	🙂	🙂	🙂	

Each 🙂 = 1 student.

Do more students like crabs and sea turtles or octopuses and jellyfish?

Addition equations:

Compare: _____ ◯ _____

More students like _____ and _____.

Show and Grow I can think deeper!

4. **Vehicles You See**

Car	◯	◯	◯	◯	◯	◯	◯	◯	◯
Van	◯	◯	◯	◯	◯	◯	◯		
Truck	◯	◯	◯						
Motorcycle	◯	◯							

Each ◯ = 1 vehicle.

Do you see more cars and motorcycles or vans and trucks?

You see more _____ and _____.

622 six hundred twenty-two

Name _____

Practice  13.2

Learning Target: Understand the data shown by a picture graph.

Favorite Vegetable

Broccoli	😊	😊	😊	😊	😊	😊	😊	😊	😊	
Carrot	😊	😊	😊	😊	😊					
Asparagus	😊	😊	😊	😊	😊	😊	😊			
Pea	😊	😊	😊	😊						

Each 😊 = 1 student.

How many students chose asparagus? __7__

Which vegetable is the most favorite? __broccoli__

1.

Favorite Fruit

Apple	😊	😊	😊	😊						
Pear	😊	😊	😊	😊	😊					
Grape	😊	😊	😊	😊	😊	😊	😊			
Banana	😊	😊	😊	😊	😊	😊	😊	😊	😊	

Each 😊 = 1 student.

Which fruit do exactly 7 students like most? _____

How many students like the fruit with the fewest votes? _____

How many more students chose banana than pear? _____

2. **Writing** Use the picture graph.

   Write two true statements about the picture graph.

   _____

   _____

Transportation to School						
Bus	🙂	🙂	🙂	🙂	🙂	🙂
Walk	🙂	🙂	🙂	🙂		
Car	🙂	🙂				
Subway	🙂	🙂	🙂	🙂	🙂	

   Each 🙂 = 1 student.

3. **Modeling Real Life** Use the picture graph.

Favorite After-School Activity									
Play outside	🙂	🙂	🙂	🙂	🙂	🙂			
Video games	🙂	🙂	🙂	🙂	🙂	🙂	🙂	🙂	🙂
Watch TV	🙂	🙂	🙂	🙂	🙂	🙂	🙂		
Read	🙂	🙂	🙂						

   Each 🙂 = 1 student.

   Do more students like to play video games and read or play outside and watch TV?

   More students like to _____ and _____.

   Review & Refresh

   4. What is the best estimate of the length of a keyboard?

      18 inches   18 feet   18 yards

Name _____

Make Picture Graphs 13.3

Learning Target: Use data to make picture graphs.

 **Explore and Grow**

Look at your color tiles. Complete the tally chart and the picture graph.

Tile Colors

Blue	
Green	
Red	
Yellow	

Tile Colors

Blue										
Green										
Red										
Yellow										

Each ◯ = 1 tile.

Chapter 13 | Lesson 3

six hundred twenty-five 625

Think and Grow

Favorite Color	
Red	||||
Blue	||||	
Yellow		
Pink	|||

Favorite Color						
Red	☺	☺	☺	☺	☺	
Blue	☺	☺	☺	☺	☺	☺
Yellow	☺					
Pink	☺	☺	☺			

Each ☺ = 1 student.

Which color is the most favorite? blue

How many more students chose red than pink? 2

Show and Grow — I can do it!

1. Complete the picture graph.

Favorite Fruit	
Orange	||||
Strawberry	||
Apple	||||	
Banana	||||

Favorite Fruit						
Orange						
Strawberry						
Apple						
Banana						

Each ☺ = 1 student.

Which fruit is the most favorite? _____

Which fruit is the least favorite? _____

How many more students chose apple than banana? ____

 Apply and Grow: Practice

2. Complete the picture graph.

Favorite Bird	
Parrot	||
Flamingo	|||||
Owl	|||
Penguin	||||| ||

Favorite Bird						
Parrot						
Flamingo						
Owl						
Penguin						

Each 🙂 = 1 student.

How many students chose the most favorite bird? _____

How many students chose flamingo or penguin? _____

3. Complete the picture graph.

Number of Coins	
You	|||||
Newton	||||
Descartes	|||||	

Number of Coins						
You						
Newton						
Descartes						

Each ◯ = 1 coin.

Newton gives 4 coins to Descartes. How many coins does Newton have now? How do you know?

_____

_____

Chapter 13 | Lesson 3

Think and Grow: Modeling Real Life

You ask 20 students to name their eye colors. 9 have brown eyes. 3 more students have brown eyes than blue eyes. The rest have green eyes. Complete the picture graph.

Check Your Work How can you check that you have the correct number of 🙂 in the picture graph?

Eye Color

Blue										
Brown										
Green										

Each 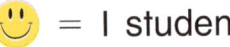 = 1 student.

Show and Grow   I can think deeper!

4. You ask 15 students which community helper is their favorite. 6 choose police officer. 2 fewer students choose doctor than police officer. The rest choose firefighter. Complete the picture graph.

Favorite Community Helper

Police officer								
Firefighter								
Doctor								

Each 🙂 = 1 student.

Communicate Clearly How did you find how many students chose firefighter?

628   six hundred twenty-eight

Name _____

Practice 13.3

Learning Target: Use data to make picture graphs.

Number of Points	
You	IIII
Your friend	IIII
Newton	III
Descartes	I

Number of Points					
You	○	○	○	○	
Your friend	○	○	○	○	○
Newton	○	○	○		
Descartes	○				

Each ○ = 1 point.

Who has the most points? **your friend**

1. Complete the picture graph.

Number of Medals	
You	IIII
Your friend	II
Newton	IIII
Descartes	IIII I

Number of Medals					
You					
Your friend					
Newton					
Descartes					

Each ○ = 1 medal.

Who has the least medals? _____

How many more medals do you have than your friend? _____

How many medals do Newton and Descartes have in all? _____

Chapter 13 | Lesson 3   six hundred twenty-nine 629

2. Complete the picture graph.

Favorite Soup	
Alphabet	|||| ||
Vegetable	|||
Tomato	||||	

Favorite Soup							
Alphabet							
Vegetable							
Tomato							

Each 🙂 = 1 student.

DIG DEEPER! How many fewer students chose vegetable soup than the other soups combined? _____

3. **Modeling Real Life** You ask 20 students about their favorite way to exercise. 4 like to walk. 6 like to swim. The rest like to bike. Complete the picture graph.

Favorite Way to Exercise								
Bike								
Walk								
Swim								

Each 🙂 = 1 student.

Communicate Clearly How did you find how many students like to bike?

_____

Review & Refresh

4.   4 1 5
　　　− 2 7 3

5.   5 8 3
　　　− 1 2 7

6.   8 9 2
　　　− 1 0 5

Name _____

Learning Target: Understand the data shown by a bar graph.

Read and Interpret Bar Graphs

13.4

Explore and Grow

How are the tally chart and the bar graph the same? How are they different?

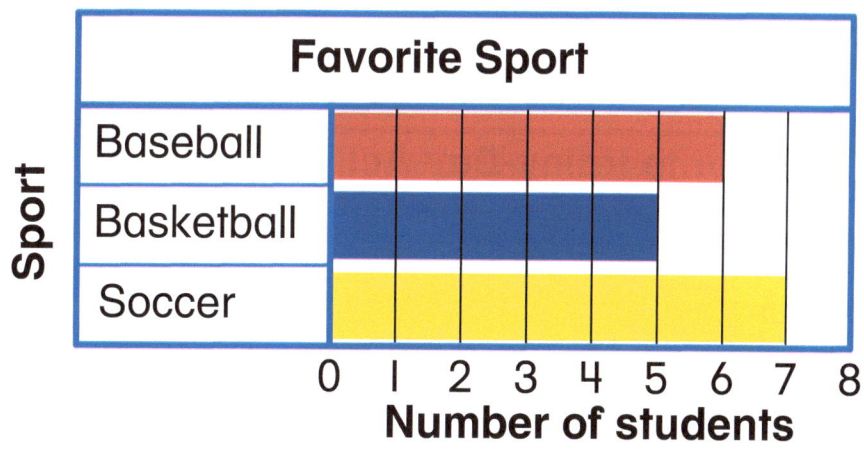

_____

_____

Chapter 13 | Lesson 4   six hundred thirty-one   631

Think and Grow

bar graph

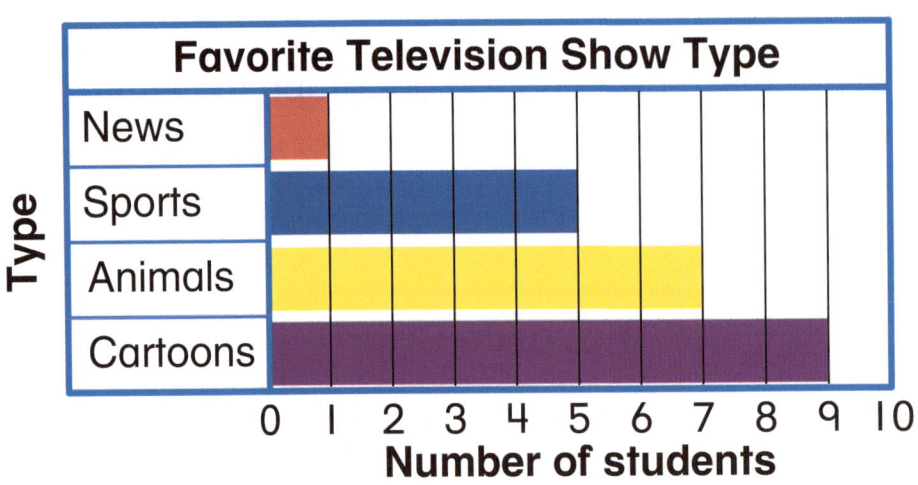

How many students chose animals? __7__

Which show type is the most favorite? __cartoons__

Show and Grow — I can do it!

1. **Favorite Rainy-Day Activity**

    How many students chose computer? _____

    Which activity is the least favorite? _____

Apply and Grow: Practice

2.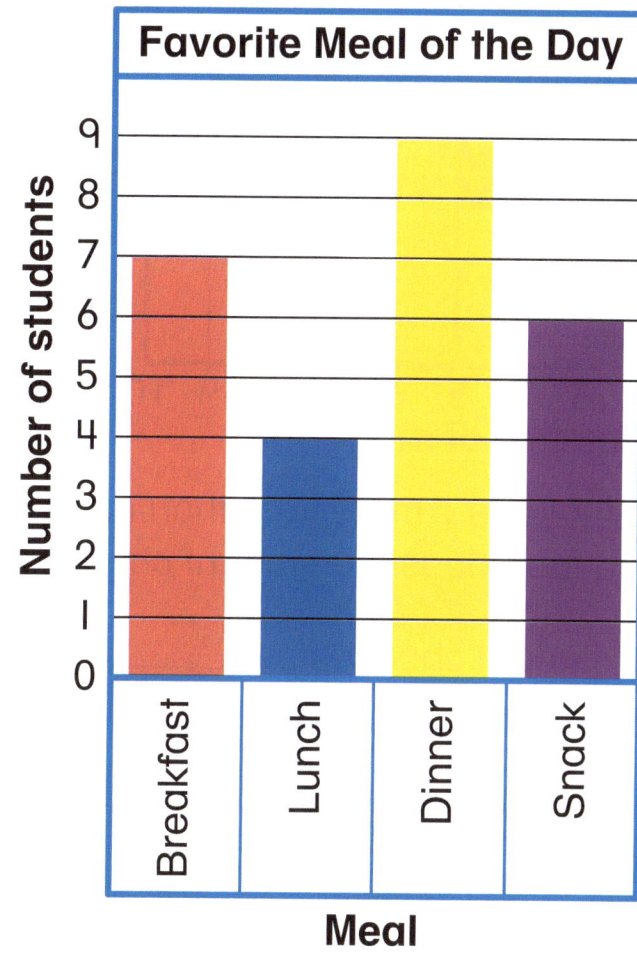

How many students chose breakfast?

_____

Which meal is the most favorite?

_____

How many students chose the meal that is least favorite?

_____

How many more students chose snack than lunch?

_____

3. **DIG DEEPER!** Order the meals in Exercise 2 from the least favorite to the most favorite.

_____, _____, _____, _____

Chapter 13 | Lesson 4

Think and Grow: Modeling Real Life

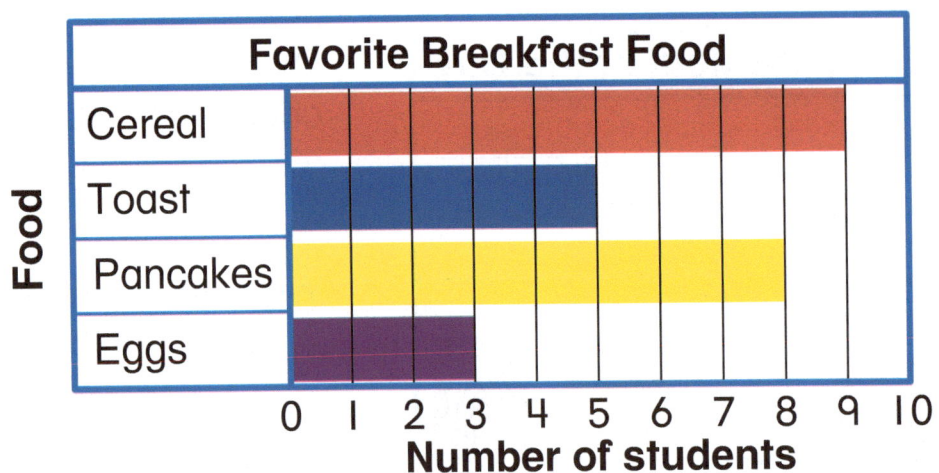

A student chooses a food that has 1 more vote than eggs and toast combined. Which food does the student choose?

The student chooses _____.

Show and Grow   I can think deeper!

4.

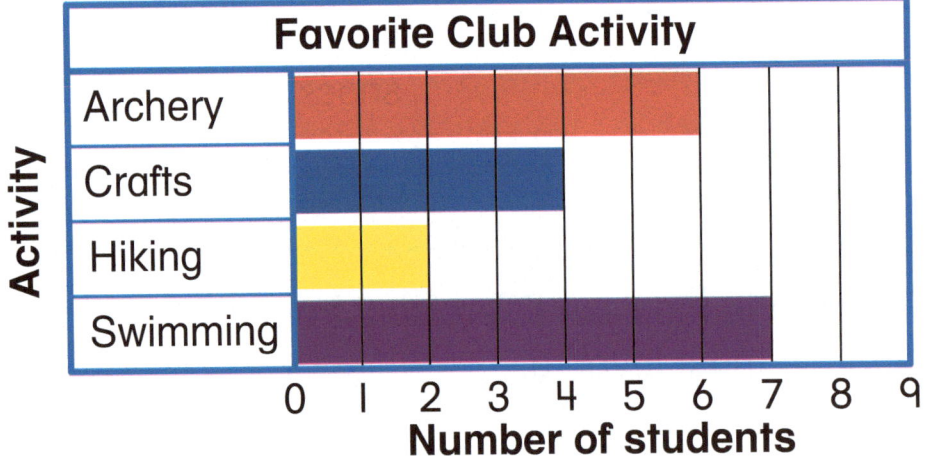

A student chooses an activity that has the same number of votes as crafts and hiking combined. Which activity does the student choose?

The student chooses _____.

Name _____

Practice 13.4

Learning Target: Understand the data shown by a bar graph.

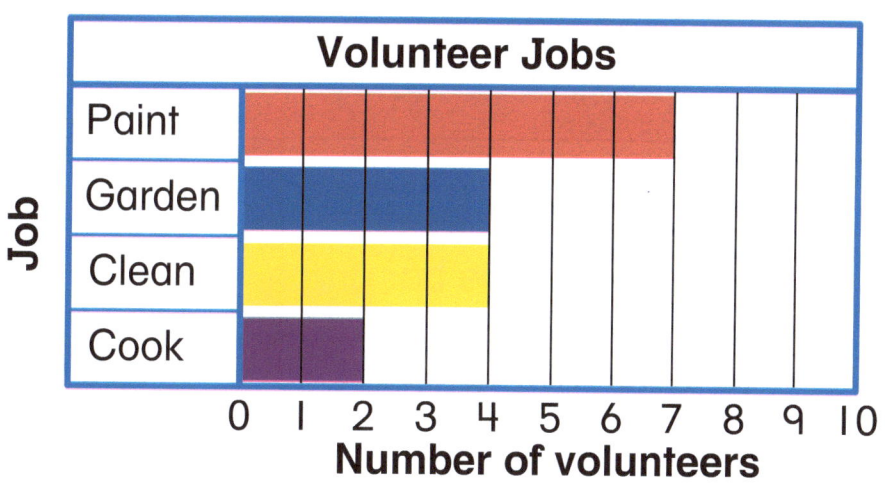

How many volunteers chose garden? __4__

Which job was picked by the fewest number of volunteers? __cook__

1.

How many students chose police officer? _____

How many more students chose teacher than nurse? _____

2. **Repeated Reasoning** How are picture graphs and bar graphs alike? How are they different?

   _____

   _____

3. **Modeling Real Life** Use the bar graph.

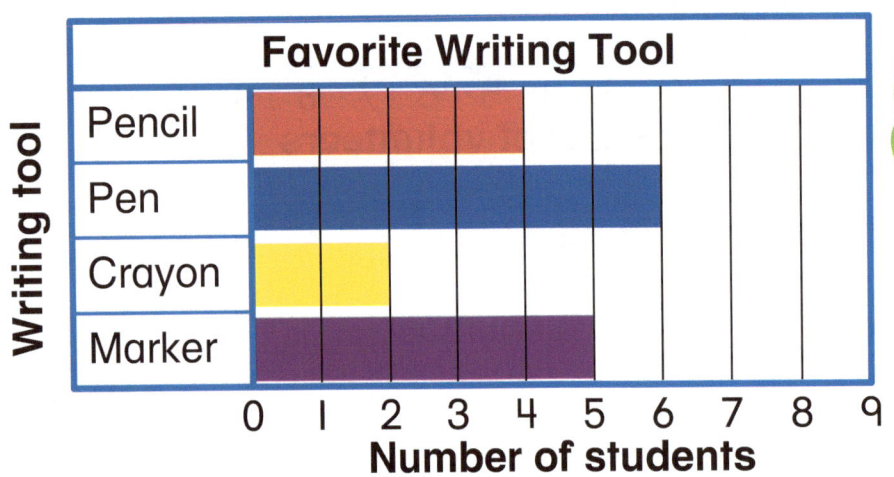

Justify a Result How did you use the bar graph to determine which writing tool the student chooses?

A student chooses a writing tool that has 3 fewer votes than crayon and marker combined. Which writing tool does the student choose?

The student chooses _____.

Review & Refresh

Find the missing number.

4.   5 7 6
   + ☐ ☐ ☐
   ─────────
       7 2 9

5.   4 3 1
   + ☐ ☐ ☐
   ─────────
       8 2 0

6.   1 2 8
   + ☐ ☐ ☐
   ─────────
       6 4 9

Name _____

Make Bar Graphs 13.5

Learning Target: Use data to make bar graphs.

 **Explore and Grow**

Look at your Instrument Cards. Complete the tally chart and the bar graph.

Band Instruments

Drum	
Trumpet	
Tuba	

Band Instruments

Instrument
- Drum
- Trumpet
- Tuba

0 1 2 3 4 5 6 7 8
Number of students

Use Math Tools
Why is it helpful to complete the tally chart before you complete the bar graph?

Chapter 13 | Lesson 5

six hundred thirty-seven 637

Think and Grow

Trees in a Park	
Pine	‖‖‖
Birch	‖
Oak	‖‖‖
Maple	‖‖‖‖ ‖‖‖

Trees in a Park (bar graph: Pine = 5, Birch = 2, Oak = 4, Maple = 8)

Which tree type is the most common? __maple__

How many more pine trees are there than oak trees? __1__

Show and Grow — I can do it!

1. Complete the bar graph.

Favorite Book Type	
History	‖‖‖
Fiction	‖‖‖‖ ‖‖
Science	‖‖‖‖
Poetry	‖‖‖‖ ‖

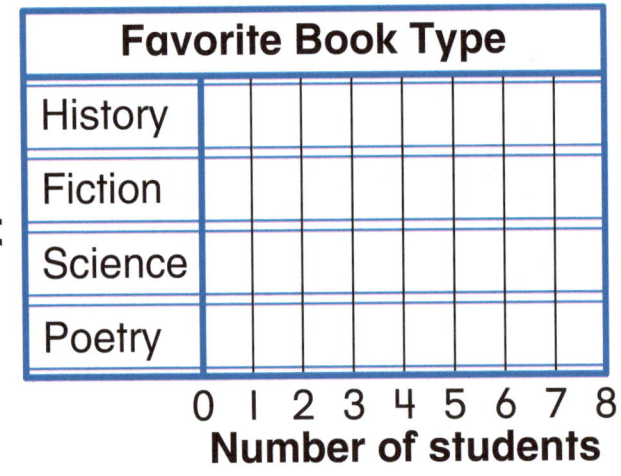

Which book type is the least favorite? _____

How many more students chose fiction than history? _____

638   six hundred thirty-eight

Apply and Grow: Practice

2. Complete the bar graph.

Trail Mix Pieces	
Peanuts	|||| ||||
Raisins	||||	
Almonds	|||| ||
Dried fruit	||||

Trail Mix Pieces — Type vs. Number of pieces (0–9)

How many raisins are there? _____

How many more almonds are there than dried fruit? _____

3. Complete the bar graph.

Drinks at a Picnic	
Water	||||
Fruit punch	||
Lemonade	|||| ||||
Iced tea	|||| |||

Drinks at a Picnic — Drink vs. Number of people (0–9)

Which drink was chosen the most? _____

How many more people chose iced tea than water? _____

Chapter 13 | Lesson 5

Think and Grow: Modeling Real Life

You classify 30 animals as fish, mammals, or reptiles. 11 are fish. 7 are reptiles. The rest are mammals. Complete the bar graph.

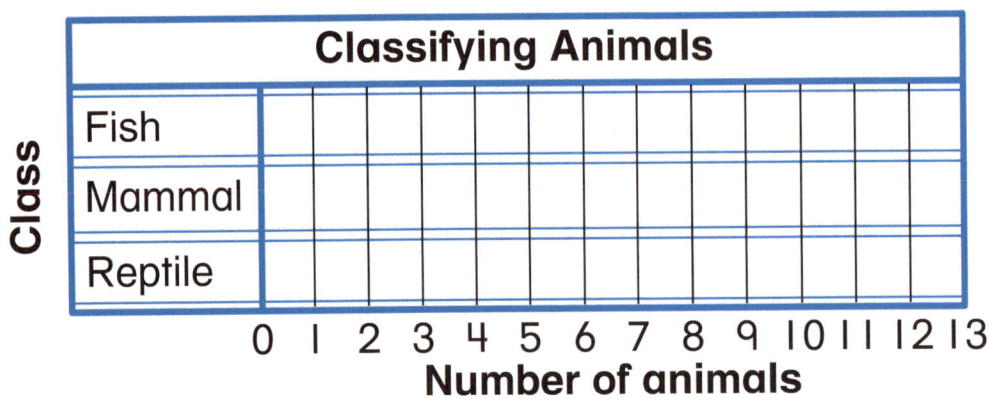

Show and Grow   I can think deeper!

4. You ask 29 students if they want to collect seashells, fossils, or stickers. 8 said fossils. 12 said stickers. The rest said seashells. Complete the bar graph.

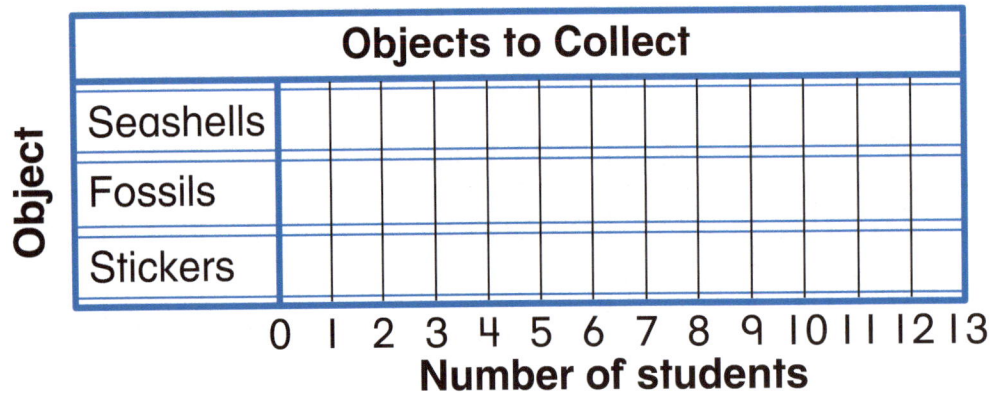

DIG DEEPER! You ask 3 more students which object they want to collect. 1 said fossils. 2 said seashells. How many fewer students chose fossils than seashells now?

_____ students

Name _____

Practice 13.5

Learning Target: Use data to make bar graphs.

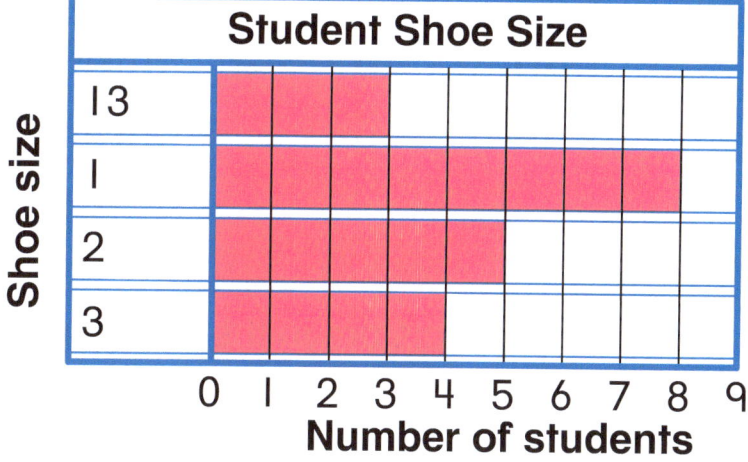

Student Shoe Size	
13	III
1	HHT III
2	HHT
3	IIII

Which shoe size is the least common? __13__

How many more students wear size 2 than size 3? __1__

1. Complete the bar graph.

Class Pet Name	
Spot	HHT IIII
Sparkle	II
Flip	HHT II
Star	HHT I

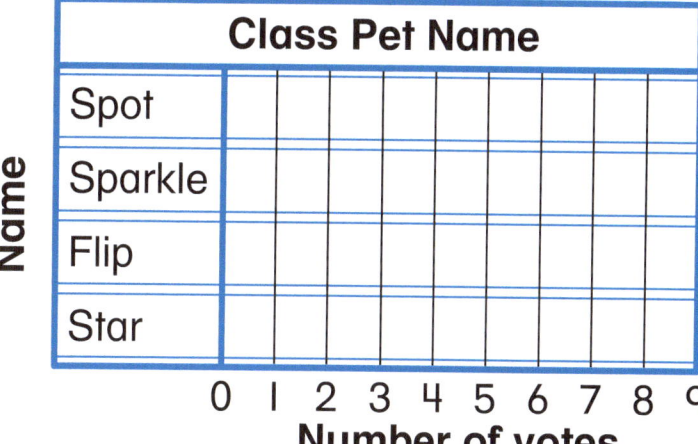

How many more votes did Spot receive than Sparkle? _____

Chapter 13 | Lesson 5

six hundred forty-one 641

2. Complete the bar graph.

Animals in a Pet Store	
Fish	‖‖‖ ‖
Hamster	‖‖‖
Snake	‖‖‖‖
Rabbit	‖‖‖‖

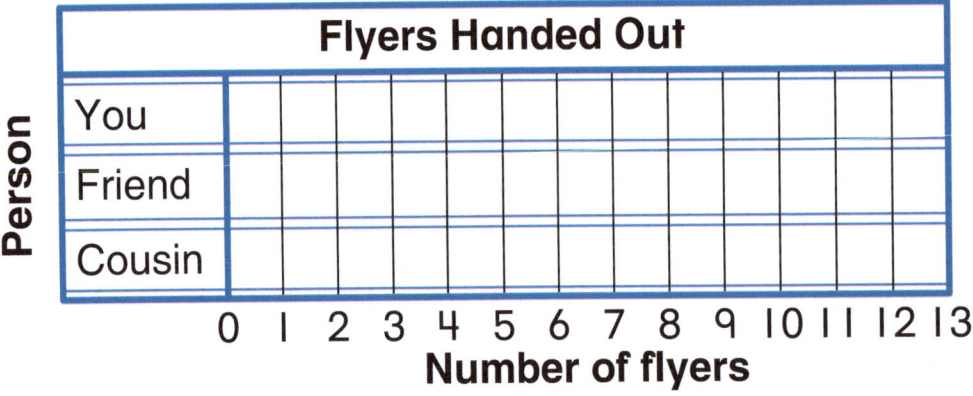

How many total animals are in the pet store? _____

3. **Modeling Real Life** You, your friend, and your cousin hand out a total of 25 flyers. You hand out 12. Your friend hands out 9. Your cousin hands out the rest. Complete the bar graph.

Flyers Handed Out

Person: You / Friend / Cousin
Number of flyers: 0 1 2 3 4 5 6 7 8 9 10 11 12 13

DIG DEEPER! You hand out 1 more flyer. Your friend hands out 4 more. How many fewer flyers does your cousin hand out than your friend now?

_____ flyers

Review & Refresh

4. 861 − 410 = _____

5. 624 − 320 = _____

Name _____

Learning Target: Use data to make line plots.

Make Line Plots 13.6

Explore and Grow

How are the thumb lengths shown on the number line?

Thumb Lengths

Thumb 1 — 4 cm	Thumb 5 — 6 cm
Thumb 2 — 5 cm	Thumb 6 — 5 cm
Thumb 3 — 3 cm	Thumb 7 — 4 cm
Thumb 4 — 4 cm	

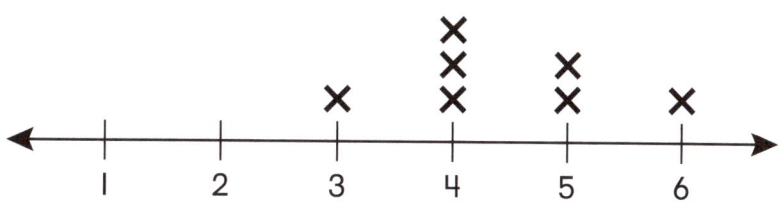

_____

_____

Chapter 13 | Lesson 6

Think and Grow

Car Lengths (feet)	
Car 1	12
Car 2	13
Car 3	14
Car 4	12
Car 5	12
Car 6	15
Car 7	14

line plot

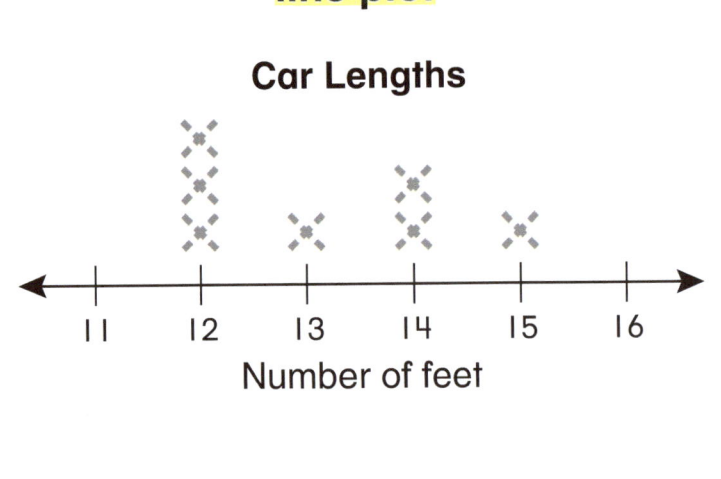

How many cars are 14 feet long? __2__

What is the most common car length? __12__ feet

Show and Grow — I can do it!

1. Complete the line plot.

Long Jump Lengths (inches)	
Child 1	41
Child 2	44
Child 3	43
Child 4	41
Child 5	45

Long Jump Lengths

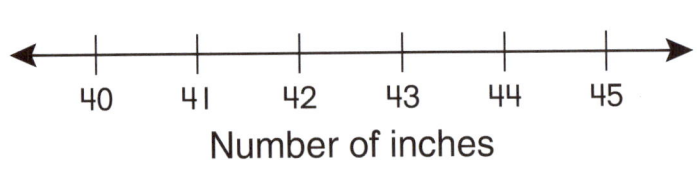

How many long jumps are 43 inches long? _____

What is the most common long jump length? _____ inches

Name _____

✓ Apply and Grow: Practice

2. Complete the line plot.

Puppy Lengths (inches)	
Puppy 1	11
Puppy 2	9
Puppy 3	10
Puppy 4	12
Puppy 5	9
Puppy 6	10
Puppy 7	10
Puppy 8	8

 **Puppy Lengths**

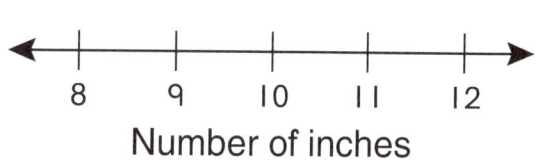
Number of inches

What is the most common puppy length? _____ inches

How many fewer puppies are 11 inches long than 10 inches long?

_____

How many puppies are 8 or 9 inches long?

_____

How many puppies are shorter than 11 inches? How do you know?

_____

_____

Chapter 13 | Lesson 6   six hundred forty-five 645

Think and Grow: Modeling Real Life

9 people measure the length of a guitar. The line plot shows the measured lengths. How long do you think the guitar is? Explain.

_____ inches

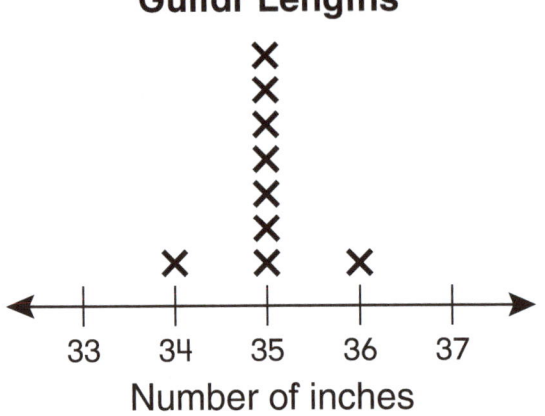

_____

_____

Show and Grow   I can think deeper!

3. 8 people measure the length of a playground. The line plot shows the measured lengths. How long do you think the playground is? Explain.

_____ meters

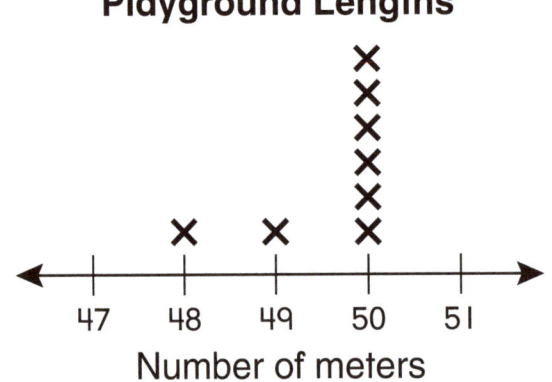

_____

DIG DEEPER! Why are the measurements different?

_____

Name _____

Practice 13.6

Learning Target: Use data to make line plots.

Complete the line plot.

Classroom Lengths (yards)	
Room 1	10
Room 2	9
Room 3	10
Room 4	10

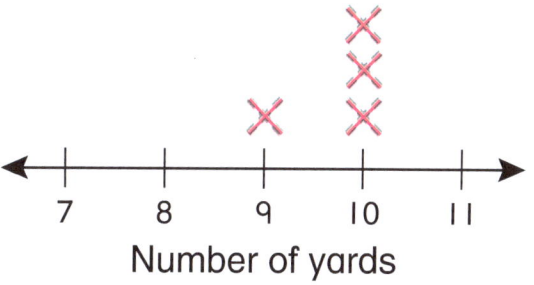

How many classrooms are 10 yards long? ___3___

1. Complete the line plot.

Leaf Lengths (centimeters)	
Leaf 1	14
Leaf 2	15
Leaf 3	15
Leaf 4	14
Leaf 5	12
Leaf 6	15

 **Leaf Lengths**

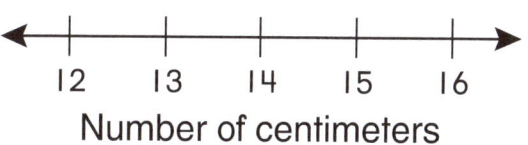

How many leaves are 13 centimeters long? _____

What is the most common leaf length? _____ centimeters

How many more leaves are 14 centimeters long than 12 centimeters long? _____

How many leaves are 14 or 15 centimeters? _____

Chapter 13 | Lesson 6

2. Complete the line plot.

Shark Lengths (feet)	
Shark 1	14
Shark 2	15
Shark 3	16
Shark 4	14
Shark 5	12
Shark 6	16

Shark Lengths

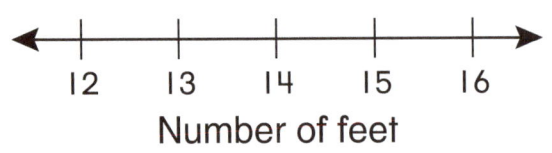

Number of feet

How many sharks are longer than 14 feet? How do you know?

_____

3. **Modeling Real Life** 8 people measure the length of a bus. The line plot shows the measured lengths. How long do you think the school bus is? Explain.

_____ meters

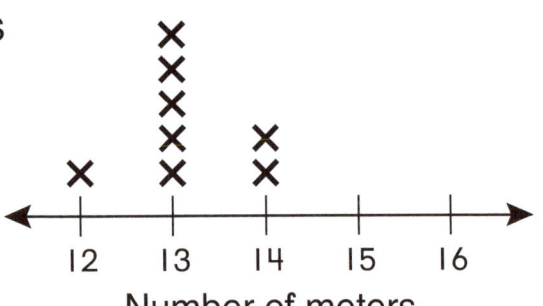

Bus Lengths

Number of meters

_____

Review & Refresh

4.
```
   3 6
     4
   2 2
 + 6 5
```

5.
```
   9 5
   6 8
 + 4 5
```

6.
```
   7 6
   5 0
   1 8
 + 8 2
```

Name _____

Learning Target: Measure objects and make line plots.

Measure Objects and Make Line Plots

13.7

Explore and Grow

Use a ruler to measure the caterpillars on Lengths of Caterpillars. Use the lengths to complete the chart and the line plot.

Caterpillar Lengths (centimeters)	
Caterpillar 1	
Caterpillar 2	
Caterpillar 3	
Caterpillar 4	
Caterpillar 5	
Caterpillar 6	
Caterpillar 7	
Caterpillar 8	

Caterpillar Lengths

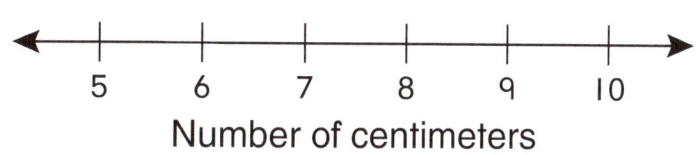

Number of centimeters

Chapter 13 | Lesson 7

six hundred forty-nine 649

Think and Grow

Crayon Lengths (centimeters)	
Crayon 1	8
Crayon 2	7
Crayon 3	5
Crayon 4	8
Crayon 5	9

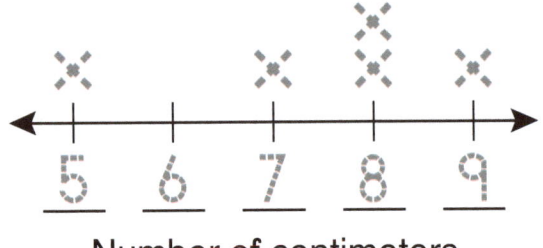

What is the length of the longest crayon? 9 centimeters

How much longer is the longest crayon than the shortest crayon? 4 centimeters

Show and Grow — I can do it!

1. Measure the lengths of 4 pencils. Complete the line plot.

Pencil Lengths (inches)	
Pencil 1	
Pencil 2	
Pencil 3	
Pencil 4	

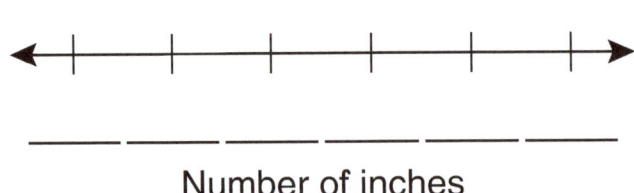

What is the length of the longest pencil? _____ inches

How much longer is the longest pencil than the shortest pencil? _____ inches

Name _____

✓ Apply and Grow: Practice

2. Measure the lengths of 8 shoes. Complete the line plot.

Shoe Lengths (inches)	
Shoe 1	
Shoe 2	
Shoe 3	
Shoe 4	
Shoe 5	
Shoe 6	
Shoe 7	
Shoe 8	

Shoe Lengths

Number of inches

What is the length of the longest shoe? _____ inches

What is the length of the shortest shoe? _____ inches

How much shorter is the shortest shoe than
the longest shoe? _____ inches

MP Structure You measure 5 more shoes and they are each 6 inches long. How does the line plot change?

_____

_____

Think and Grow: Modeling Real Life

A fire station is building a new garage for emergency vehicles. Complete the sentence. Explain.

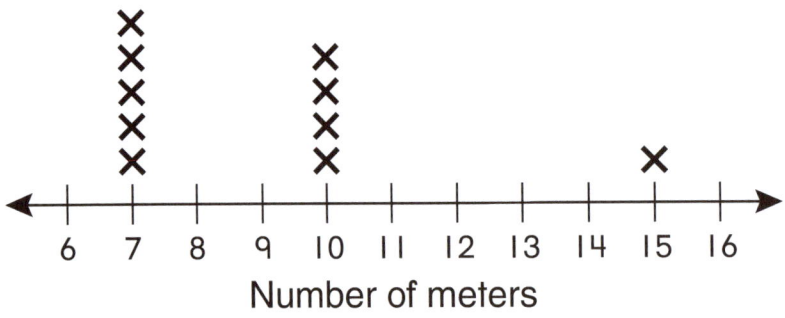

The garage should be more than _____ meters long.

_____

Show and Grow I can think deeper!

3. You want to put some school supplies in a pencil box. Complete the sentence. Explain.

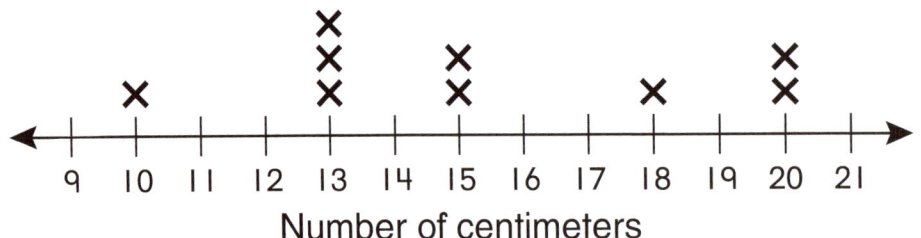

The pencil box should be more than _____ centimeters long.

_____

652 six hundred fifty-two

Name _____

Practice

Learning Target: Measure objects and make line plots.

Measure the lengths of 4 pieces of chalk. Complete the line plot.

Chalk Lengths (centimeters)	
Chalk 1	9
Chalk 2	8
Chalk 3	7
Chalk 4	8

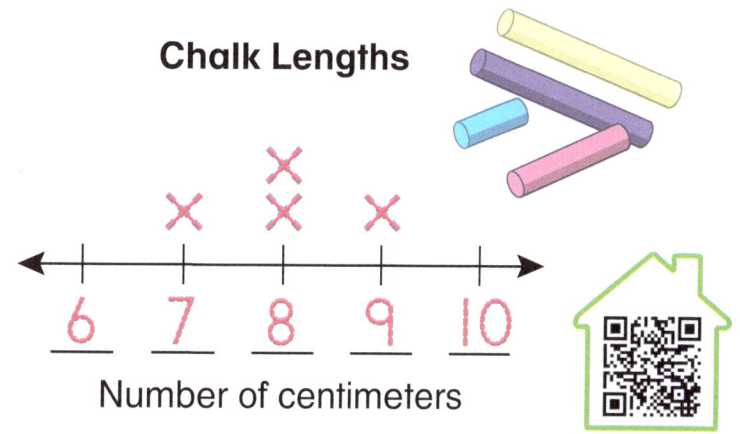

1. Measure the lengths of 5 socks. Complete the line plot.

Sock Lengths (inches)	
Sock 1	
Sock 2	
Sock 3	
Sock 4	
Sock 5	

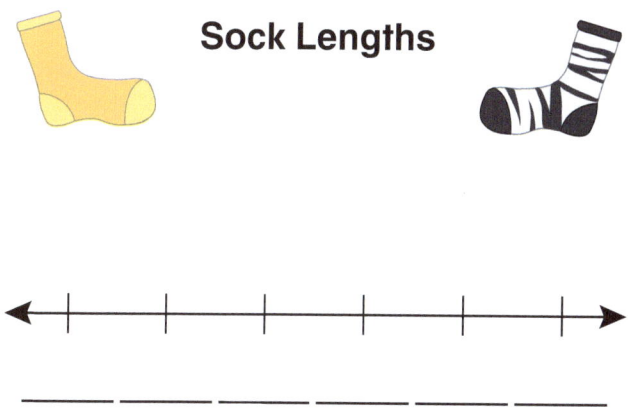

What is the length of the longest sock? _____ inches

What is the length of the shortest sock? _____ inches

How much longer is the longest sock than the shortest sock? _____ inches

Chapter 13 | Lesson 7   six hundred fifty-three   653

2. Measure the lengths of 4 hands. Complete the line plot.

Hand Lengths (inches)	
Hand 1	
Hand 2	
Hand 3	
Hand 4	

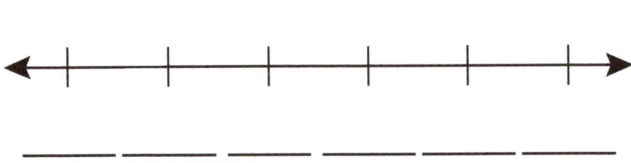

Hand Lengths

Number of inches

How many hands are longer than 5 inches? How do you know?

_____

_____

3. **Modeling Real Life** Newton wants to put his dog bones in a box. Complete the sentence. Explain.

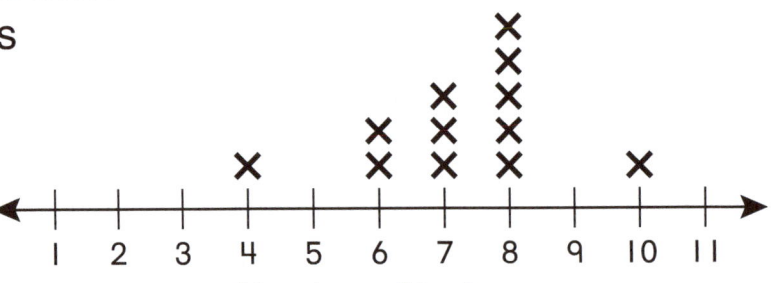

The box should be more than _____ inches long.

_____

Review & Refresh

4. 10 more than 347 is _____.

5. 100 less than 926 is _____.

Name _____

Performance Task 13

You measure the lengths of 8 writing tools. The tools and their lengths are shown.

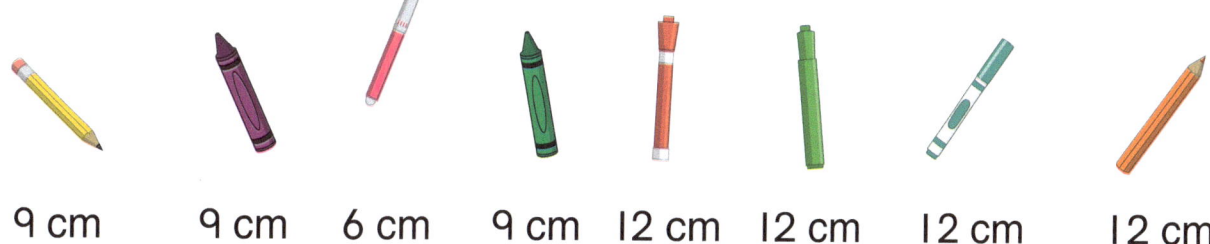

9 cm   9 cm   6 cm   9 cm   12 cm   12 cm   12 cm   12 cm

1. Organize the writing tool lengths on the line plot.

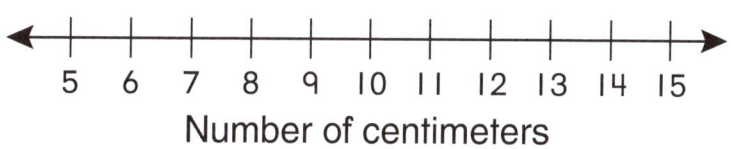

Number of centimeters

2. Use the line plot to complete the equation. Why is the sum 8?

   _____ + _____ + _____ = 8

3. Measure your pencil. Add the length of your pencil to the line plot in Exercise 1.

4. Compare the lengths of your pencil and one of the writing tools above.

_____

Chapter 13   six hundred fifty-five   655

Spin and Graph

To Play: Spin 10 times. Complete the tally chart. Then complete the bar graph. Answer the Spin and Graph Questions about your graph.

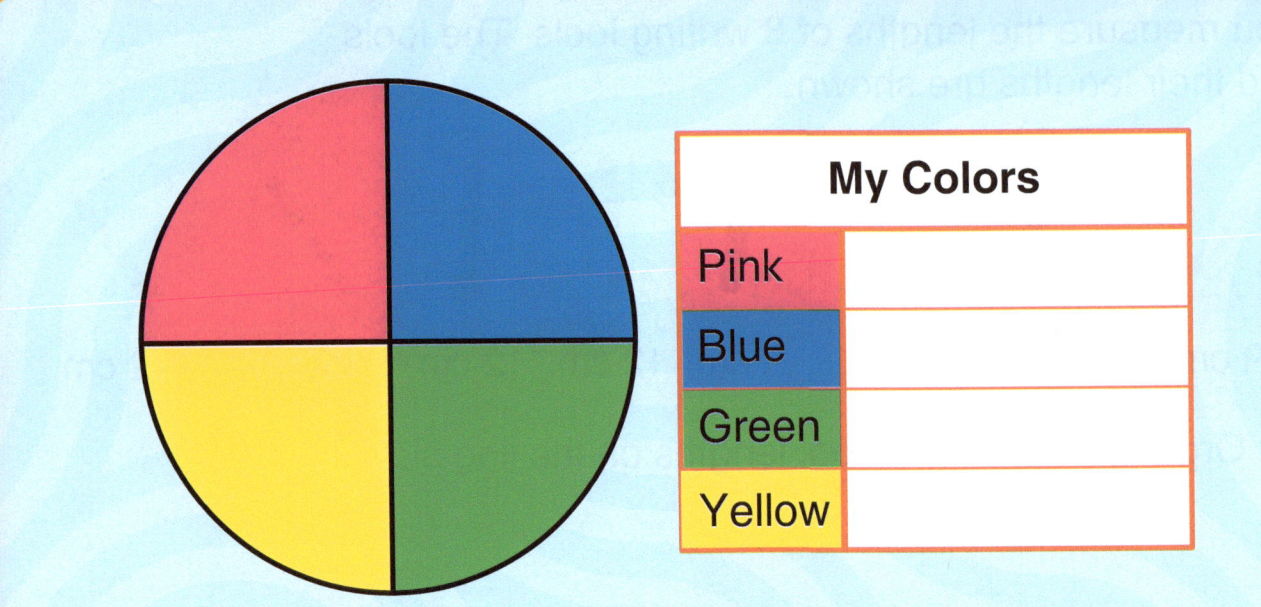

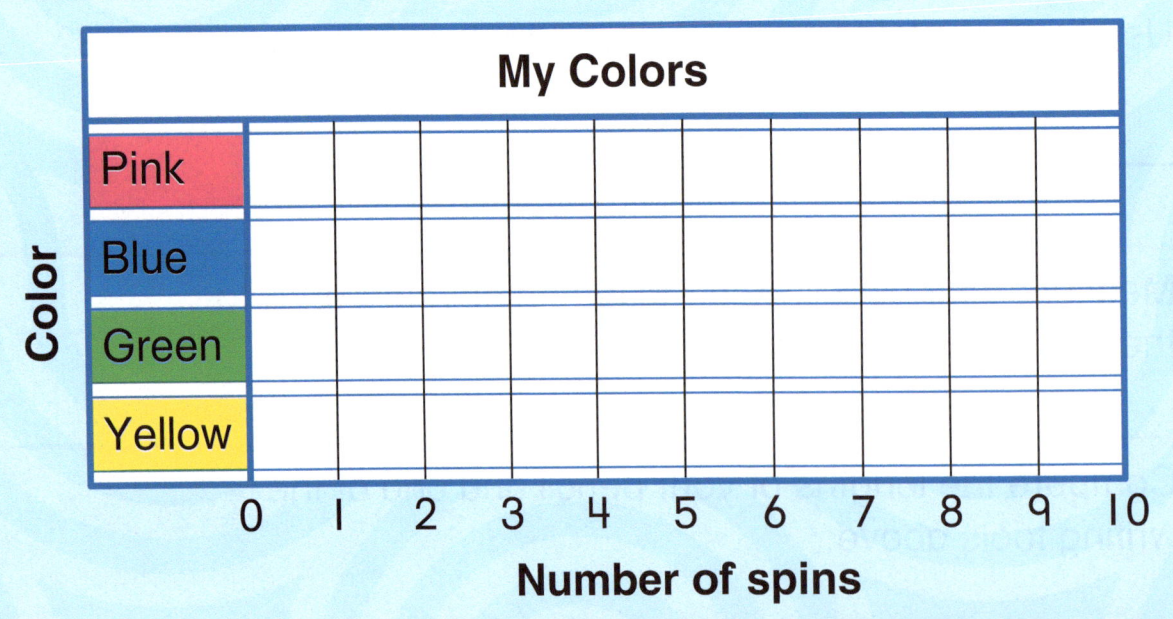

Chapter 13 Practice

13.1 Sort and Organize Data

1. Use the data to complete the tally chart.

face painting	face painting
games	magic show
dancing	games
magic show	face painting
magic show	magic show
face painting	magic show

Favorite Festival Event	
Magic show	
Games	
Face painting	
Dancing	

   How many students chose magic show? _____

   Which event is the least favorite? _____

2. **Modeling Real Life** You want to survey 30 students. How many more students do you need to ask?

Hair Color	
Blonde	⧗⧗ IIII
Brown	⧗⧗ ⧗⧗
Black	⧗⧗
Red	II

   _____ students

   How many more students need to have red hair so that the numbers of students with red hair and blonde hair are equal?

   _____ students

13.2 Read and Interpret Picture Graphs

3.

Favorite Type of Book									
Comics	😊	😊	😊	😊	😊	😊	😊		
Fiction	😊	😊	😊	😊					
Nonfiction	😊	😊	😊	😊	😊				
Magazine	😊	😊	😊	😊	😊	😊	😊		

Each 😊 = 1 student.

Which type of book do exactly 7 students like best? _____

How many more students chose magazine than fiction? _____

13.3 Make Picture Graphs

4. Complete the picture graph.

Favorite Cat	
Tiger	III
Lion	IIII
Cheetah	HHT II
Panther	HHT

Favorite Cat							
Tiger							
Lion							
Cheetah							
Panther							

Each 😊 = 1 student.

How many fewer students chose tiger than cheetah? _____

How many students chose the least favorite cat? _____

How many students chose panther or lion? _____

13.4 Read and Interpret Bar Graphs

5.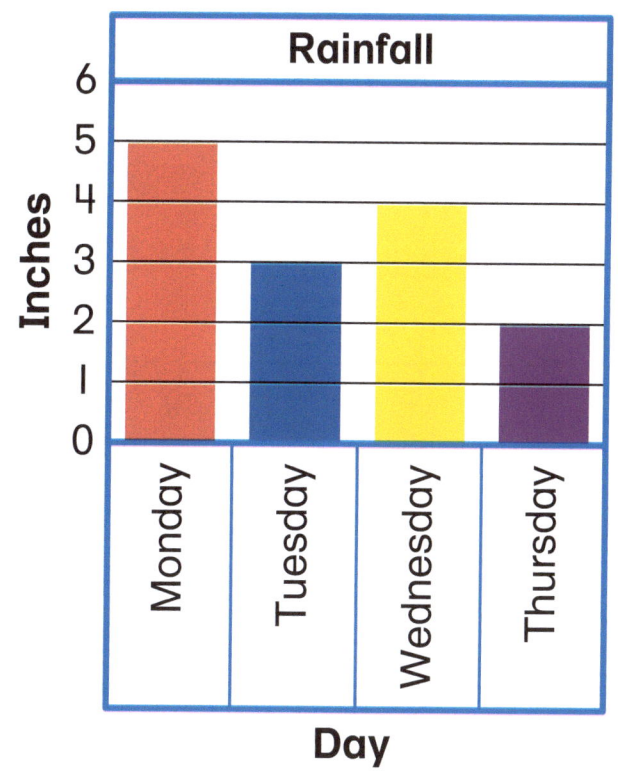

How much rain fell on Tuesday?

_____

Which day did it rain the least?

_____

How much more rain fell on Monday than Wednesday?

_____

13.5 Make Bar Graphs

6. Complete the bar graph.

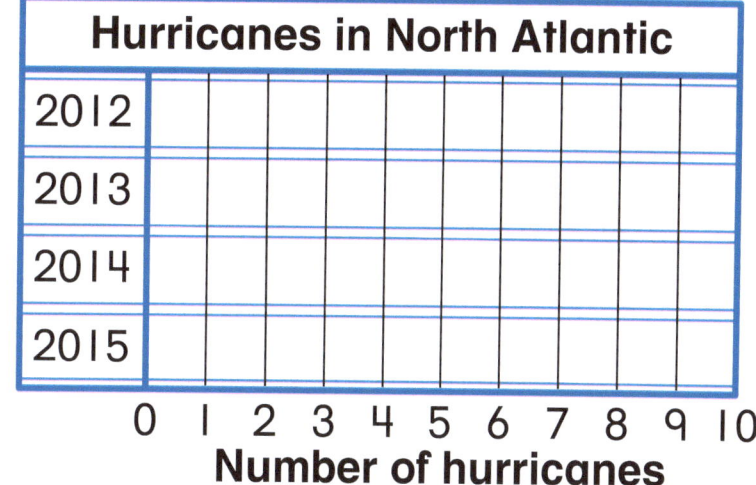

How many hurricanes were there in 2012 and 2013? _____

13.6 Read and Interpret Line Plots

7. Complete the line plot.

Feather Lengths (centimeters)	
Feather 1	14
Feather 2	13
Feather 3	15
Feather 4	12

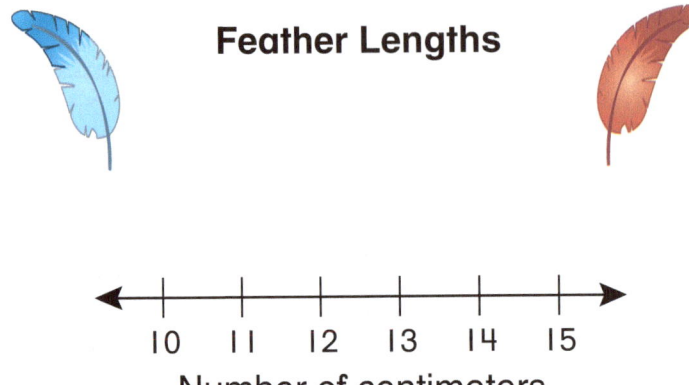

Feather Lengths

Number of centimeters

How many feathers are longer than 13 centimeters?
How do you know?

_____

_____

13.7 Measure Objects and Make Line Plots

8. Use an inch ruler to measure the lengths of 5 toys to the nearest inch. Then complete the line plot.

Toy Lengths (inches)	
Toy 1	
Toy 2	
Toy 3	
Toy 4	
Toy 5	

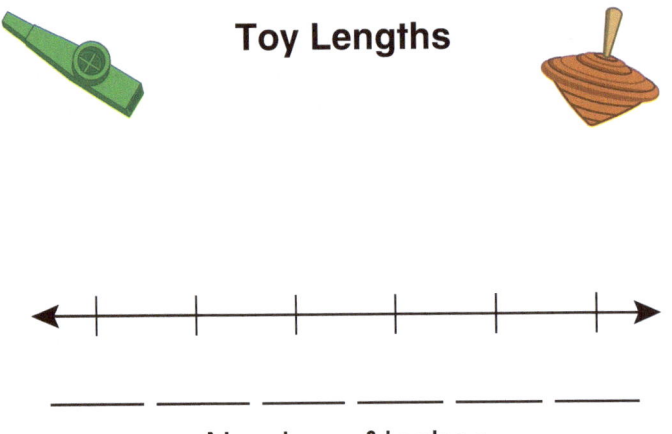

Toy Lengths

Number of inches

What is the length of the longest toy? _____ inches

14 Money and Time

- What are some types of public transportation?
- The next subway arrives at 7:30. How many minutes are there until the next subway arrives?

Chapter Learning Target:
Understand money and time.

Chapter Success Criteria:
- I can identify the values of coins and bills and times on a clock.
- I can choose a strategy to solve money and time problems.
- I can compare the value of one coin to another and tell the time.
- I can solve money and time problems.

Name _____

Vocabulary

Review Words
analog clock
hour hand
minute hand

Organize It

Use the review words to complete the graphic organizer.

Define It

Use your vocabulary cards to complete the puzzle.

Across

1.

2.

Down

3.

4.

662   six hundred sixty-two

Chapter 14 Vocabulary Cards

$1 bill	$5 bill
$10 bill	$20 bill
a.m.	cents
cent sign	dime

$5 bill

$1 bill

$20 bill

$10 bill

1 cent or 1¢   25 cents or 25¢

 go to school

 8:00 a.m.

A **dime** is 10 cents or 10¢.

¢

Chapter 14 Vocabulary Cards

dollar	dollar sign
half past	midnight
nickel	noon
penny	p.m.

$

A **dollar** is $1 or 100¢.

Midnight is 12:00 at night.

half past 3

Noon is 12:00 in the daytime.

A **nickel** is 5 cents or 5¢.

go to sleep

8:00 p.m.

A **penny** is 1 cent or 1¢.

Chapter 14 Vocabulary Cards

quarter

quarter past

quarter to

15 minutes after 8 or
quarter past 8

A **quarter** is 25 cents or 25¢.

15 minutes before 8 or
quarter to 8

Name _____

Find Total Values of Coins 14.1

Learning Target: Find the total value of a group of coins.

Explore and Grow

Sort your coins.

Explain how you sorted.

_____

_____

_____

_____

Chapter 14 | Lesson 1

six hundred sixty-three 663

Think and Grow

penny
1 cent
1¢

nickel
5 cents
5¢

dime
10 cents
10¢

quarter
25 cents
25¢

¢ is the **cent sign**.

25¢, 50¢, 60¢, 70¢, 75¢, 80¢, 81¢, 82¢

The total value is 82¢.

Show and Grow   I can do it!

Count on to find the total value.

1.

_____, _____, _____, _____, _____   Total value: _____

2.

_____, _____, _____, _____, _____, _____   Total value: _____

 **Apply and Grow: Practice**

Count on to find the total value.

3.

_____, _____, _____   Total value: _____

4.

_____, _____, _____, _____, _____, _____

Total value: _____

5.

Total value: _____

6. **Reasoning** You have 27¢. Which groups of coins could you have?

Chapter 14 | Lesson 1

Think and Grow: Modeling Real Life

You have 2 quarters, 1 dime, 4 nickels, and 1 penny. How many cents do you have? Do you have enough money to buy the airplane?

Draw:

_____ Yes   No

Show and Grow — I can think deeper!

7. You have 5 dimes, 3 nickels, and 2 pennies. How many cents do you have? Do you have enough money to buy the coloring book?

_____ Yes   No

8. You have 4 dimes, 1 nickel, and 3 pennies. How many more cents do you need to buy the whistle? Draw and label the coins you need.

_____ more cents

9. **DIG DEEPER!** You have 3 quarters, 2 nickels, and 3 pennies. Your friend has 1 quarter and 5 dimes. Who has more money? How much more?

You   Friend   _____ more cents

Name _____

Practice **14.1**

Learning Target: Find the total value of a group of coins.

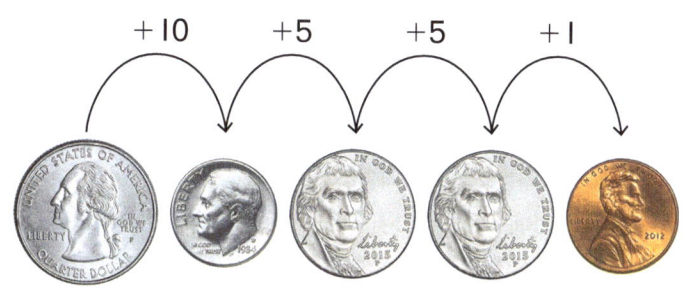

25¢, 35¢, 40¢, 45¢, 46¢

The total value is 46¢.

Count on to find the total value.

1.

_____, _____, _____, _____, _____   Total value: _____

2.

_____, _____, _____, _____, _____, _____   Total value: _____

3.

Total value: _____

Chapter 14 | Lesson 1

4. **DIG DEEPER!** You had 52¢. You lost a coin. Now you have the 5 coins shown. What coin did you lose?

_____

5. **MP Precision** Circle coins to show 80¢.

6. **MP Modeling Real Life** You have 3 quarters, 1 nickel, and 4 pennies. How many cents do you have? Do you have enough money to buy the boomerang?

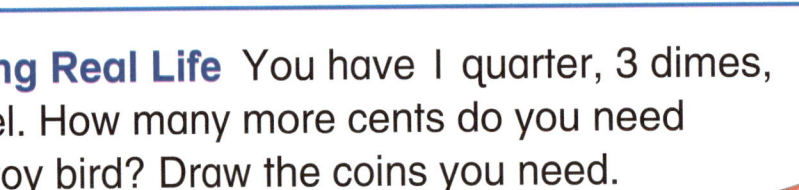

_____ Yes   No

7. **MP Modeling Real Life** You have 1 quarter, 3 dimes, and 1 nickel. How many more cents do you need to buy the toy bird? Draw the coins you need.

_____ more cents

Review & Refresh

Compare.

8. 324 ◯ 317

9. 426 ◯ 206

10. 546 ◯ 564

11. 931 ◯ 842

Name _____

Learning Target: Order a group of coins to find the total value.

Order to Find Total Values of Coins

14.2

Explore and Grow

Order your coins from the greatest value to the least value. Draw and label each coin with its value. What is the total value of all the coins?

Total: _____ ¢

Explain how ordering the coins helped you find the total.

_____

_____

_____

_____

Chapter 14 | Lesson 2

six hundred sixty-nine

Think and Grow

Draw and label the coins from the greatest value to the least value. Then find the total value.

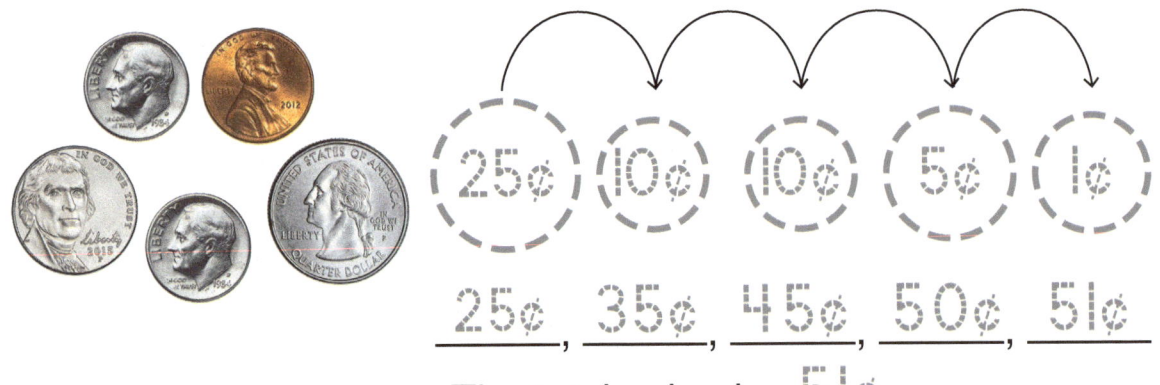

25¢, 35¢, 45¢, 50¢, 51¢

The total value is 51¢.

Show and Grow   I can do it!

Draw and label the coins from the greatest value to the least value. Then find the total value.

1.

   Total value: _____

2.

   Total value: _____

3.

   Total value: _____

Name _____

✓ Apply and Grow: Practice

Draw and label the coins from the greatest value to the least value. Then find the total value.

4.

Total value: _____

5.

Total value: _____

6.

Total value: _____

7. **Reasoning** You have a dime, a nickel, and one other coin. The total value is 40¢. What is your third coin?

Chapter 14 | Lesson 2

Think and Grow: Modeling Real Life

You have 3 nickels and 4 pennies in one pocket. You have 2 dimes and 2 quarters in your other pocket. How much money do you have in all? Do you have enough money to buy the car?

Draw:

_____   Yes   No

Show and Grow — I can think deeper!

8. You have 30¢. You find 2 nickels, 1 dime, and 3 pennies in your room. How much money do you have now? Do you have enough money to buy the yo-yo?

_____   Yes   No

9. You have 1 nickel, 1 quarter, and 4 dimes. How many more cents do you need to buy the stuffed animal? Draw and label the coin you need.

_____ more cents

10. **DIG DEEPER!** You have 65¢. You give your friend a dime. You have 3 coins left. Draw and label the coins you have left.

672   six hundred seventy-two

Name _____

Practice 14.2

Learning Target: Order a group of coins to find the total value.

Draw and label the coins from the greatest value to the least value. Then find the total value.

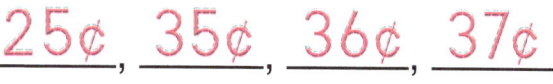

25¢, 35¢, 36¢, 37¢

The total value is 37¢ .

Draw and label the coins from the greatest value to the least value. Then find the total value.

1.

Total value: _____

2.

Total value: _____

3.

Total value: _____

Chapter 14 | Lesson 2   six hundred seventy-three

4. **Open-Ended** Draw and label four coins that have a total value of 40¢.

5. **Modeling Real Life** You have 46¢. You find 4 pennies and 1 nickel in your room. How much money do you have now? Do you have enough money to buy the app?

_____ Yes   No

6. **Modeling Real Life** You have 1 dime, 2 quarters, and 2 nickels. How many more cents do you need to buy the slime? Draw and label the coins you need.

_____ more cents

7. **DIG DEEPER!** You have some nickels and dimes. You have 1 more nickel than dimes. The total value of your coins is 50¢. How many nickels and dimes do you have?

_____ nickels   _____ dimes

Review & Refresh

8. Which fruit is the least favorite?

_____

Favorite Fruit	
Orange	|||||
Cherry	||
Apple	||||

674 six hundred seventy-four

Name _____

Learning Target: Show money amounts in different ways.

Show Money Amounts in Different Ways 14.3

 **Explore and Grow**

Use your coins to show 25 cents in two different ways. Draw and label the coins.

Did everyone in your class use the same coins?

_____

_____

_____

_____

Chapter 14 | Lesson 3   six hundred seventy-five   **675**

 Think and Grow

Show 35¢ in two different ways.

One Way:

Another Way:

Fewer coins!

Show and Grow   I can do it!

Show the amount in two different ways.

1.

2.

3.

Name _____

✓ Apply and Grow: Practice

Show the amount in two different ways.

4.

5.

6.

7. **Structure** You have 55¢. You have no quarters. Draw to show what coins you might have.

8. **YOU BE THE TEACHER** Newton says he drew the fewest number of coins to show 66¢. Is he correct? Explain.

    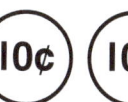  

Chapter 14 | Lesson 3   six hundred seventy-seven   677

Think and Grow: Modeling Real Life

Newton has 2 dimes, 1 nickel, and 1 penny. Descartes uses the fewest number of coins to make the same amount. Draw and label their coins.

Newton   Descartes

Show and Grow   I can think deeper!

9. Newton has 3 dimes and 2 pennies. Descartes uses the fewest number of coins to make the same amount. Draw and label their coins.

    Newton   Descartes

10. You use fewer than 5 coins to buy the pack of gum. Draw and label coins to show how you pay.

11. **DIG DEEPER!** You have 2 quarters. Newton and Descartes each have 5 coins and the same amount of money as you. Their coins are different. Draw and label their coins.

    Newton   Descartes

Name _____

Practice 14.3

Learning Target: Show money amounts in different ways.

Show 31¢ in two different ways.

One Way:

Another Way:

Show the amount in two different ways.

1.

2.

3.

4. **Reasoning** Draw to show 60¢ with only 3 coins.

5. **Structure** Draw to show 42¢ without using dimes.

6. **Modeling Real Life** Newton has 6 dimes and 1 nickel. Descartes uses the fewest number of coins to make the same amount. Draw and label their coins.

   Newton　　　　　　　　　　　Descartes

7. **DIG DEEPER!** You have 3 quarters. Newton and Descartes each have 6 coins and the same amount of money as you. Their coins are different. Draw and label their coins.

   Newton　　　　　　　　　　　Descartes

Review & Refresh

8. A green scarf is 50 inches long. An orange scarf is 40 inches long. A red scarf is 38 inches long. How much longer is the green scarf than the red scarf?

   _____ inches

Name _____

Make One Dollar 14.4

Learning Target: Use coins to make one dollar.

Explore and Grow

Newton has 4 coins. The total value is 100¢. Draw and label his coins.

Descartes has 10 coins. The total value is 100¢. Draw and label his coins.

Chapter 14 | Lesson 4 six hundred eighty-one 681

Think and Grow

One **dollar** has the same value as 100 cents.

1 dollar

$1 bill

$1 = 100¢

$ is the **dollar sign**.

You have 45¢. Draw coins to make $1. How many cents do you need?

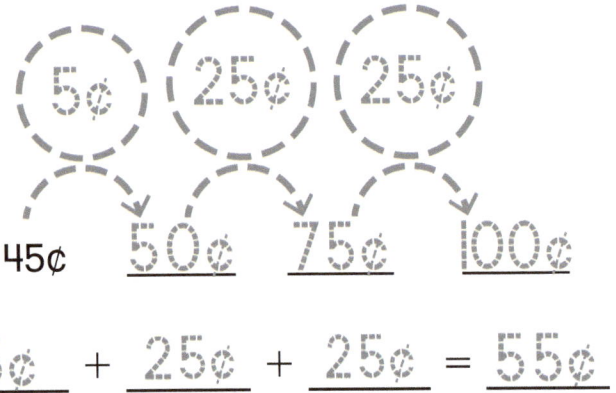

45¢ → 50¢ → 75¢ → 100¢

5¢ + 25¢ + 25¢ = 55¢

Is there another way?

You need 55¢.

Show and Grow   I can do it!

Draw coins to make $1. How many cents do you need?

1. 25¢

2. 80¢

You need _____.

You need _____.

682   six hundred eighty-two

Name _____

 **Apply and Grow: Practice**

Draw coins to make $1. How many cents do you need?

3. 35¢

You need _____.

4. 72¢

You need _____.

5.

You need _____.

6.

You need _____.

7. **Maintain Accuracy** Circle coins to make $1.

Chapter 14 | Lesson 4

six hundred eighty-three

Think and Grow: Modeling Real Life

You have 1 quarter, 3 pennies, and 1 dime in one pocket. You have 2 pennies, 2 nickels, and 4 dimes in your other pocket. How many more cents do you need to make $1?

Draw:

_____

Show and Grow I can think deeper!

Use Math Tools
How can you use a hundred chart to help solve?

8. You have 2 dimes and 1 nickel in your desk. You have a quarter and 10 pennies in your backpack. How many more cents do you need to make $1?

_____

9. A notebook costs $1. You have 5 dimes and 4 pennies. How much more money do you need to buy the notebook?

_____

10. **DIG DEEPER!** You have a $1 bill. You have 33 more cents than your friend. How much money does your friend have?

_____

Name _____

Practice  14.4

Learning Target: Use coins to make one dollar.

You have 78¢. Draw coins to make $1. How many cents do you need?

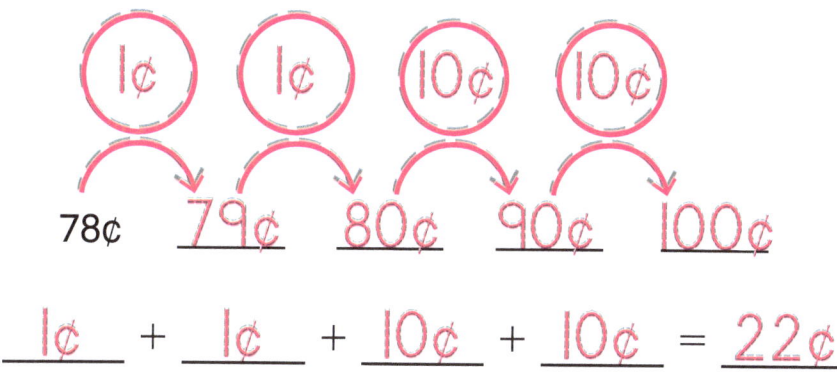

78¢ 79¢ 80¢ 90¢ 100¢

__1¢__ + __1¢__ + __10¢__ + __10¢__ = __22¢__

You need __22¢__.

Draw coins to make $1. How many cents do you need?

1. 54¢

2. 38¢

You need _____.   You need _____.

3.

4.

You need _____.   You need _____.

Chapter 14 | Lesson 4 — six hundred eighty-five — 685

5. **Structure** Show $1 using only nickels and dimes.

6. **Structure** How many nickels make $1?

_____ nickels

7. **Modeling Real Life** You have 1 dime and 4 nickels in a jar. You have 1 quarter and 3 pennies in your pocket. How many more cents do you need to make $1?

_____

8. **DIG DEEPER!** A snack costs 50¢. You have 2 quarters and 2 dimes. How much more money do you need to buy 2 snacks?

_____

Review & Refresh

9. 100 − 54 = _____

10. 200 − 134 = _____

Name _____

Make Change from One Dollar 14.5

Learning Target: Solve word problems to make change from one dollar.

Explore and Grow

Model the story.
Newton buys a bag of fish crackers for 45¢. He pays with a $1 bill. What is his change?

_____ cents

Communicate Clearly Explain how you solved.

_____

_____

_____

_____

Chapter 14 | Lesson 5   six hundred eighty-seven   687

Think and Grow

You buy a balloon for 29¢. You pay with a $1 bill. What is your change?

One Way: Count back.

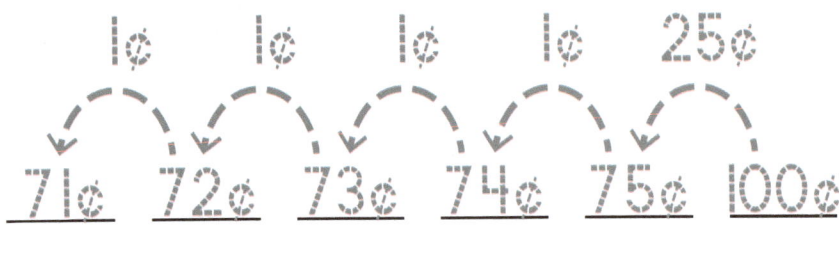

Start at 100. Count back 29.

Your change is ___71¢___.

Another Way: 100¢ − 29¢ = ?

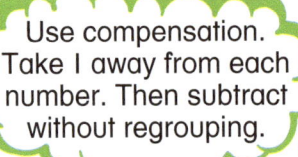

Use compensation. Take 1 away from each number. Then subtract without regrouping.

99¢ − 28¢ = 71¢

Your change is ___71¢___.

Show and Grow — I can do it!

You buy the item shown. You pay with a $1 bill. What is your change?

1.

   Your change is _____.

2.

   Your change is _____.

Name _____

Apply and Grow: Practice

You buy the item shown. You pay with a $1 bill. What is your change?

3.

Your change is _____.

4.

Your change is _____.

5.

Your change is _____.

6.

Your change is _____.

7. **Reasoning** Newton buys a notebook for 34¢. Descartes buys one for 52¢. You buy one for 48¢. You each pay with $1. Who gets back the most amount of money? How do you know?

_____

_____

_____

Think and Grow: Modeling Real Life

You pay for some school supplies with $1. Your change is 17¢. How much money did you spend?

Equation:

Show and Grow   I can think deeper!

8. You pay for some erasers with $1. Your change is 38¢. How much money did you spend?

9. You buy a toy ring. You pay with $1. You get back 1 quarter, 2 dimes, 1 nickel, and 1 penny. How much does the toy ring cost?

10. You buy a banana for 25¢ and an orange for 45¢. You pay with $1. What is your change?

Name _____

Practice **14.5**

Learning Target: Solve word problems to make change from one dollar.

You buy a pack of crayons for 52¢. You pay with a $1 bill. What is your change?

Count back.

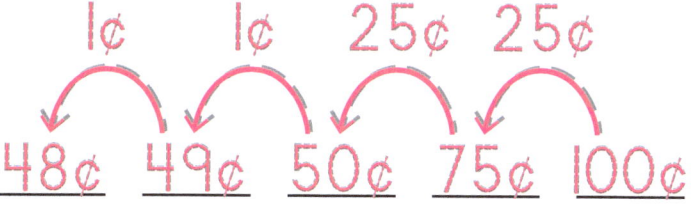

Start at 100. Count back 52.

Your change is __48¢__.

You buy the item shown. You pay with a $1 bill. What is your change?

1.

Your change is _____.

2.

Your change is _____.

3.

Your change is _____.

4.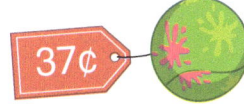

Your change is _____.

Chapter 14 | Lesson 5   six hundred ninety-one   **691**

5. **Reasoning** A puzzle costs 68¢. Newton pays for it with a $1 bill. Draw to show his change in two ways.

6. **Modeling Real Life** You buy a pencil sharpener. You give the cashier $1. You get back 2 quarters, 1 nickel, and 3 pennies. How much does the pencil sharpener cost?

_____

7. **DIG DEEPER!** You buy an onion for 36¢, a red pepper for 35¢, and a green pepper for 22¢. You pay with a $1 bill. Is it possible to get a quarter back in your change? Explain.

_____

Review & Refresh

8. 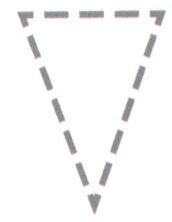 _____ straight sides

   _____ vertices

9. 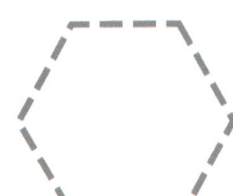 _____ straight sides

   _____ vertices

Name _____

Find Total Values of Bills 14.6

Learning Target: Find the total value of a group of bills.

Explore and Grow

Model the story.
Descartes has three $5 bills and three $1 bills. How much money does he have in all?

_____ dollars

Communicate Clearly Explain how you solved.

_____

_____

_____

_____

Chapter 14 | Lesson 6   six hundred ninety-three   693

Think and Grow

$5 bill $10 bill $20 bill

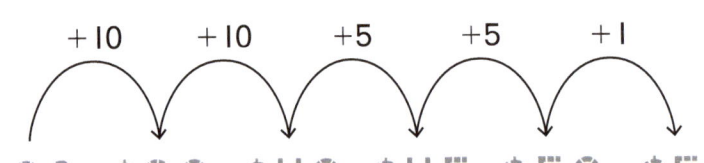

Count on from the greatest bill to the least bill.

+10   +10   +5   +5   +1

$20 $30 $40 $45 $50 $51

The total value is $51.

Show and Grow — I can do it!

Count on to find the total value.

1.

Total value: _____

2.

Total value: _____

Name _____

 **Apply and Grow: Practice**

Count on to find the total value.

3.      Total value: _____

4.
       Total value: _____

5.
        Total value: _____

6. **Which One Doesn't Belong?** Which group of bills does *not* belong with the other two?

Chapter 14 | Lesson 6   six hundred ninety-five 695

Think and Grow: Modeling Real Life

You buy some T-shirts for $39. Draw and label bills to show two different ways to pay for the T-shirts. One way should use the fewest number of bills.

Draw:

Show and Grow I can think deeper!

7. You buy a pair of sneakers for $24. Draw and label bills to show two different ways to pay for the sneakers. One way should use the fewest number of bills.

8. Newton has three $20 bills, one $10 bill, one $5 bill, and three $1 bills. Does he have enough money to buy a new doghouse that costs $80? Explain.

_____

_____

9. **Repeated Reasoning** Explain why you would order a group of bills from the greatest value to the least value to find the total value.

_____

_____

696   six hundred ninety-six

Name _____

Practice

Learning Target: Find the total value of a group of bills.

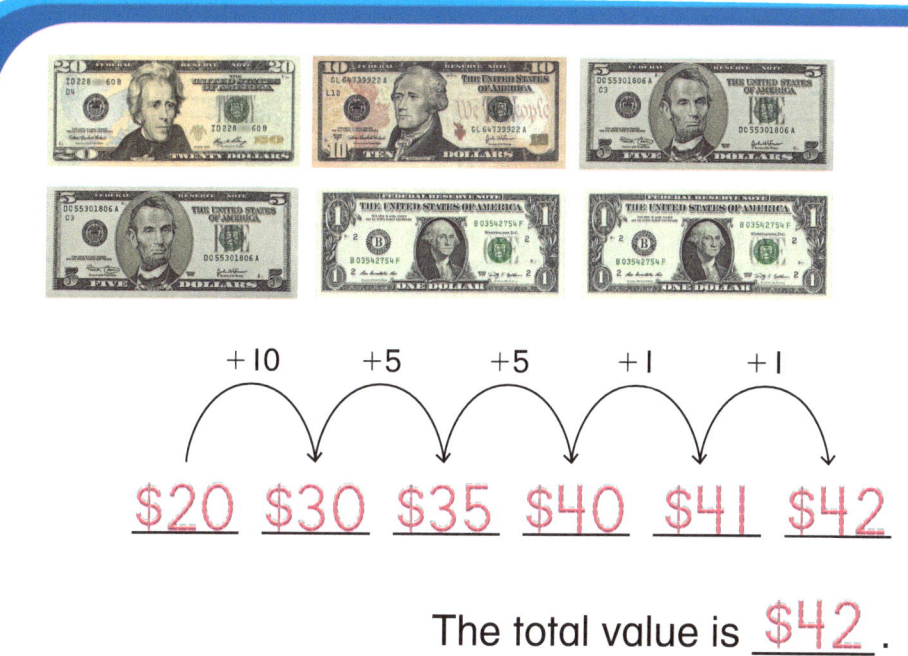

The total value is $42.

Count on to find the total value.

1.

   Total value: _____

2.

   Total value: _____

3.

   Total value: _____

Chapter 14 | Lesson 6   six hundred ninety-seven   697

4. **YOU BE THE TEACHER** Newton says he drew the fewest number of bills to show $35. Is he correct? Explain.

$10	$10
$10	$5

_____

_____

5. **Modeling Real Life** A pair of headphones costs $88. Draw and label bills to show two different ways to pay for the headphones. One way should use the fewest number of bills.

6. **DIG DEEPER!** Descartes buys a wakeboard for $74 with 9 bills. Draw and label the bills he uses.

Make a Plan What is your first step to solve?

Review & Refresh

7. A photo album has 3 rows of photos. There are 4 photos in each row. How many photos are there in all?

____ + ____ + ____ = ____   ____ photos

Name _____

Problem Solving: Money

14.7

Learning Target: Solve money word problems.

Explore and Grow

Model the story.
You buy a book for 60¢. Your friend buys a book for 33¢. How much do you and your friend spend in all?

_____ cents

Check Your Work
Should your answer be greater than or less that 90¢? Explain.

Communicate Clearly Explain how you solved.

_____

_____

_____

_____

Chapter 14 | Lesson 7

Think and Grow

Newton has a $20 bill, a $5 bill, and two $1 bills. How much more money does he need to buy a present that costs $40?

Think: What do you know? What do you need to find?

Step 1: Find how much money Newton has.

$20 | $1
$5 | $1

$20 + $5 + $2 = $27

Step 2: Subtract to find how much more he needs.

$40
$27 | ?

$40 − $27 = $13

Newton needs $13.

Show and Grow — I can do it!

1. Descartes has two $10 bills and two $5 bills. He has $21 more than Newton. How much money does Newton have?

   Step 1:   **Step 2:**

2. Descartes has some coins in a jar. He puts in 4 dimes, 1 nickel, and 1 penny. Now he has $1. How many cents were in the jar to start?

700 seven hundred

Name _____

Apply and Grow: Practice

3. Newton has some money. He loses a $10 bill and three $1 bills. Now he has $19. How much money did he have to start?

    _____

4. Descartes has one $20 bill, three $10 bills, and three $5 bills. He spends $50. How much money does he have left?

    _____

5. A joke book costs $1. You have 2 quarters and 1 nickel. How much more money do you need to buy the joke book?

    _____

6. **YOU BE THE TEACHER** Your friend says that 3 dimes and 2 nickels is 50¢. Is your friend correct? Explain.

    _____

    _____

Think and Grow: Modeling Real Life

You have a $20 bill and a $5 bill. Your friend has $10 less than you. Do you and your friend have enough money to buy a $38 skateboard? Explain.

Step 1:

Step 2:

_____

_____

Show and Grow   I can think deeper!

7. You have 1 quarter, 2 dimes, and 3 pennies. Your friend has 4 nickels and 2 pennies. Do you and your friend have enough money to buy a 75¢ bottle of orange juice? Explain.

_____

_____

8. Descartes buys a board game for $19. He has three $5 bills and two $1 bills left over. How much money did he have before he bought the game?

_____

9. **DIG DEEPER!** You have 25¢ in your desk, 18¢ in your backpack, and 50¢ in your pocket. You spend 43¢ and lose a quarter. How much money do you have left?

_____

Name _____

Practice 14.7

Learning Target: Solve money word problems.

Newton has a $10 bill, two $5 bills, and a $1 bill. How many more dollars does he need to buy a coat that costs $35?

Think: What do you know? What do you need to find?

Step 1: Find how much money Newton has.

$10	$5
$5	$1

$10 + $5 + $5 + $1 = $21

Step 2: Subtract to find how much more he needs.

$35	
$21	?

$35 − $21 = $14

Newton needs $14.

1. Newton has $30. Descartes has a $20 bill, a $10 bill, and two $1 bills. How much more money does Descartes have?

   _____

2. You have some money. You spend 2 quarters and 3 dimes at the cafeteria. Now you have 20¢. How much money did you have to start?

   _____

Chapter 14 | Lesson 7   seven hundred three   **703**

3. **Writing** Write and solve a two-step word problem that has an answer of $45.

   _____

   _____

4. **Modeling Real Life** You have 12 pennies, 2 dimes, and 1 nickel. Your friend has 20¢ more than you. Do you and your friend have enough money to buy a toy car that costs $1? Explain.

   _____

   _____

5. **Modeling Real Life** Descartes has $45. He spends a $20 bill and a $1 bill. He earns two $5 bills and a $10 bill. How much money does he have now?

   _____

Review & Refresh

6. Which time does not belong with the other three?

      half past 3

Name _____

Learning Target: Tell time to the nearest five minutes.

Tell Time to the Nearest Five Minutes

Explore and Grow

Label the missing minutes around the clock. Then tell the time.

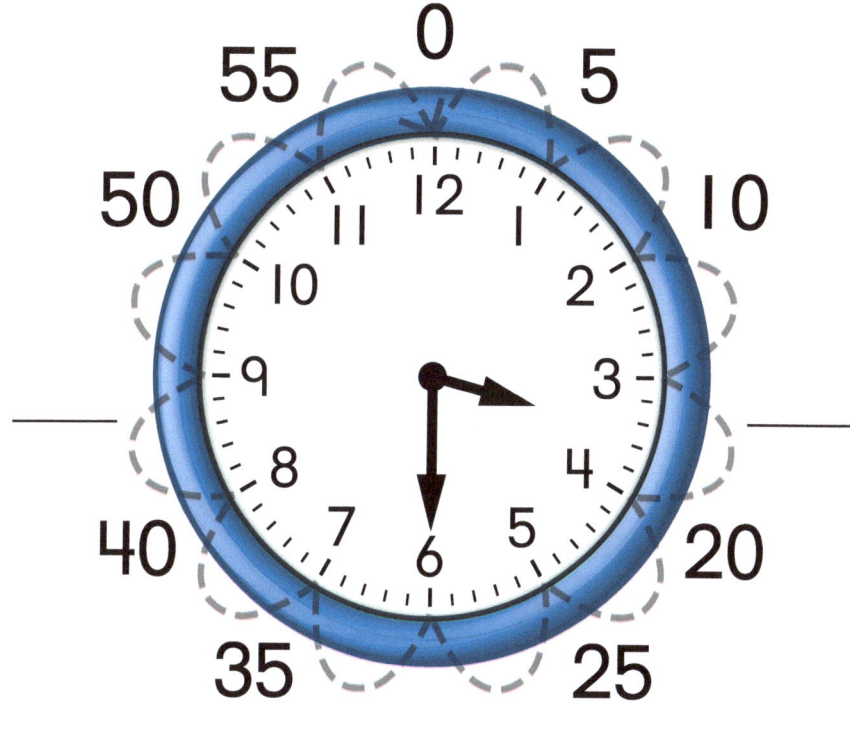

The time is _____ : _____ .

Chapter 14 | Lesson 8

Think and Grow

Show and Grow I can do it!

Write the time.

1.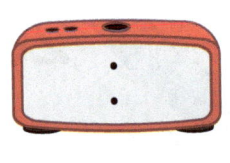

2.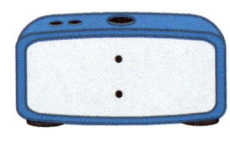

3.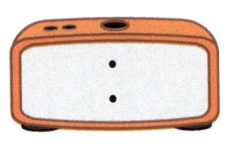

4.

Name _____

 **Apply and Grow: Practice**

Write the time.

5.

6.

7.

Draw to show the time.

8.

7:05

9.

9:25

10.

12:55

11. **Patterns** Write the next time in the pattern.

   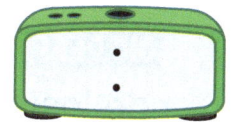

12. **Precision** The hour hand points between the 4 and the 5. The minute hand points to the 4. What time is it?

_____ : _____

Chapter 14 | Lesson 8   seven hundred seven   707

Think and Grow: Modeling Real Life

Baseball practice lasts 40 minutes. Show and write the time practice ends.

Start

End

 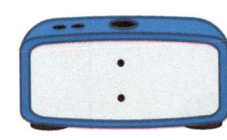

Show and Grow I can think deeper!

13. Recess lasts 25 minutes. Show and write the time recess ends.

    Start

    End

     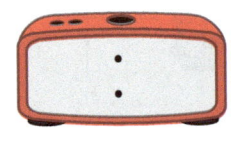

14. **DIG DEEPER!** A train ride starts at 6:40. The ride lasts 45 minutes. What time does the ride end?

    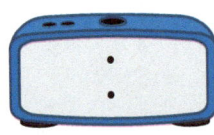

708 seven hundred eight

Name _____

Practice

Learning Target: Tell time to the nearest five minutes.

Write the time.

1.

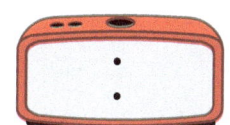

2.

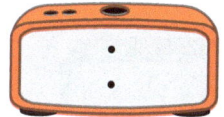

3.

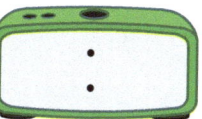

Draw to show the time.

4.

5.

6.

Chapter 14 | Lesson 8

seven hundred nine

7. **Reasoning** The minute hand points to the 7. What number will it point to in 10 minutes?

_____

8. **Precision** The hour hand points between the 11 and the 12. In 25 minutes it will be the next hour. What time is it now?

_____:_____

9. **Modeling Real Life** Your walk to school lasts 15 minutes. Show and write the time your walk ends.

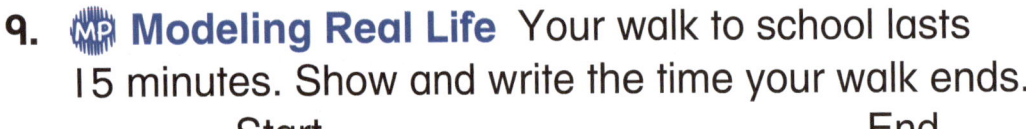

Start   End

  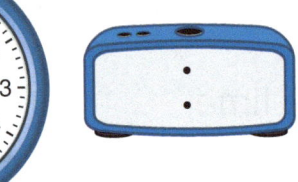

10. **DIG DEEPER!** Your swimming lesson starts at 5:30. It lasts 35 minutes. What time does the lesson end?

Review & Refresh

11. The crayon is about 7 centimeters long. What is the best estimate of the length of the toothpick?

6 centimeters

4 centimeters

8 centimeters

710   seven hundred ten

Name _____

Learning Target: Describe the time before or after the hour in different ways.

Tell Time Before and After the Hour

Explore and Grow

Write each time on the digital clocks. How much time has passed?

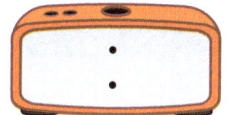
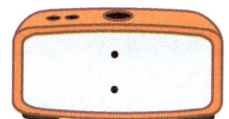

_____ minutes

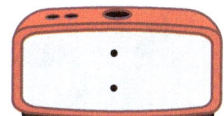
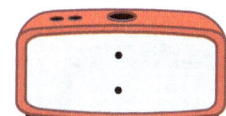

_____ minutes

Chapter 14 | Lesson 9

Think and Grow

  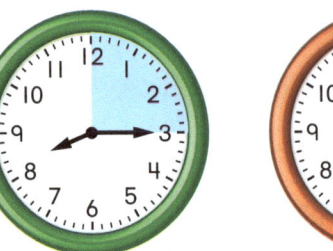 

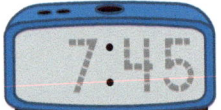 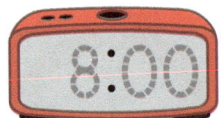 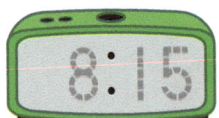 

15 minutes before 8 or **quarter to** 8

8 o'clock

15 minutes after 8 or **quarter past** 8

30 minutes after 8 or half past 8

Show and Grow I can do it!

Write the time. Circle another way to say the time.

1.

half past 4

quarter past 4

2.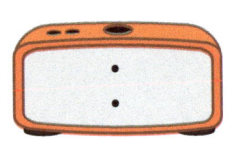

half past 11

30 minutes after 12

3.

quarter past 2

quarter to 3

4.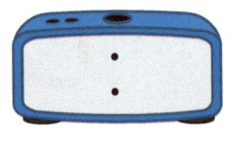

40 minutes after 9

20 minutes after 9

Name _____

 **Apply and Grow: Practice**

Write the time. Circle another way to say the time.

5.

quarter past 1

half past 1

6.

10 minutes after 7

20 minutes after 7

Show and write the time.

7. quarter to 11

8. quarter past 5

 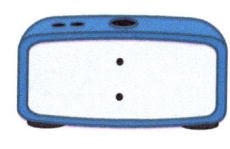

9. **Which One Doesn't Belong?** Which time does *not* belong with the other three?

quarter past 7   6:45   45 minutes after 6   quarter to 7

10. **Precision** Is it time for homework or dinner?

Homework: quarter to 6
Dinner: quarter after 6

Homework

Dinner

Chapter 14 | Lesson 9   seven hundred thirteen   713

Think and Grow: Modeling Real Life

School starts at quarter past 8. Are you early or late to school? Explain.

Arrive

_____

_____

_____

Show and Grow   I can think deeper!

11. A movie starts at quarter to 6. Are you early or late to the movie? Explain.

Arrive

_____

_____

_____

12. **DIG DEEPER!** You arrive at the bus station 20 minutes before 12. Which is the first bus you can board? How many minutes are there until it leaves?

the _____ bus

_____ minutes

Bus Schedule	
Bus	**Time**
Red	11:35
Blue	11:55
Yellow	12:15
Green	12:35
Orange	12:55

Name _____

Practice

Learning Target: Describe the time before or after the hour in different ways.

15 minutes before 7 or quarter to 7

15 minutes after 7 or quarter past 7

30 minutes after 7 or half past 7

Write the time. Circle another way to say the time.

1.

    quarter to 12

    quarter to 11

2.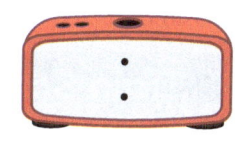

    25 minutes after 8

    40 minutes after 5

Show and write the time.

3. half past 3

     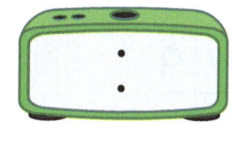

4. quarter past 12

     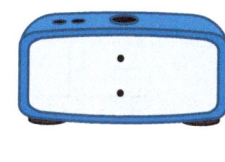

Chapter 14 | Lesson 9

seven hundred fifteen   715

5. **YOU BE THE TEACHER** Newton says it is 2:45, or quarter to 3. Is he correct? Explain.

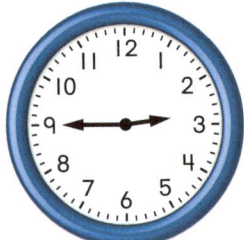

_____

_____

6. **Modeling Real Life** A show starts at quarter to 7. Are you early or late to the show? Explain.

Arrive

_____

_____

_____

7. **DIG DEEPER!** You arrive at the metro station 10 minutes after 2. Which is the first train you can board? How many minutes are there until it leaves?

Train Schedule	
Train	Time
Green	2:00
Yellow	2:30
Orange	3:00

the _____ train

_____ minutes

Review & Refresh

8.
```
  6 2 0
− 4 5 8
```

9.
```
  9 0 6
− 7 2 9
```

10.
```
  7 0 0
− 2 5 4
```

Name _____

Relate A.M. and P.M. 14.10

Learning Target: Describe the time using a.m. and p.m.

Explore and Grow

Describe what you do in the morning. Show and write the time. Describe what you do in the evening. Show and write the time.

Morning	Evening
 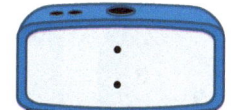	 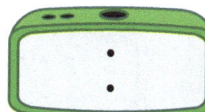

Chapter 14 | Lesson 10

seven hundred seventeen 717

# Think and Grow

Times after midnight and before noon are written with *a.m.*

Sleep

 p.m.

12:00 a.m. is **midnight**.

Times after noon and before midnight are written with *p.m.*

Eat lunch

a.m.

12:00 p.m. is **noon**.

Show and Grow — I can do it!

Write the time. Circle *a.m.* or *p.m.*

1. Eat breakfast

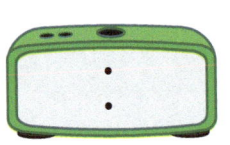

a.m.   p.m.

2. Eat dinner

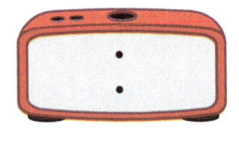

a.m.   p.m.

3. Go to art class

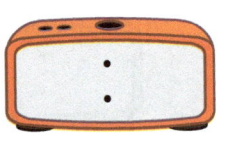

a.m.   p.m.

4. Do homework

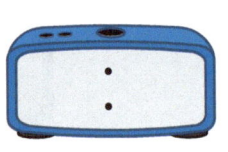

a.m.   p.m.

Name _____

 Apply and Grow: Practice

Write the time. Circle *a.m.* or *p.m.*

5. Ride the bus to school

a.m.　　p.m.

6. Go to a party

a.m.　　p.m.

Draw to show the time. Circle *a.m.* or *p.m.*

7. Read before bed

a.m.　　p.m.

8. Sunrise

a.m.　　p.m.

9. **Reasoning** Use the times in the list to complete the story.

You arrive at school at

_____. Your class goes

to music at _____. After

school, you read a book at

_____.

| 10:15 a.m. |
| 5:20 p.m. |
| 8:30 a.m. |

Chapter 14 | Lesson 10　　　　seven hundred nineteen　719

Think and Grow: Modeling Real Life

Use the times to complete the timeline. Write something you might do at those times.

2:50 p.m.
4:10 p.m.
8:45 a.m.

7:15 a.m. [ ]   11:25 a.m. [ ]   [ ]   8:30 p.m.

Show and Grow   I can think deeper!

10. Use the times to complete the timeline. Write something you might do at those times.

7:30 a.m.
7:35 p.m.
9:55 a.m.

[ ]   8:05 a.m.   [ ]   1:20 p.m.   6:50 p.m.   [ ]

11. DIG DEEPER! Use the times to complete the timeline. Then rewrite each time digitally below, including *a.m.* or *p.m.*

quarter past 3
half past 6
10 minutes after 11

20 minutes before 7   [ ]   noon   [ ]   [ ]   20 minutes after 8

720   seven hundred twenty

Name _____

Practice

Learning Target: Describe the time using a.m. and p.m.

Write the time. Circle *a.m.* or *p.m.*

1. Look at the stars

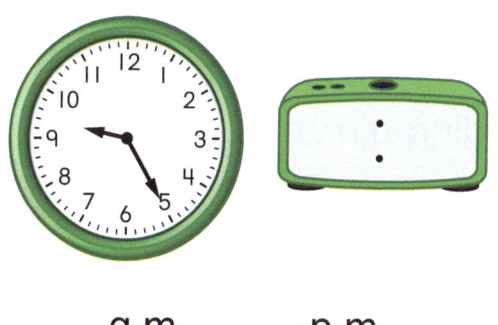

a.m.   p.m.

2. Get ready for school

a.m.   p.m.

Draw to show the time. Circle *a.m.* or *p.m.*

3. Eat lunch

a.m.   p.m.

4. Walk the dog

a.m.   p.m.

Chapter 14 | Lesson 10

5. **Reasoning** Right now, it is p.m. In 10 minutes it will be a.m. What time is it now? Explain.

_____

_____

6. **Modeling Real Life** Use the times to complete the timeline. Write something you might do at those times.

| 8:15 p.m.   11:55 a.m.   8:15 a.m. |

[ ]   10:30 a.m.   [ ]   4:10 p.m.   6:15 p.m.   [ ]

_____   _____   _____

7. **DIG DEEPER!** Use the times to complete the timeline. Then rewrite each time digitally below, including *a.m.* or *p.m.*

| noon   half past 9   quarter to 8 |

[ ]   20 minutes after 8   quarter past 11   [ ]   10 minutes after 2   [ ]

___ ___ ___ ___ ___

Review & Refresh

8. 65 + 36 = _____

9. 56 + 18 = _____

722 seven hundred twenty-two

Name _____

Performance Task 14

1. a. You have two $1 bills, 1 quarter, 5 dimes, 3 nickels, and 2 pennies. How much more money do you need to buy a subway pass?

_____ cents

b. You find a dime. Do you have enough money to buy the pass now?

Yes   No

2. A weekly subway pass is $32. A customer pays with a $50 bill. Use tally marks to show three different ways that the customer can receive change. What is the total change?

Change		
$10 bill	$5 bill	$1 bill

Total change: _____

3. You arrive at the subway station at quarter to 3. What times will the subways arrive?

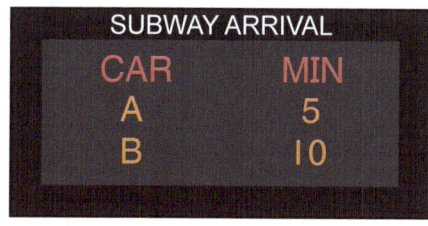

Subway A: _____

Subway B: _____

Flip and Find

To Play: Place the Flip and Find Cards face down in the boxes. Take turns flipping 2 cards. If your cards show the same time or value, keep the cards. If your cards show different times or values, flip the cards back over. Play until all matches are made.

Name _____

Chapter Practice 14

14.1 Find Total Values of Coins

1. Count on to find the total value.

Total value: _____

2.  **Modeling Real Life** You have 2 quarters, 2 dimes, and 1 penny. How many cents do you have? Do you have enough money to buy the frozen fruit bar?

_____   Yes   No

14.2 Order to Find Total Values of Coins

3. Draw and label the coins from the greatest value to the least value. Then find the total value.

Total value: _____

Chapter 14   seven hundred twenty-five   725

14.3 Show Money Amounts in Different Ways

4. Draw and label coins to show the amount in two different ways.

14.4 Make One Dollar

Draw coins to make $1. How many cents do you need?

5. 79¢

6.

You need _____.   You need _____.

14.5 Make Change from One Dollar

7. **Reasoning** Newton buys a toy for 21¢. Descartes buys one for 94¢. You buy one for 57¢. You each pay with $1. Who gets back the least amount of money? How do you know?

_____

_____

14.6 Find Total Values of Bills

8. Count on to find the total value.

Total value: _____

14.7 Problem Solving: Money

9. Newton has five $10 bills. He has $32 more than Descartes. How much money does Descartes have?

_____

14.8 Tell Time to the Nearest Five Minutes

Write the time.

10.
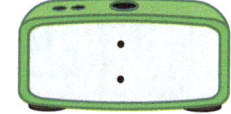

11.
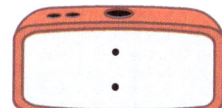

12.
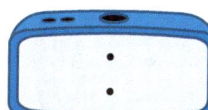

 **14.9 Tell Time Before and After the Hour**

Write the time. Circle another way to say the time.

13.

quarter past 5

quarter to 5

14.

half past 9

quarter to 10

15. **Modeling Real Life** Soccer practice starts at half past 1. Are you early or late to soccer practice? Explain.

Arrive

_____

_____

_____

14.10 Relate A.M. and P.M.

Draw to show the time. Circle *a.m.* or *p.m.*

16. Sunset

a.m.   p.m.

17. Eat breakfast

a.m.   p.m.

728   seven hundred twenty-eight

15 Identify and Partition Shapes

- Have you ever seen a stained glass window?
- What shapes do you see in the window?

Chapter Learning Target:
Understand shapes.

Chapter Success Criteria:
- I can name shapes.
- I can explain information about shapes.
- I can compare one shape to another.
- I can draw different shapes.

15 Vocabulary

Name _____

Review Words
equal shares
unequal shares

Organize It

Use the review words to complete the graphic organizer.

Define It

Use your vocabulary cards to identify the word. Find the word in the word search.

1.

2.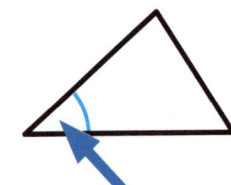

3.

```
N R P E L B I Y
K Y G Y S A U M
A R N T O N F W
O P O L Y G O N
X A I H S L A T
L V G E P E Q H
S U D A T O E N
T H I R D S J X
```

Chapter 15 Vocabulary Cards

angle	cube
edge	face
fourths	halves
hexagon	octagon

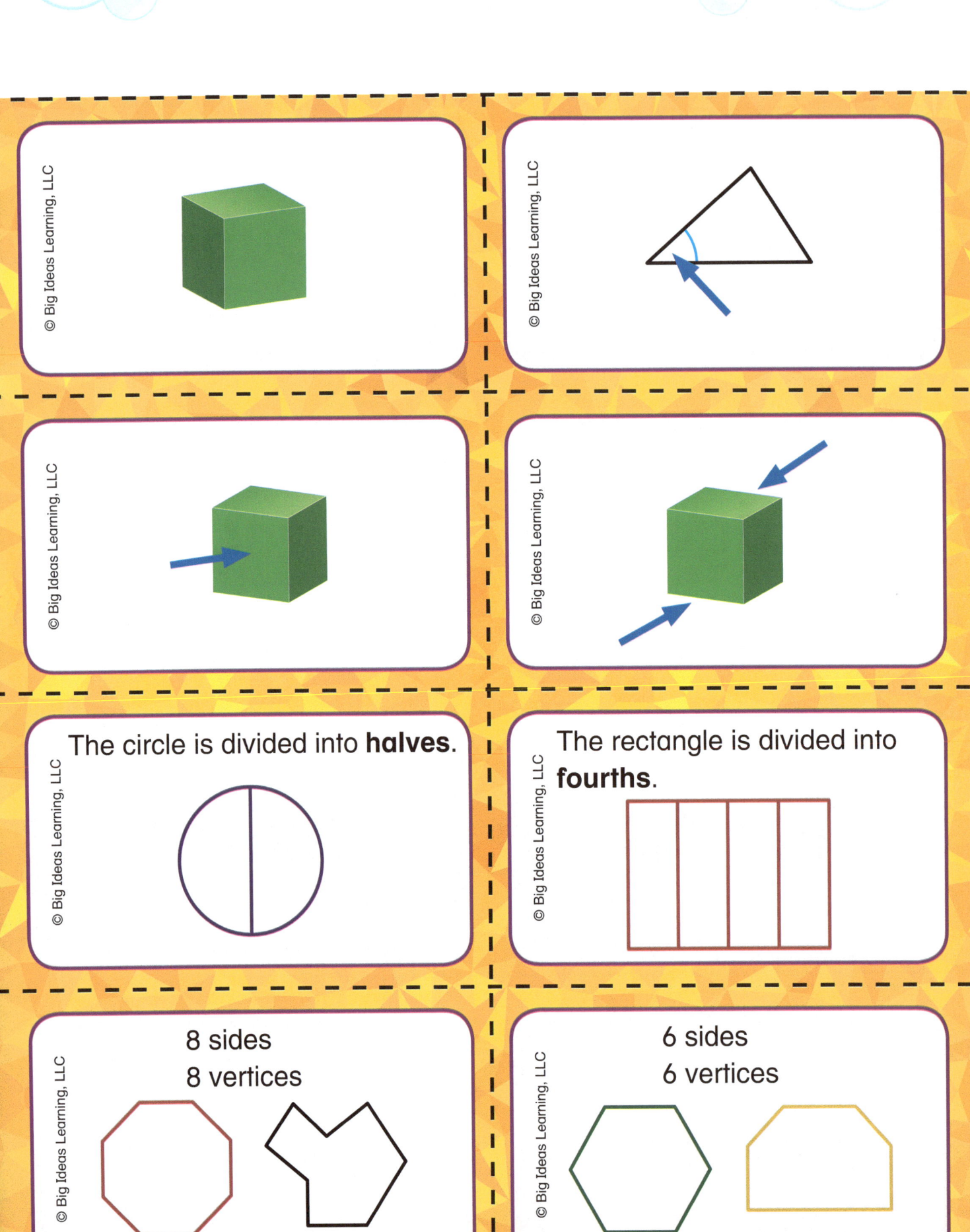

Chapter 15 Vocabulary Cards

pentagon	polygon
quadrilateral	rhombus
right angle	side
thirds	vertex

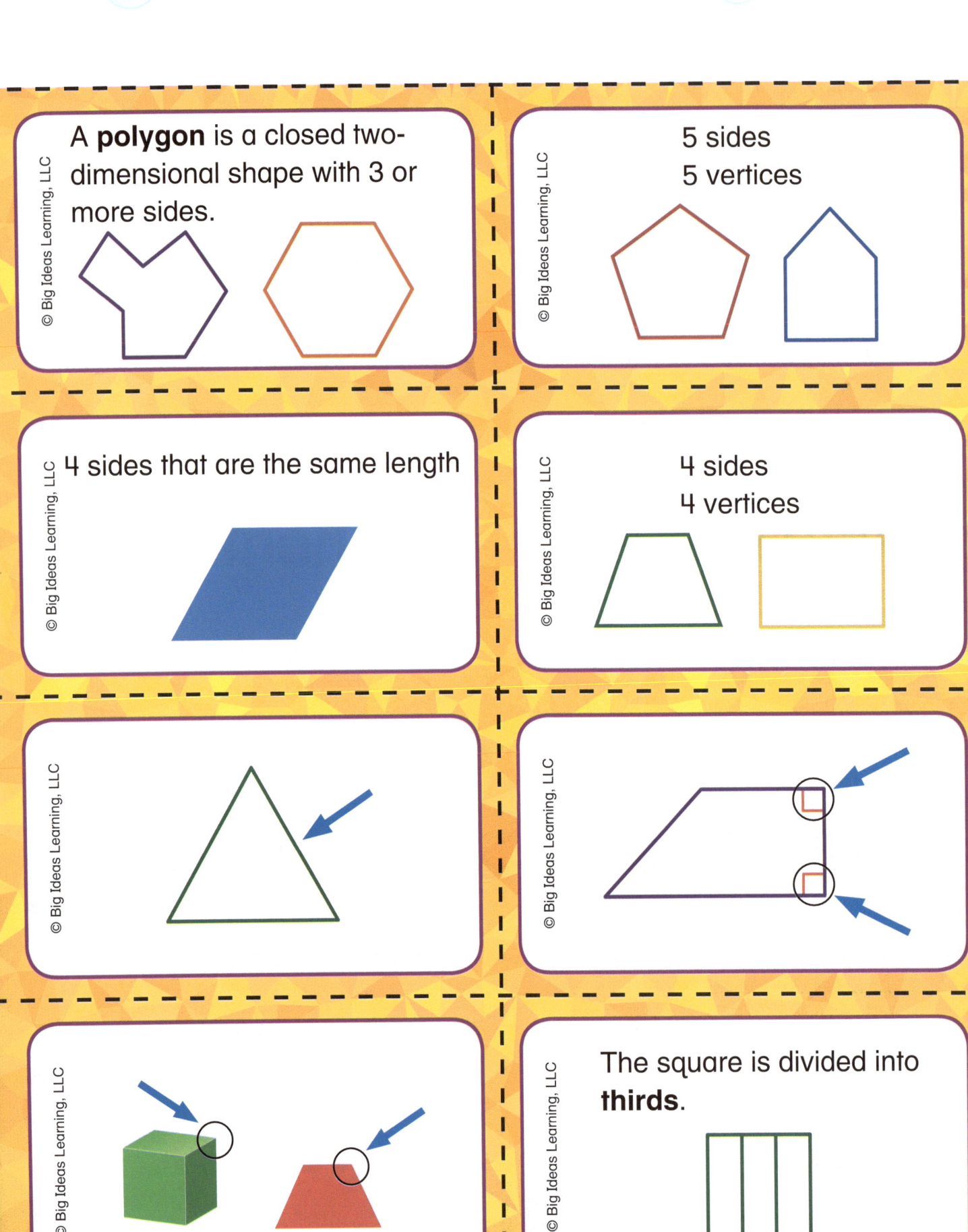

Name _____

Learning Target: Identify and describe two-dimensional shapes.

Describe Two-Dimensional Shapes
15.1

 **Explore and Grow**

Create a shape with 3 sides on your geoboard. Draw your shape. Did everyone in your class make the same shape?

Circle the word that makes the sentence true.

_____ are shapes with 3 sides.

Circles   Squares   Triangles

Think and Grow

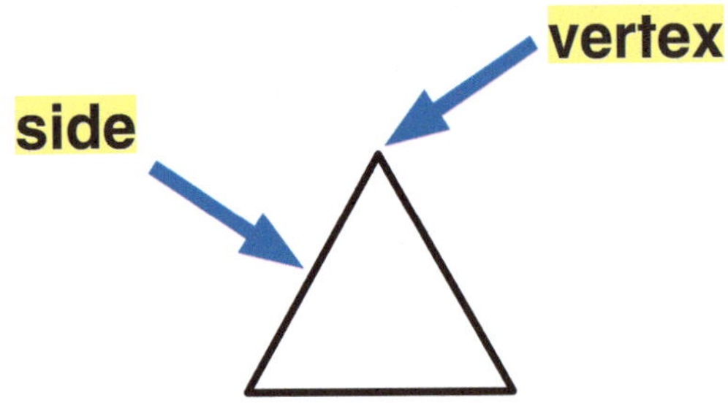

side → △ ← **vertex**

triangles — 3 sides, 3 vertices

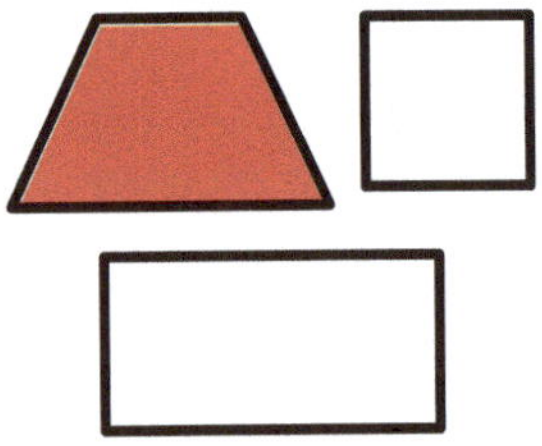

quadrilaterals — 4 sides, 4 vertices

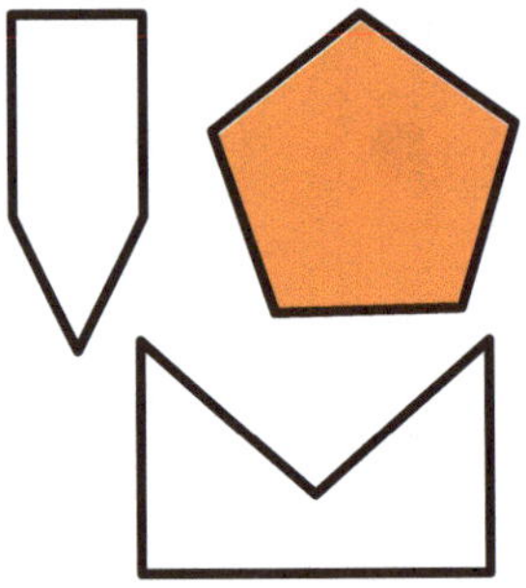

pentagons — 5 sides, 5 vertices

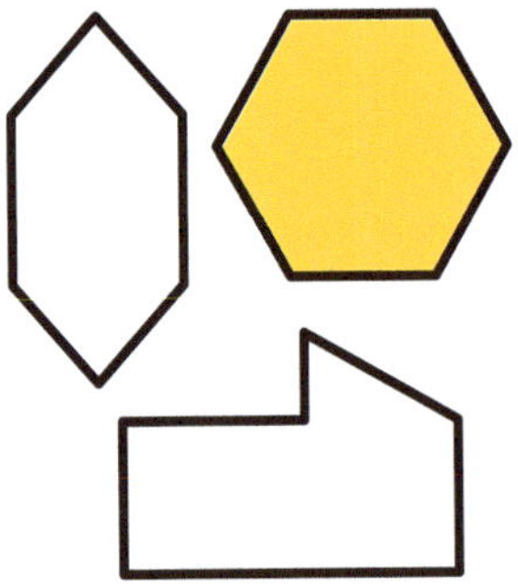

hexagons — 6 sides, 6 vertices

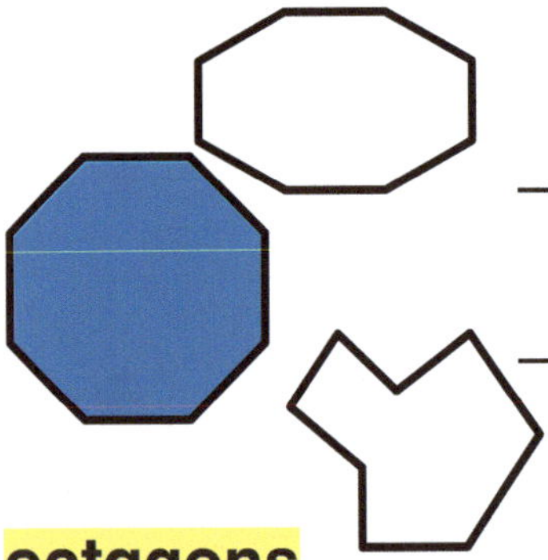

octagons — 8 sides, 8 vertices

Show and Grow I can do it!

1. 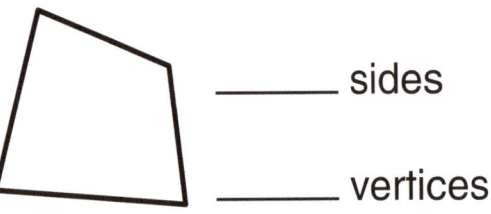 ___ sides ___ vertices

Shape: _____

2. 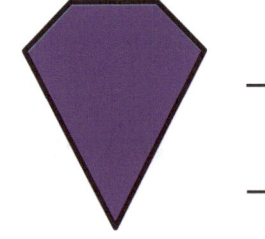 ___ sides ___ vertices

Shape: _____

732   seven hundred thirty-two

Name _____

✓ Apply and Grow: Practice

3. 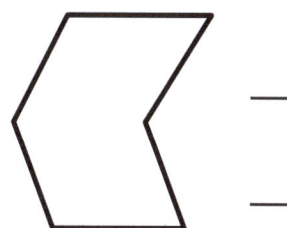 _____ sides

   _____ vertices

   Shape: _____

4. 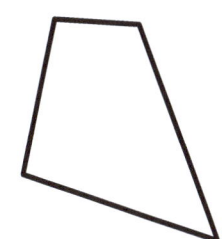 _____ sides

   _____ vertices

   Shape: _____

5.  _____ sides

   _____ vertices

   Shape: _____

6.  _____ sides

   _____ vertices

   Shape: _____

7.  _____ sides

   _____ vertices

   Shape: _____

8.  _____ sides

   _____ vertices

   Shape: _____

9. **Writing** How are a pentagon and an octagon different?

   _____

   _____

Chapter 15 | Lesson 1 seven hundred thirty-three 733

Think and Grow: Modeling Real Life

Draw a pentagon to make a house. Draw 2 quadrilaterals to make windows and 1 quadrilateral to make a door. Draw an octagon to make a chimney.

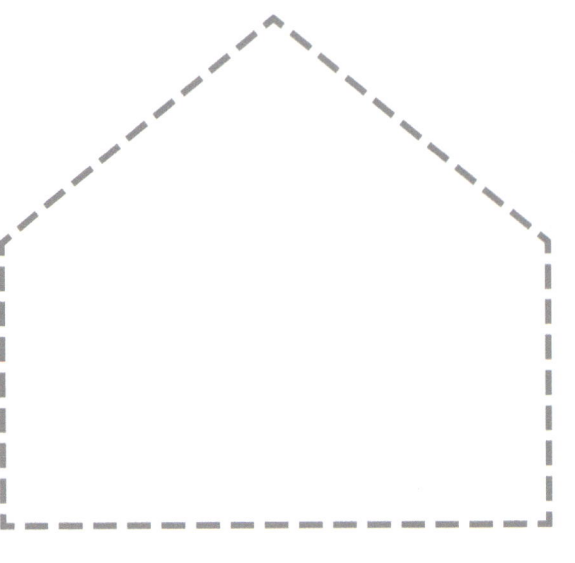

Show and Grow — I can think deeper!

10. Draw a pentagon to make a fish. Draw 4 triangles to make the fins. Draw a hexagon to make an eye.

11. You draw 5 quadrilaterals. How many sides and vertices do you draw in all?

    _____ sides   _____ vertices

12. **DIG DEEPER!** You draw an octagon and two pentagons. How many sides and vertices do you draw in all?

    _____ sides   _____ vertices

Name _____

Practice 15.1

Learning Target: Identify and describe two-dimensional shapes.

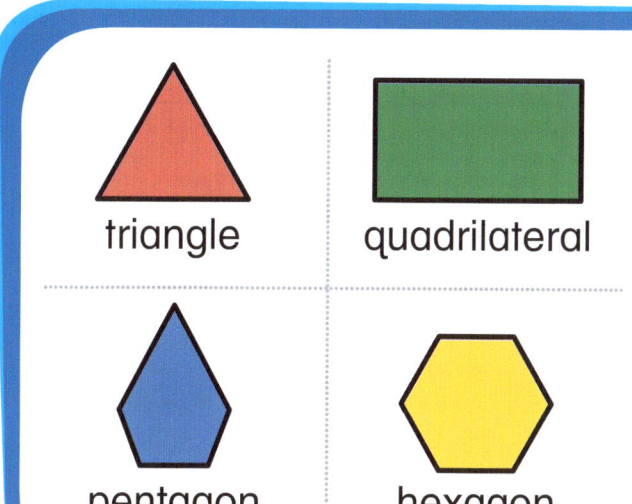

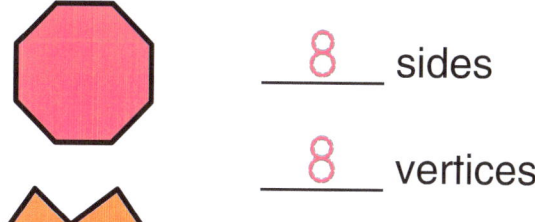

_8_ sides

_8_ vertices

1.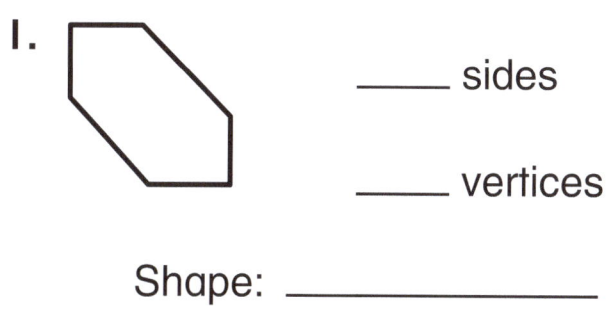

___ sides

___ vertices

Shape: _____

2.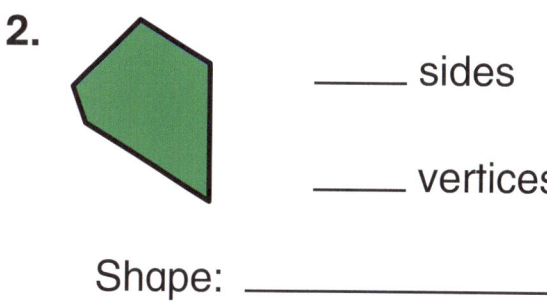

___ sides

___ vertices

Shape: _____

3.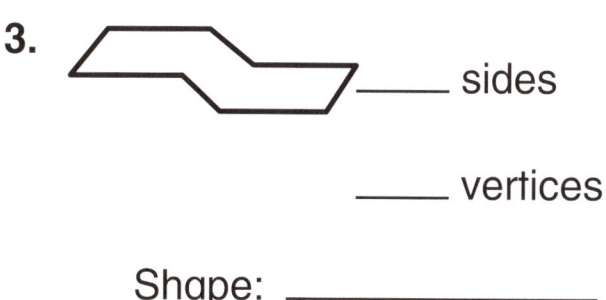

___ sides

___ vertices

Shape: _____

4.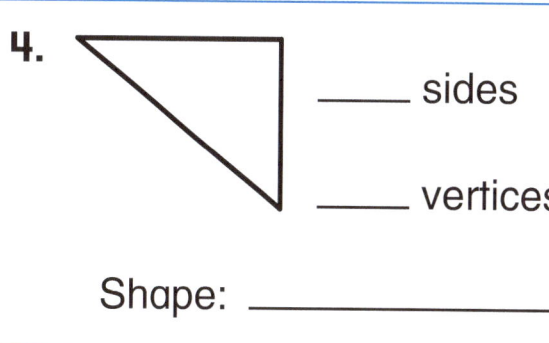

___ sides

___ vertices

Shape: _____

5.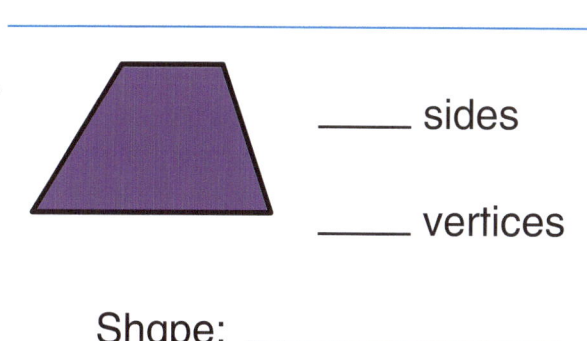

___ sides

___ vertices

Shape: _____

6.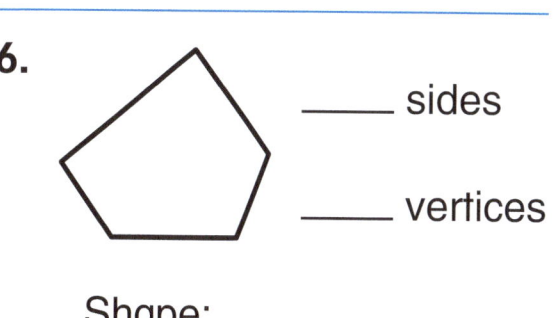

___ sides

___ vertices

Shape: _____

Chapter 15 | Lesson 1   seven hundred thirty-five   735

7. **Precision** Describe the shape in 3 ways.

_____

_____

_____

8. **Modeling Real Life** Draw a hexagon to make a dog's body. Draw quadrilaterals for the head and tail. Draw two triangles for the ears.

9. **DIG DEEPER!** You draw a triangle and two hexagons. How many sides and vertices do you draw in all?

_____ sides   _____ vertices

Review & Refresh

10. You are building a 34-foot fence. You build 15 feet on Saturday and 13 feet on Sunday. How many feet are left to build?

_____ feet

Name _____

Identify Angles of Polygons 15.2

Learning Target: Identify angles of a polygon.

Explore and Grow

Color the triangle blue. Color the quadrilateral red. Color the pentagon green. Color the hexagon orange.

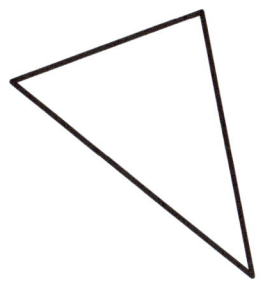
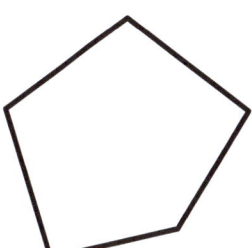
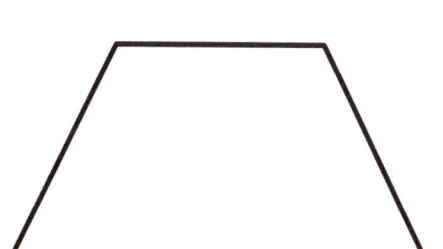
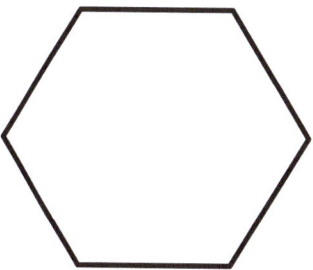

Analyze a Problem Which shape is not colored? How is it different from the other shapes?

_____

_____

_____

Chapter 15 | Lesson 2

Think and Grow

A **polygon** is a closed two-dimensional shape with 3 or more sides. When two sides meet, they form an **angle**.

angle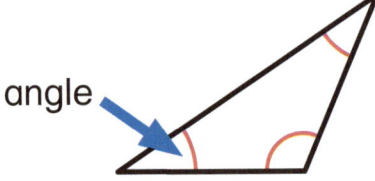

A triangle has __3__ angles.

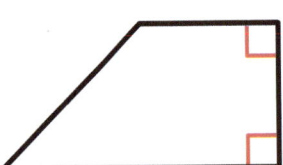

A **right angle** forms an L-shaped vertex. The symbol ∟ shows a right angle.

This quadrilateral has __4__ angles.

Two of those angles are __right__ angles.

Show and Grow — I can do it!

1.  ____ angles

   How many right angles? ____

   Shape: _____

2. 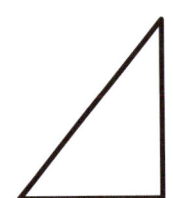 ____ angles

   How many right angles? ____

   Shape: _____

3.  ____ angles

   How many right angles? ____

   Shape: _____

4.  ____ angles

   How many right angles? ____

   Shape: _____

Name _____

✓ Apply and Grow: Practice

5. 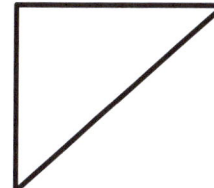 ____ angles

How many right angles? ____

Shape: _____

6. 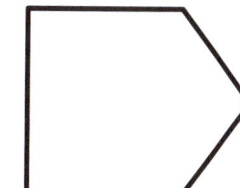 ____ angles

How many right angles? ____

Shape: _____

7. 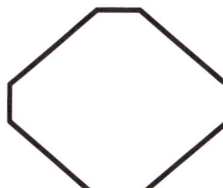 ____ angles

How many right angles? ____

Shape: _____

8. 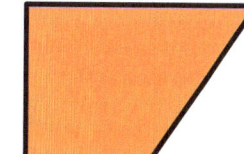 ____ angles

How many right angles? ____

Shape: _____

9. Draw and name a polygon with 6 angles.

_____

10. Draw and name a polygon with 2 right angles.

_____

11. **Repeated Reasoning** Can you draw a polygon with 4 sides and 5 angles? Explain.

_____

_____

Chapter 15 | Lesson 2   seven hundred thirty-nine   739

Think and Grow: Modeling Real Life

You are designing a road sign. The new sign must be a pentagon with only 2 right angles. Which signs might be yours?

Show and Grow — I can think deeper!

12. You are making a sign for your lemonade stand. Your sign must be a quadrilateral with 4 right angles. Which signs might be yours?

13. You draw 3 pentagons. How many angles do you draw in all?

_____ angles

14. **DIG DEEPER!** You draw a quadrilateral and three triangles. Your friend draws an octagon and a hexagon. Who draws more angles in all? How many more?

You   Friend   _____ more angles

Name _____

Practice 15.2

Learning Target: Identify angles of a polygon.

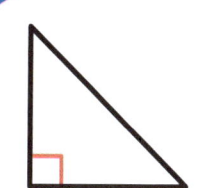 __3__ angles

How many right angles? __1__

Shape: __triangle__

 __5__ angles

How many right angles? __0__

Shape: __pentagon__

1.  ____ angles

   How many right angles? ____

   Shape: _____

2. 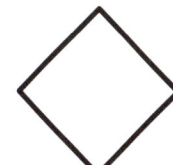 ____ angles

   How many right angles? ____

   Shape: _____

3.  ____ angles

   How many right angles? ____

   Shape: _____

4. 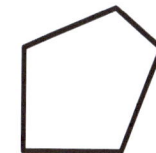 ____ angles

   How many right angles? ____

   Shape: _____

5. Draw and name a polygon with 4 sides and 1 right angle.

   _____

6. Draw and name a polygon with 6 angles.

   _____

Chapter 15 | Lesson 2   seven hundred forty-one

7. **DIG DEEPER!** Draw two polygons that have 9 angles in all.

8. **Modeling Real Life** You are designing a company logo. Your logo must be a hexagon with 2 right angles. Which logos might be yours?

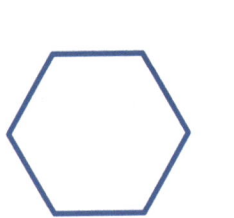    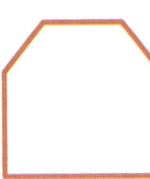 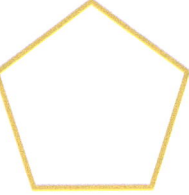

9. **DIG DEEPER!** You draw an octagon and two triangles. Your friend draws two quadrilaterals and a pentagon. Who draws more angles in all? How many more?

You _____   Friend _____   _____ more angles

Review & Refresh

Draw to show the time.

10.

11.

12.

Name _____

Draw Polygons 15.3

Learning Target: Draw shapes given a description.

Compare the shapes.

 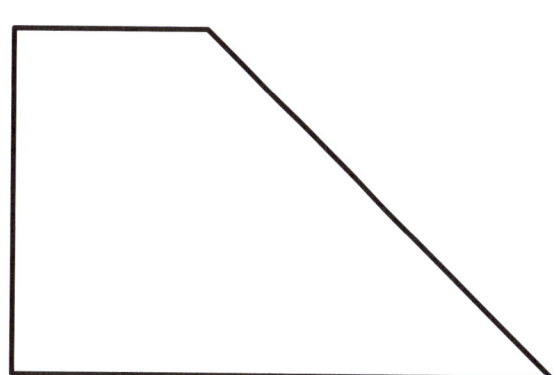

Structure How are the shapes the same? How are they different?

_____

_____

_____

Chapter 15 | Lesson 3

Think and Grow

Draw a polygon with 4 sides that are the same length.

I drew a rhombus. A **rhombus** is a quadrilateral. It has 4 sides that are the same length.

__4__ angles
Polygon: rhombus

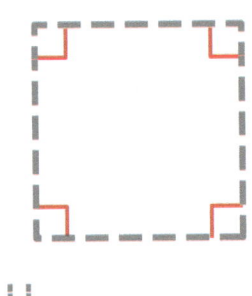

I drew a square. A square is a quadrilateral. It has 4 sides that are the same length and 4 right angles.

__4__ right angles
Polygon: square

Show and Grow — I can do it!

1. Draw a polygon with 6 sides. Two of the sides are the same length.

   _____ angles

   Polygon: _____

2. Draw a polygon with 5 angles. One of the angles is a right angle.

   _____ sides

   Polygon: _____

744 seven hundred forty-four

Name _____

Apply and Grow: Practice

3. Draw a polygon with 3 angles. One of the angles is a right angle.

_____ sides

Polygon: _____

4. Draw a polygon with 1 more side than a triangle. No sides are equal.

_____ sides

Polygon: _____

5. Draw a polygon with 4 fewer angles than an octagon. All sides are equal. All angles are right angles.

_____ sides

Polygon: _____

6. Draw a polygon with 4 sides. Two pairs of sides are the same length.

_____ angles

Polygon: _____

7. **Precision** Which is *not* a polygon with only 4 angles?

square   rectangle   rhombus

trapezoid   pentagon   quadrilateral

Chapter 15 | Lesson 3   seven hundred forty-five   **745**

Think and Grow: Modeling Real Life

You have 9 straws. You use all the straws to create two polygons. Draw two polygons you can create. Write the names of the polygons.

Polygon 1: _____   Polygon 2: _____

Show and Grow   I can think deeper!

8. You have 7 clay balls and some toothpicks. You create two polygons using the clay balls as vertices and the toothpicks as sides. Draw two polygons you can create. Write the names of the polygons.

Polygon 1: _____   Polygon 2: _____

9. **DIG DEEPER!** You draw two different polygons. One of the polygons is a pentagon. You draw 11 sides in all. Draw a possible shape for your other polygon. Write the name of the polygon.

Polygon: _____

Name _____

Practice 15.3

Learning Target: Draw shapes given a description.

Draw a polygon with 3 angles. All sides are the same length.

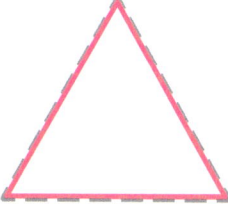

___3___ sides

Polygon: __triangle__

1. Draw a polygon with 4 angles. There are no right angles. No sides are equal.

_____ sides

Polygon: _____

2. Draw a polygon with 8 sides. Two of the angles are right angles.

_____ angles

Polygon: _____

3. Draw a polygon with 2 more angles than a quadrilateral. Two of the angles are right angles.

_____ sides

Polygon: _____

4. Draw a polygon with 3 fewer sides than an octagon.

_____ angles

Polygon: _____

Chapter 15 | Lesson 3   seven hundred forty-seven   **747**

5. **Patterns** Draw 3 shapes. The first shape is a quadrilateral. The number of angles in each shape increases by two.

Name the third shape. _____

6. **Modeling Real Life** You have 9 apples and some sticks. You create two polygons using the apples for vertices and the sticks for sides. Draw two polygons you can create. Write the names of the polygons.

Polygon 1: _____   Polygon 2: _____

7. **DIG DEEPER!** You draw two different polygons. One of the polygons is an octagon. You draw 14 sides in all. Draw a possible shape for your other polygon. Write the name of the polygon.

Polygon: _____

Review & Refresh

8.

Favorite Subject

How many more students chose math than science? _____

Name _____

Identify and Draw Cubes

15.4

Learning Target: Identify, draw, and describe cubes.

Explore and Grow

Draw an X on the shapes with curved surfaces. Circle the remaining shape with flat surfaces that are all the same.

Name the shape you circled.

_____

Chapter 15 | Lesson 4   seven hundred forty-nine   749

Think and Grow

Each face of a **cube** is a square.

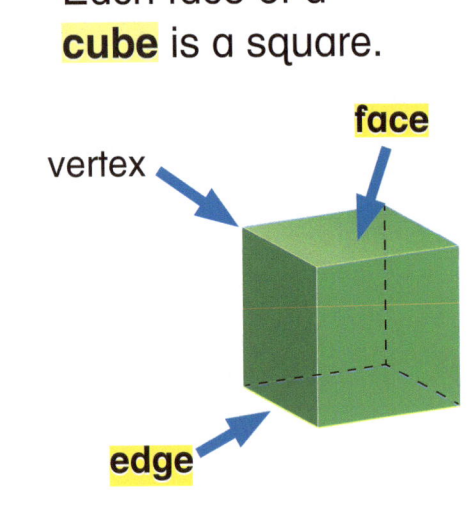

You can use dot paper to draw a cube.

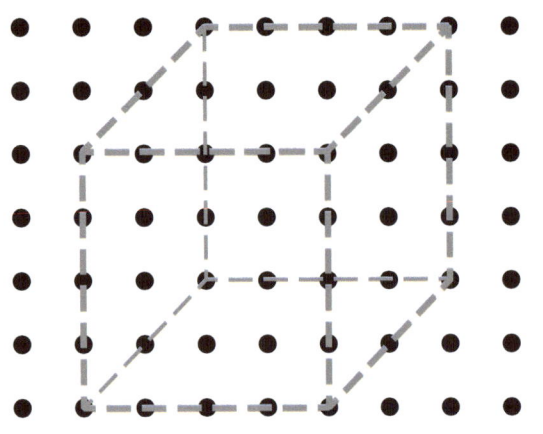

Show and Grow   I can do it!

1.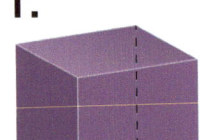

   _____ faces

   _____ vertices

   _____ edges

   Is it a cube?   Yes   No

2.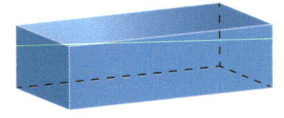

   _____ faces

   _____ vertices

   _____ edges

   Is it a cube?   Yes   No

3. Use the dot paper to draw a cube.

Name _____

 **Apply and Grow: Practice**

4. Which shapes are cubes?

5. Use the dot paper to draw a cube.

6. How many faces do two cubes have in all?

_____ faces

7. **MP Structure** Which two-dimensional shape makes up a cube? Name the shape.

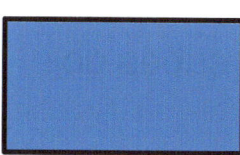   

A cube is made up of _____.

Chapter 15 | Lesson 4

Think and Grow: Modeling Real Life

You make a ballot box for a school election. Your box is in the shape of a cube. Each face of the ballot box is a different color. How many colors do you use?

_____ colors

Show and Grow I can think deeper!

8. You construct a cube. You use clay balls for the vertices and straws for the edges. How many clay balls do you make? How many straws do you use?

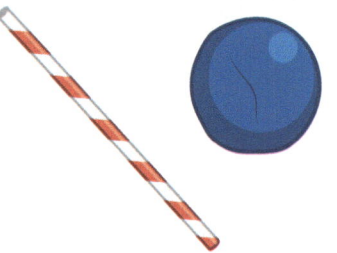

_____ clay balls   _____ straws

9. The faces of the number cube are numbered, starting with 1. Draw and label all the faces of the number cube.

10. **DIG DEEPER!** You have 48 toothpicks and 32 grapes. You use all of the materials to make cubes using the toothpicks as edges and the grapes as vertices. How many cubes do you make?

_____ cubes

Name _____

Practice

Learning Target: Identify, draw, and describe cubes.

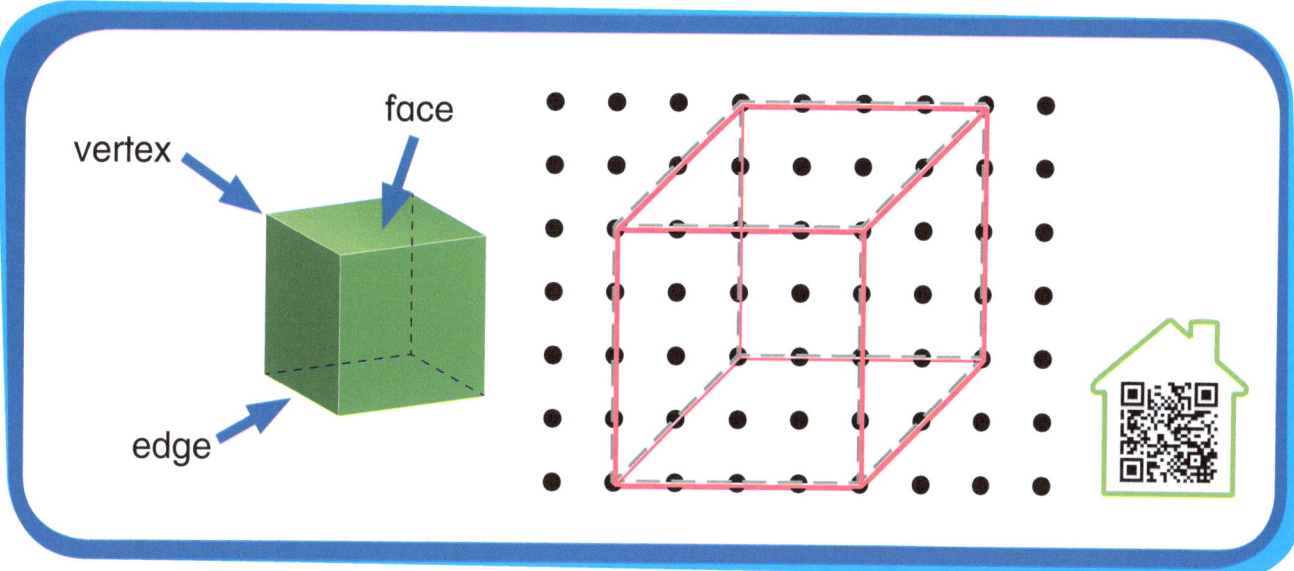

1. _____ faces
   _____ vertices
   _____ edges

   Is it a cube? Yes   No

2. _____ faces
   _____ vertices
   _____ edges

   Is it a cube? Yes   No

3. Use the dot paper to draw a cube.

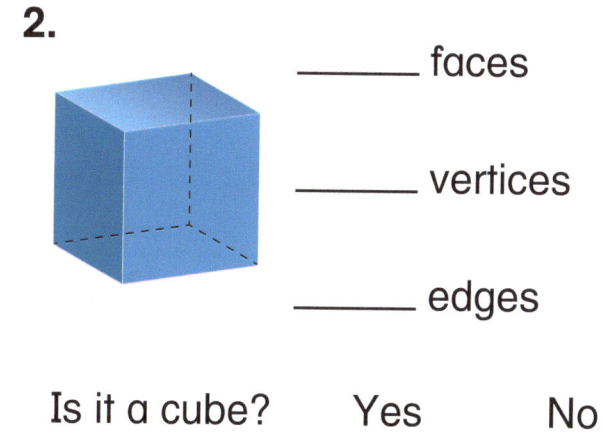

Chapter 15 | Lesson 4 seven hundred fifty-three 753

4. How many vertices do two cubes have in all?

_____ vertices

5. **YOU BE THE TEACHER** Newton says the cube has 3 faces. Is he correct? Explain.

_____

_____

6. **Modeling Real Life** You construct a cube. You use marshmallows for the vertices and pretzel rods for the edges. How many marshmallows do you use? How many pretzel rods do you use?

_____ marshmallows   _____ pretzel rods

7. **DIG DEEPER!** You have 24 cotton balls and 36 toothpicks. You use all of the materials to make cubes using the cotton balls as vertices and the toothpicks as edges. How many cubes do you make?

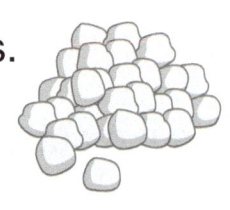

_____ cubes

Review & Refresh

8. 43 − 5 = _____

9. 62 − 6 = _____

10. _____ = 41 − 4

11. _____ = 44 − 7

754   seven hundred fifty-four

Name _____

Compose Rectangles

Learning Target: Show a rectangle as equal squares.

How many square tiles do you need to cover the rectangle?

_____ squares

Use Equations Write an equation to match your model.

Chapter 15 | Lesson 5

Think and Grow

You can add the square tiles by rows or by columns.

How many square tiles cover this rectangle?

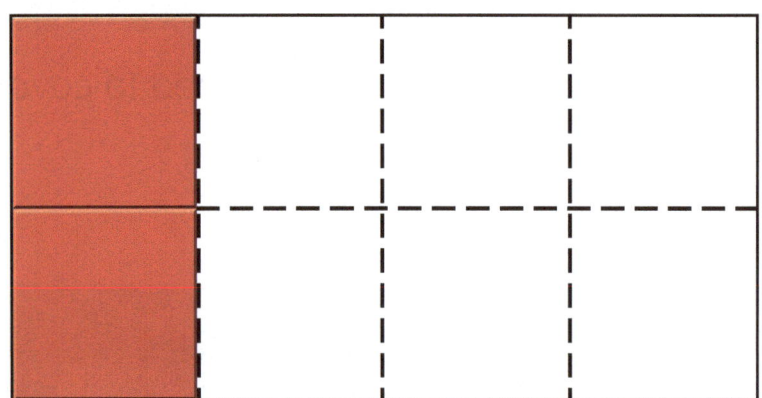

Number of rows: __2__   Number of columns: __4__

Add by rows: __4__ + __4__ = __8__

Add by columns: __2__ + __2__ + __2__ + __2__ = __8__

Total square tiles: __8__

Show and Grow   I can do it!

1. Use square tiles to cover the rectangle. Draw to show your work.

Complete the statements.

Add by rows:

____ + ____ + ____ = ____

Add by columns: ____ + ____ = ____

Total square tiles: ____

756   seven hundred fifty-six

Name _____

 **Apply and Grow: Practice**

2. Use square tiles to cover the rectangle. Draw to show your work.

Complete the statements.

Add by rows: ____ + ____ + ____ = ____

Add by columns: ____ + ____ + ____ + ____ + ____ = ____

Total square tiles: ____

3. **Precision** Divide the rectangle into 6 equal parts.

Chapter 15 | Lesson 5

seven hundred fifty-seven 757

Think and Grow: Modeling Real Life

You use foam mats to cover the entire floor of a square room. You fit 4 mats across one side of the room. How many rows and columns of mats will you have?

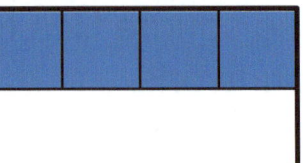

_____ rows   _____ columns

How many foam mats do you use to cover the entire floor?

Addition equation:

_____ foam mats

Show and Grow   I can think deeper!

4. You use square tiles to cover the floor of a square room. You fit 5 tiles across one side of the room. How many rows and columns of tiles will you have?

   _____ rows   _____ columns

   DIG DEEPER! How many tiles do you use to cover the entire floor?

   _____ tiles

Name _____

Practice 15.5

Learning Target: Show a rectangle as equal squares.

How many square tiles cover this rectangle?

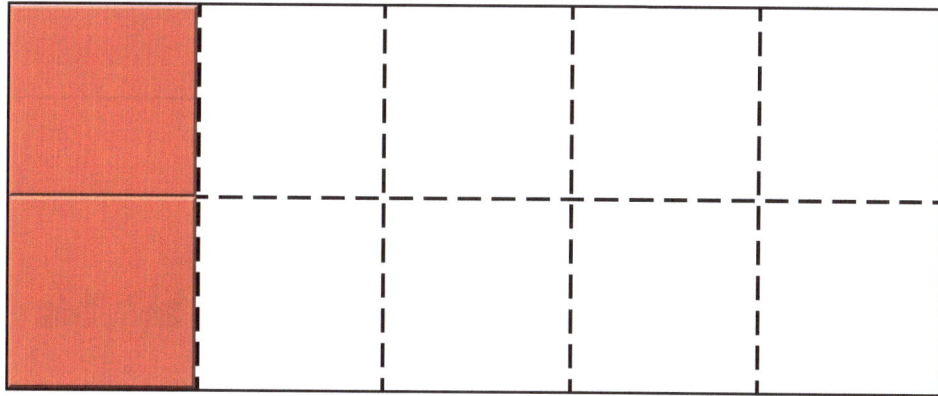

Number of rows: __2__   Number of columns: __5__

Add by rows: __5__ + __5__ = __10__

Add by columns: __2__ + __2__ + __2__ + __2__ + __2__ = __10__

__10__ total square tiles

1. Use square tiles to cover the rectangle. Draw to show your work.

Complete the statements.

Add by rows: ____ = ____   Total square tiles: ____

Add by columns:

____ + ____ + ____ + ____ + ____ + ____ = ____

Chapter 15 | Lesson 5

2. **Writing** Newton wants to cover the rectangle with square tiles. Explain what he is doing wrong.

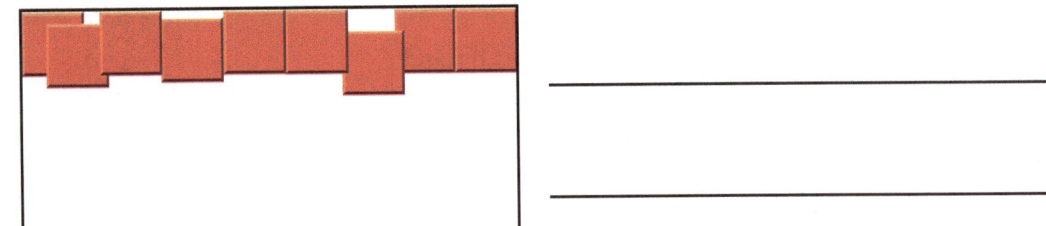

_____

_____

3. **Modeling Real Life** You use square glass tiles to make a square mosaic picture. You fit 6 tiles across one side of the picture. How many rows and columns of tiles will you have?

_____ rows _____ columns

DIG DEEPER! How many glass tiles do you use to cover the entire picture?

_____ glass tiles

Review & Refresh

4. Circle *a.m.* or *p.m.*

   Take the bus to school   Sunset

   a.m.   p.m.   a.m.   p.m.

Name _____

Learning Target: Identify shapes that show halves, thirds, and fourths.

Identify Two, Three, or Four Equal Shares 15.6

Explore and Grow

Sort the Equal Share Cards.

Two Equal Shares	Three Equal Shares
Four Equal Shares	**Unequal Shares**

Chapter 15 | Lesson 6

seven hundred sixty-one 761

 # Think and Grow

The rectangle has 2 equal shares, or **halves**. Half of the rectangle is one of the equal shares.

The rectangle has 3 equal shares, or **thirds**. A third of the rectangle is one of the equal shares.

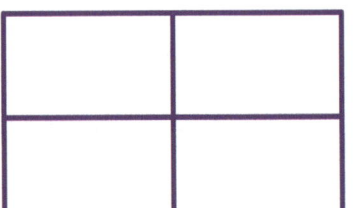

The rectangle has 4 equal shares, or **fourths**. A fourth of the rectangle is one of the equal shares.

Show and Grow   I can do it!

Circle the shape that shows halves.

1.

2.

Circle the shape that shows thirds.

3.

4.

Circle the shape that shows fourths.

5.

6.

Name _____

 Apply and Grow: Practice

7. Which shapes show halves?

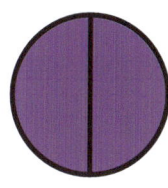 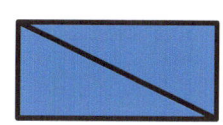  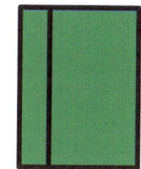

8. Which shapes show thirds?

9. Which shapes show fourths?

  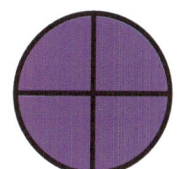 

10. Color a third of the shape.

11. Color half of the shape.

12. Color a fourth of the shape.

13. **YOU BE THE TEACHER** Newton says the shape shows fourths. Is he correct? Explain.

_____

_____

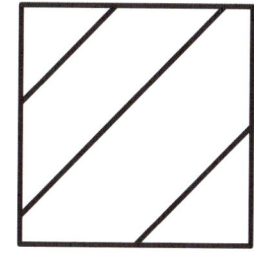

Chapter 15 | Lesson 6   seven hundred sixty-three   **763**

Think and Grow: Modeling Real Life

You want to play 3 games in the pool. Each game needs an equal share of the pool. Show how you could divide the pool.

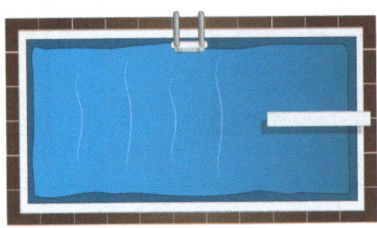

Show and Grow — I can think deeper!

14. 2 friends are making crafts. Each friend wants an equal share of the table. Show how the friends could divide the table.

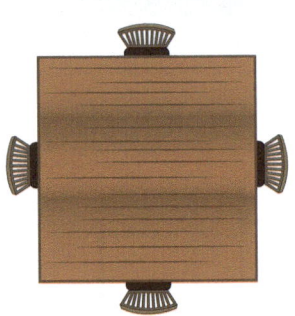

15. You and 3 friends want to share the piece of watermelon. Show how to cut the piece of watermelon so you and your friends each get an equal share.

Justify a Result How did you know how many equal shares to cut?

_____

_____

Name _____

Practice  15.6

Learning Target: Identify shapes that show halves, thirds, and fourths.

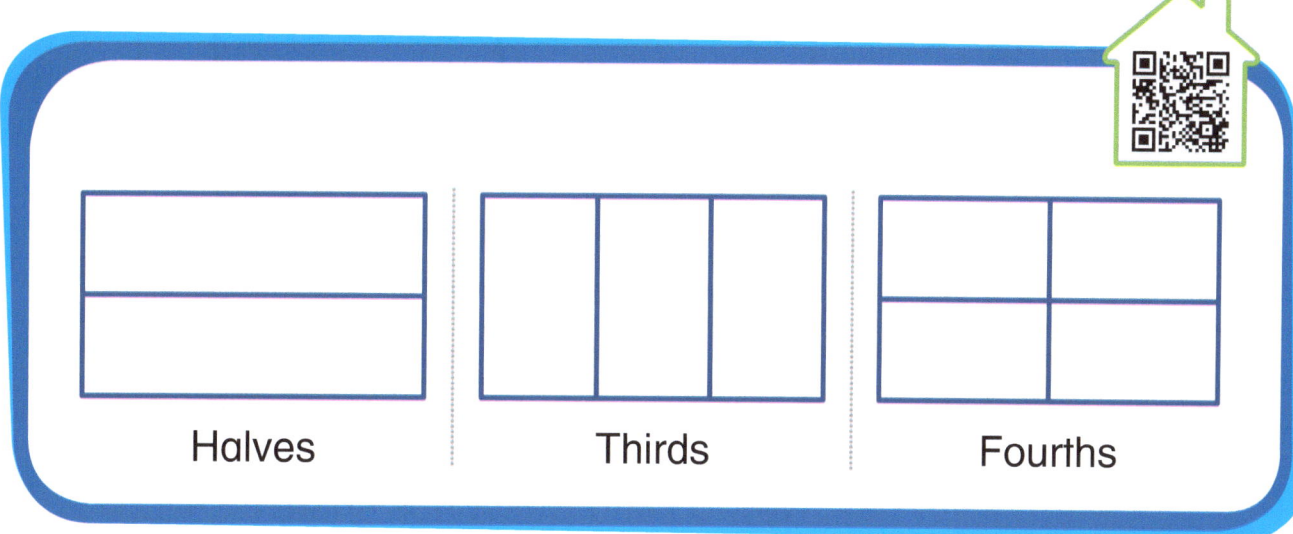

1. Which shapes show halves?

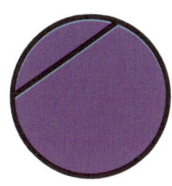         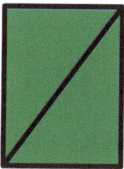

2. Which shapes show thirds?

3. Which shapes show fourths?

   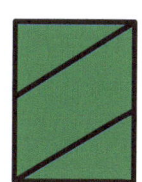      

Chapter 15 | Lesson 6

4. Color a third of the shape.

5. Color half of the shape.

6. Color a fourth of the shape.

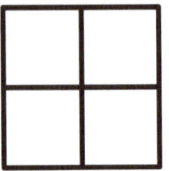

7. **Patterns** Draw what comes next.

8. **Modeling Real Life** Newton and Descartes share a bedroom. Show how they could divide their room into equal shares.

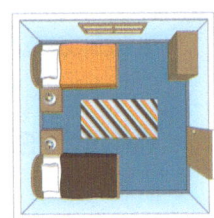

9. **Modeling Real Life** You and 2 friends are making a poster. Each friend wants an equal share of the poster. Show how the friends could divide the poster.

Analyze a Problem How else can you divide the poster? Which way do you prefer? Explain.

_____

Review & Refresh

10. A pen is 16 centimeters tall. A pen holder is 11 centimeters tall. How much taller is the pen than the pen holder?

_____ centimeters

Name _____

Learning Target: Draw lines to show halves, thirds, and fourths of a shape.

Partition Shapes into Equal Shares 15.7

Explore and Grow

Which pattern blocks can you use to model equal shares of the hexagon?

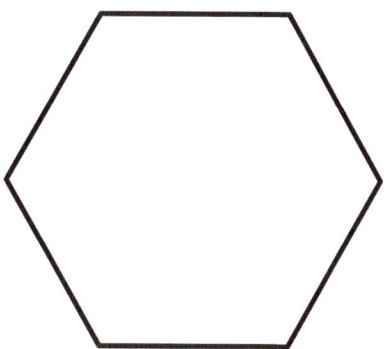

Shape	Equal Shares	Number of Equal Shares
(red trapezoid)	Yes No	
(blue rhombus)	Yes No	
(orange square)	Yes No	

Chapter 15 | Lesson 7

seven hundred sixty-seven 767

Think and Grow

Draw lines to show equal shares. Complete the sentences.

halves

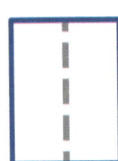

Each share is a ___half___ of the whole.

The whole is ___2 halves___.

thirds

Each share is a ___third___ of the whole.

The whole is ___3 thirds___.

fourths

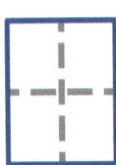

Each share is a ___fourth___ of the whole.

The whole is ___4 fourths___.

Show and Grow   I can do it!

Draw lines to show equal shares. Complete the sentences.

1. fourths

Each share is a _____ of the whole.

The whole is _____.

2. halves

Each share is a _____ of the whole.

The whole is _____.

Name _____

✓ Apply and Grow: Practice

3. Draw lines to show equal shares. Complete the sentences.

thirds

Each share is a _____ of the whole.

The whole is _____.

Draw lines to show equal shares. Which word describes the parts?

4. 4 equal parts

halves

thirds

fourths

5. 3 equal parts

halves

thirds

fourths

6. 2 equal parts

halves

thirds

fourths

7. 3 equal parts

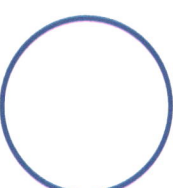

halves

thirds

fourths

---

8. **Precision** Draw lines to show thirds. Color 3 thirds.

Chapter 15 | Lesson 7

Think and Grow: Modeling Real Life

You have 2 towels that are the same size. Half of one towel is green. A fourth of the other towel is yellow. Is the green share or the yellow share larger? Explain.

Draw to show:

Which share is larger?   Green share   Yellow share

_____

_____

_____

Show and Grow   I can think deeper!

9. You have 2 rugs that are the same size. A fourth of one rug is red. A third of the other rug is blue. Is the red share or the blue share smaller? Explain.

_____

_____

Name _____

Practice 15.7

Learning Target: Draw lines to show halves, thirds, and fourths of a shape.

halves

Each share is a __half__ of the whole.

The whole is __2 halves__.

thirds

Each share is a __third__ of the whole.

The whole is __3 thirds__.

fourths

Each share is a __fourth__ of the whole.

The whole is __4 fourths__.

Draw lines to show equal shares. Complete the sentences.

1. thirds

   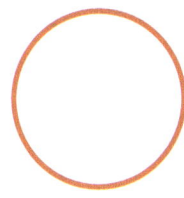

   Each share is a _____ of the whole.

   The whole is _____.

2. halves

   Each share is a _____ of the whole.

   The whole is _____.

Chapter 15 | Lesson 7   seven hundred seventy-one   771

Draw lines to show equal shares. Complete the sentences.

3. fourths

Each share is a _____ of the whole.

The whole is _____.

4. **Logic** Complete the sentences.

   I whole is _____ halves.

   I whole is _____ thirds.

   I whole is _____ fourths.

5. **DIG DEEPER!** Descartes cuts a pizza into fourths. How can he cut the pizza to feed 8 friends?

_____

_____

6. **Modeling Real Life** You have 2 blankets that are the same size. A third of one blanket is yellow. A half of the other blanket is purple. Is the yellow share or the purple share smaller? Explain.

_____

_____

Review & Refresh

7. 150 + 610 = _____

8. 553 + 250 = _____

Name _____

Learning Target: Draw to show halves, thirds, and fourths in different ways.

Analyze Equal Shares of the Same Shape

15.8

Explore and Grow

Color the squares that show equal shares.

 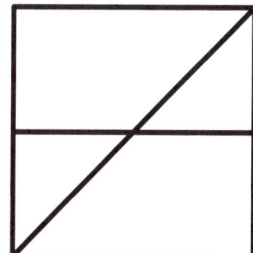 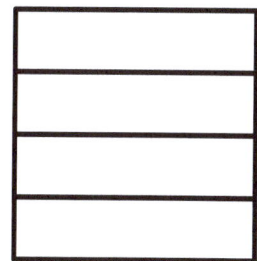

 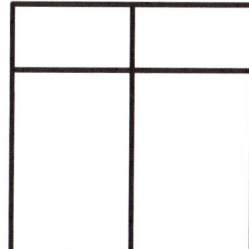 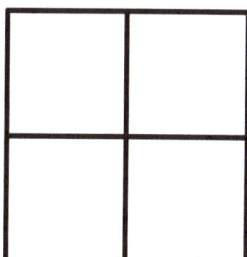

Analyze a Problem How are the squares you colored the same? How are they different?

_____

_____

_____

Chapter 15 | Lesson 8   seven hundred seventy-three   773

Think and Grow

Wow! Equal shares of a shape do not have to be the same shape.

Draw lines to show fourths in two different ways. Color one-fourth of each square.

One-fourth of this square is a rectangle.

One-fourth of this square is a triangle.

Show and Grow — I can do it!

1. Draw lines to show halves in two different ways. Color one-half of each circle.

   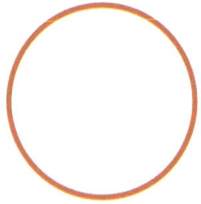 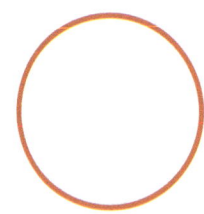

   Think: How are the halves of each circle the same? How are they different?

2. Draw lines to show thirds in two different ways. Color one-third of each rectangle.

   Think: How are the thirds of each rectangle the same? How are they different?

Name _____

 **Apply and Grow: Practice**

3. Draw lines to show fourths two different ways. Color one-fourth of each circle.

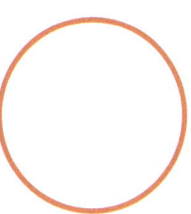 

4. Draw lines to show thirds two different ways. Color one-third of each square.

5. Draw lines to show halves two different ways. Color one-half of each rectangle.

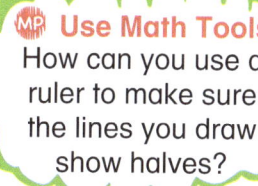
Use Math Tools
How can you use a ruler to make sure the lines you draw show halves?

6. **DIG DEEPER!** Explain how you know each color is a fourth of the whole square.

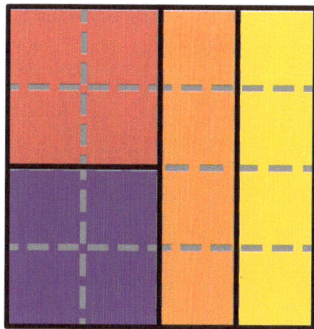

_____
_____
_____

Chapter 15 | Lesson 8   seven hundred seventy-five   775

Think and Grow: Modeling Real Life

You and your friend each cut a sandwich into fourths different ways. The sandwiches are the same size. Show how you and your friend can cut the sandwiches.

Show and Grow   I can think deeper!

7. You, Newton, and Descartes each cut a granola bar into halves different ways. The granola bars are the same size. Show how you, Newton, and Descartes can cut the granola bars.

   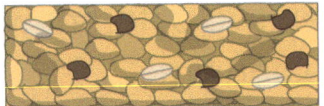   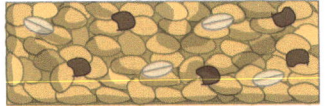

8. **DIG DEEPER!** There are 2 pizzas that are the same size. 6 friends each want an equal share of the pizzas. Should the pizzas be cut into halves, thirds, or fourths? Explain.

Halves   Thirds   Fourths

_____

_____

776   seven hundred seventy-six

Name _____

Practice 15.8

Learning Target: Draw to show halves, thirds, and fourths in different ways.

Draw lines to show halves two different ways.
Color one-half of each square.

Wow! Equal shares of a shape do not have to be the same shape!

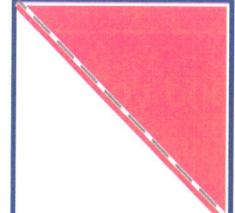 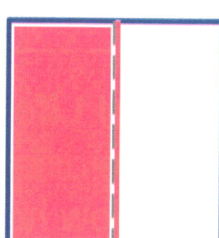

1. Draw lines to show fourths two different ways.
   Color one-fourth of each rectangle.

   Think: How are the fourths of each rectangle the same? How are they different?

2. Draw lines to show thirds two different ways.
   Color one-third of each circle.

      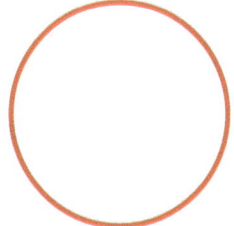

Chapter 15 | Lesson 8   seven hundred seventy-seven   777

3. **Reasoning** Descartes says there are only two ways to divide a rectangle into 3 equal shares. Is he correct? Explain.

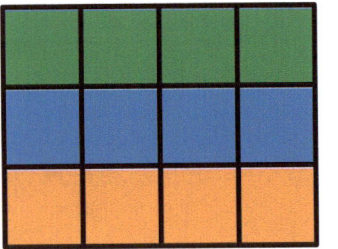 

_____
_____
_____

4. **Modeling Real Life** You and your friend each cut a loaf of bread into thirds different ways. The loaves of bread are the same size. Show how you and your friend can cut the loaves of bread.

5. **DIG DEEPER!** There are 2 quesadillas that are the same size. 8 friends each want an equal share of the quesadillas. Should the quesadillas be cut into halves, thirds, or fourths? Explain.

Halves

Thirds

Fourths

_____

Review & Refresh

6. 841 − 603 = _____

7. 439 − 210 = _____

Name _____

Performance Task 15

You paint a square suncatcher in art class.

1. You paint each shape a different color. Color to show how you paint the sun catcher.

   a. Each triangle is red.
   b. Each octagon is orange.
   c. Each pentagon with more than 1 right angle is yellow.
   d. The rest of the pentagons are green.
   e. Each shape with 6 angles is blue.
   f. Each quadrilateral with all right angles is purple.
   g. The rest of the quadrilaterals are pink.

2. The length of one side of the suncatcher is 12 inches. What are the lengths of the other sides?

   _____ inches

3. Your friend paints a rectangular suncatcher.

   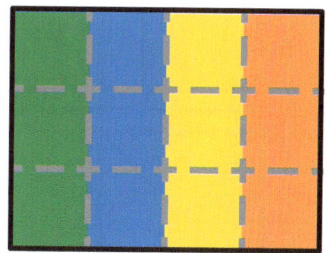

   a. What share of your friend's design is blue?

   _____

   b. What share of your friend's design is orange or yellow?

   _____

Chapter 15   seven hundred seventy-nine   779

Three In a Row: Equal Shares

To Play: Players take turns. On your turn, spin the spinner. Cover a square that matches your spin. Continue playing until a player gets three in a row.

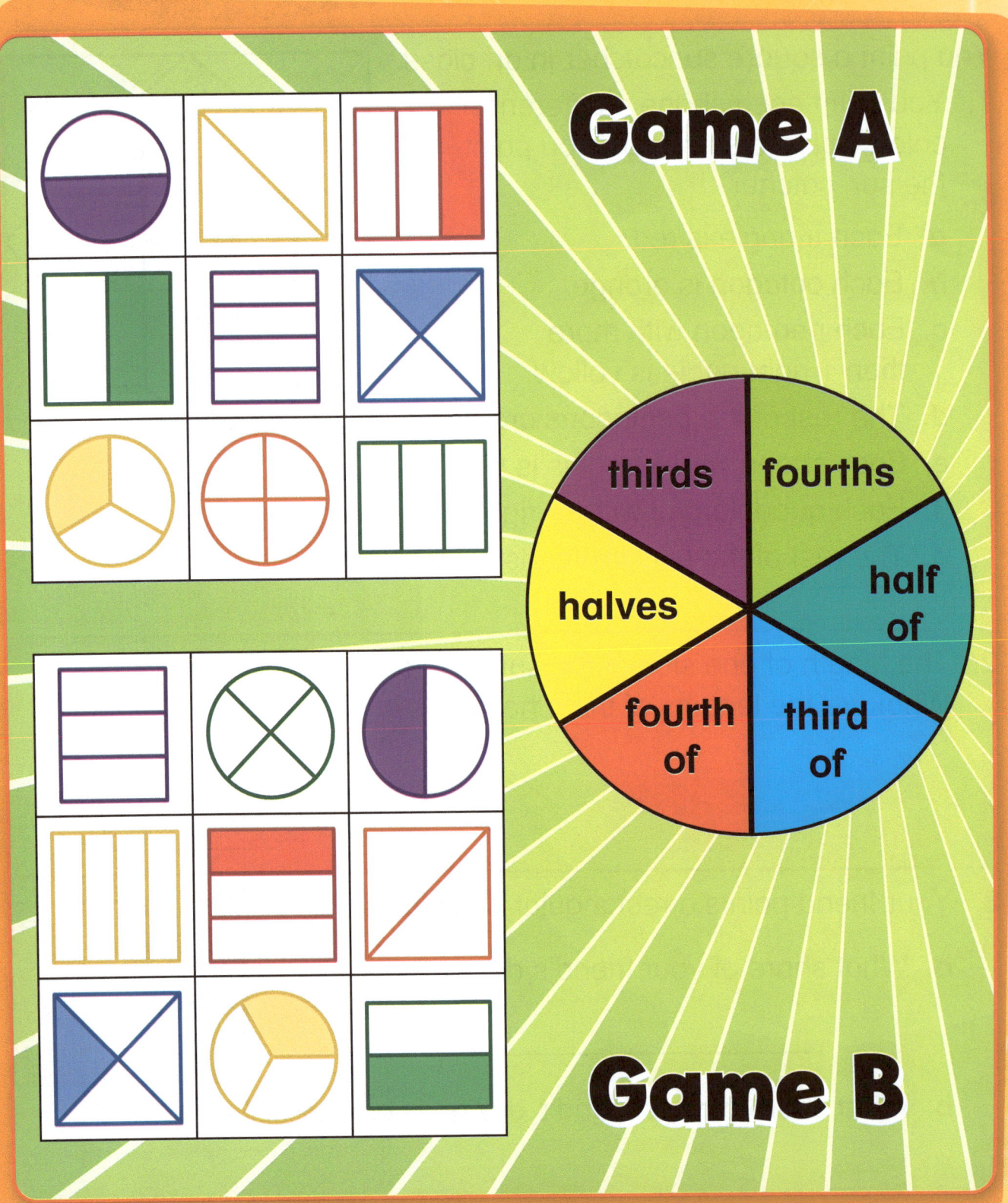

Name _____

Chapter Practice 15

15.1 Describe Two-Dimensional Shapes

1.  _____ sides

   _____ vertices

   Shape: _____

2.  _____ sides

   _____ vertices

   Shape: _____

3. **Modeling Real Life** You draw three quadrilaterals and an octagon. How many sides and vertices do you draw in all?

   _____ sides   _____ vertices

15.2 Identify Angles of Polygons

4.  _____ angles

   How many right angles? _____

   Shape: _____

5. 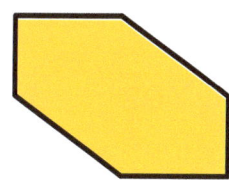 _____ angles

   How many right angles? _____

   Shape: _____

6. Draw and name a shape with 2 right angles.

   _____

Chapter 15   seven hundred eighty-one   781

15.3 Draw Polygons

7. Draw a polygon with 4 angles. All sides are equal length.

_____ sides

Polygon: _____

8. Draw a polygon with 5 sides. Two of the angles are right angles.

_____ angles

Polygon: _____

15.4 Identify and Draw Cubes

9.

_____ faces

_____ vertices

_____ edges

Is it a cube?   Yes   No

10.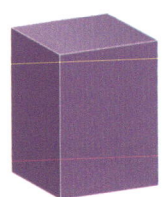

_____ faces

_____ vertices

_____ edges

Is it a cube?   Yes   No

11. Use the dot paper to draw a cube.

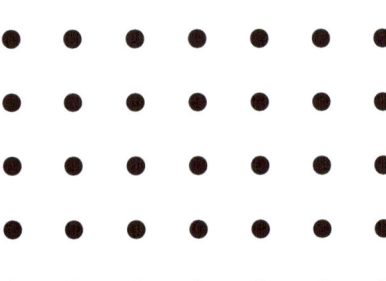

15.5 Compose Rectangles

12. Use square tiles to cover the rectangle. Draw to show your work.

Complete the statements.

Add by rows:

_____ + _____ = _____

Add by columns:

_____ + _____ = _____

Total square tiles: _____

15.6 Identify Two, Three, or Four Equal Shares

13. Which shapes show halves?

 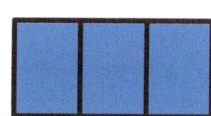  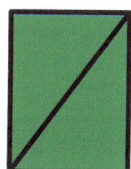

14. Which shapes show thirds?

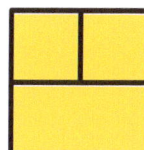 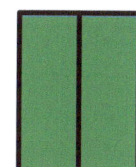  

15. Which shapes show fourths?

  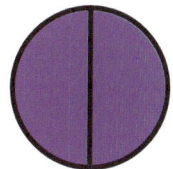 

Chapter 15   seven hundred eighty-three

15.7 Partition Shapes into Equal Shares

Draw lines to show equal parts. Complete the sentences.

16. thirds

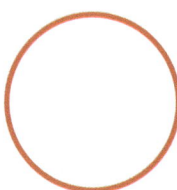

Each share is a _____ of the whole.

The whole is _____.

17. halves

Each share is a _____ of the whole.

The whole is _____.

18. fourths

Each share is a _____ of the whole.

The whole is _____.

15.8 Analyze Equal Shares of the Same Shape

19. **Modeling Real Life** There are 3 bagels that are the same size. 6 friends each want an equal share of the bagels. Should the bagels be cut into halves, thirds, or fourths? Explain.

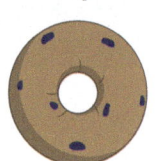
Halves

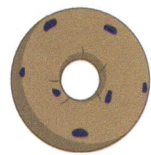
Thirds

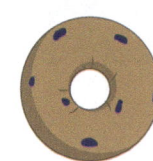
Fourths

_____

_____

784   seven hundred eighty-four

Name _____

Cumulative Practice 1–15

1. Your bed is 39 inches long. Your comforter is 66 inches long. How much longer is the comforter than the bed?

   ○ 105 inches   ○ 37 inches

   ○ 33 inches   ○ 27 inches

2. Find each difference.

   700 − 465 = _____   910 − 186 = _____   302 − 176 = _____

3. A dog park is 48 yards long. Your dog enters the park and runs 29 yards. You run 13 yards. How far is your dog from the other end of the park?

   ○ 19 yards   ○ 35 yards

   ○ 90 yards   ○ 6 yards

Chapter 15   seven hundred eighty-five   785

4. Which shapes show thirds?

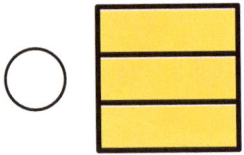   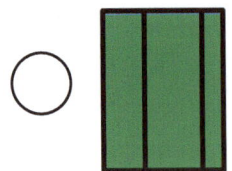

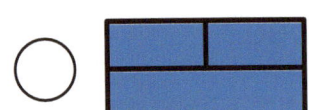   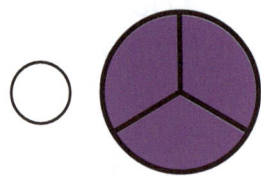

5. The girls' soccer team raises $237. The boys' soccer team raises $113 more. How much money do both teams raise in all?

○ $113   ○ $350

○ $587   ○ $124

6. Complete the bar graph.

Team Mascot	
Knight	卌 II
Tiger	III
Shark	卌 I
Warrior	卌 I

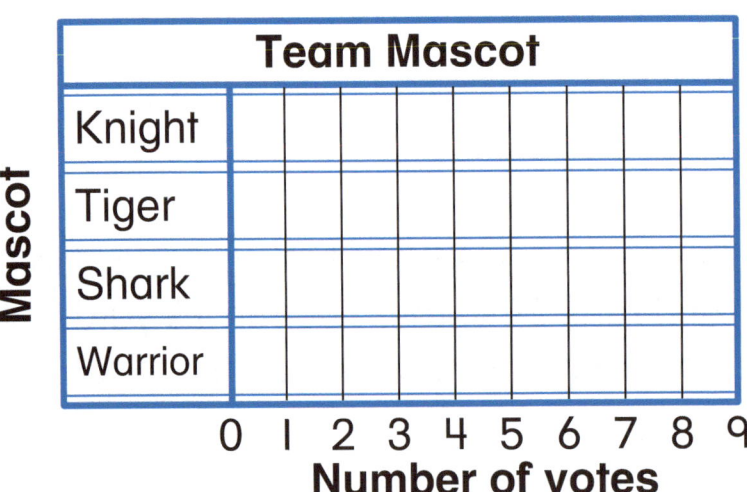

What mascot got the most votes? _____

How many more votes did Warrior get than Tiger? _____

7. Count on to find the total value.

Total value: _____

8. Which expressions have a difference of 34?

◯ 60 − 34 ◯ 86 − 50 − 2

◯ 40 − 6 ◯ 54 − 20

9. Complete the line plot. Then choose all of the statements that are true.

Child Heights (Inches)	
Child 1	44
Child 2	47
Child 3	45
Child 4	49
Child 5	45
Child 6	45
Child 7	49
Child 8	47

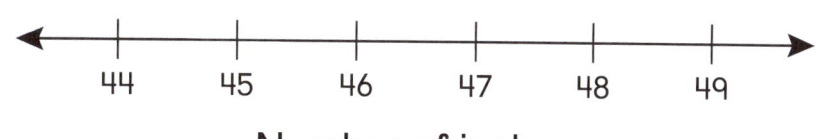

◯ Three students are 45 inches tall.

◯ Two students are taller than 46 inches.

◯ The most common height is 47 inches.

◯ Five students are 45 inches or 49 inches tall.

10. Which clock shows 10:40?

11. The phone is about 12 centimeters long. What is the best estimate for the length of the tablet?

○ 6 centimeters ○ 24 centimeters

○ 36 centimeters ○ 15 centimeters

12.

_____ sides

_____ vertices

Shape: _____

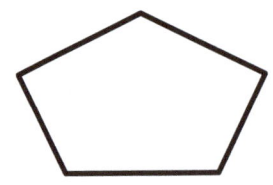

_____ sides

_____ vertices

Shape: _____

788   seven hundred eighty-eight

Glossary

A

a.m. [a.m.]

 go to school

 8:00 a.m.

---

addends [sumandos]

4 + 3 = 7

---

angle [ángulo]

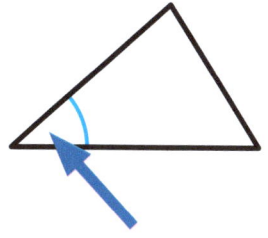

---

array [formación]

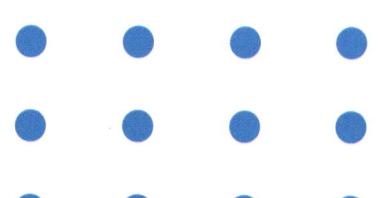

B

bar graph [gráfica de barras]

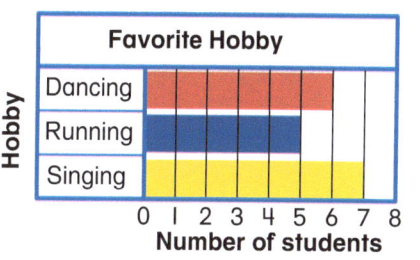

C

cent sign [signo de centavo]

¢

---

centimeter [centímetro]

centimeter (cm)

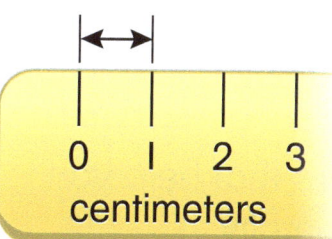

---

cents [centavos]

1 cent or 1¢   25 cents or 25¢

A1

column [columna]

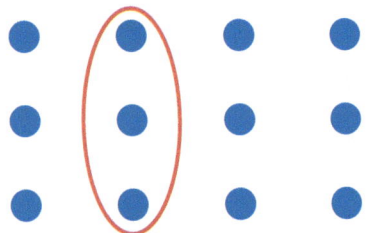

compare [comparar]

The symbols used to *compare* numbers are <, >, and =.

732 > 399   399 < 732

399 = 399

compatible numbers [números compatibles]

```
  4  2            3  7
  2  3            2  4
  3  5   10       3  1   8
+ 2  7          + 2  4
```

numbers that help you add mentally

compensation [compensación]

A strategy used to make a ten to help add and subtract numbers

cube [cubo]

D

data [datos]

Favorite Hobby
dancing dancing singing
running dancing running
running running singing
singing singing dancing
singing dancing dancing
singing running singing

decrease [disminución]

542 → 532 → 522

These numbers *decrease* by 10.

difference [diferencia]

8 − 3 = 5

dime [moneda de diez centavos]

A **dime** is 10 cents or 10¢.

A2

dollar [dólar]

A **dollar** is $1 or 100¢.

dollar sign [signo de dólar]

$

doubles minus 1 [dobles menos 1]

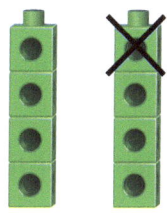

4 + 4 = 8, so 4 + 3 = 7.

doubles plus 1 [dobles más 1]

4 + 4 = 8, so 4 + 5 = 9.

edge [arista]

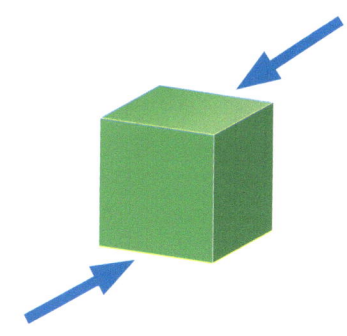

equal groups [grupos iguales]

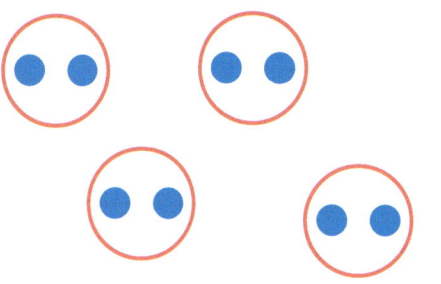

equal to (=) [igual a]

399 = 399

399 is equal to 399.

equation [ecuación]

10 − 4 = 6

5 + 5 = 10

A3

estimate [estimación]

even [par]

can be shown as equal groups

expanded form
[forma expandida]

$$300 + 20 + 9$$

expression [expresión]

$$4 + 7 \qquad 7 - 4$$

face [cara]

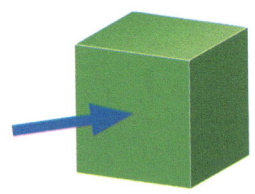

$5 bill [billete de $5]

$5 bill

foot [pie]

foot (ft)

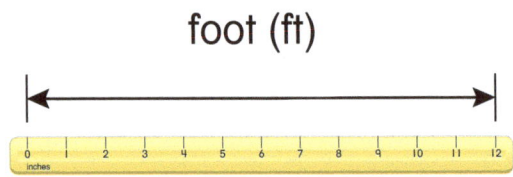

There are 12 inches in 1 foot.

fourths [cuartos]

The rectangle is divided into **fourths**.

greater than (>) [mayor que]

$$732 > 399$$

732 is greater than 399.

half past [y media]

half past 3

halves [mitades]

The circle is divided into **halves**.

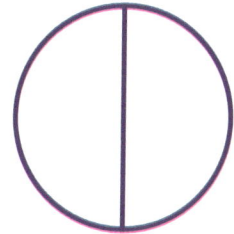

hexagon [hexágono]

6 sides
6 vertices

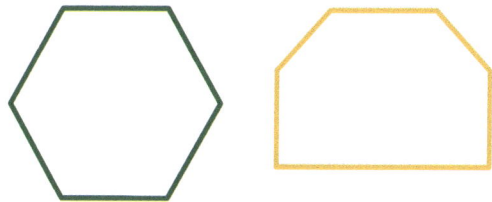

hundred [cien]

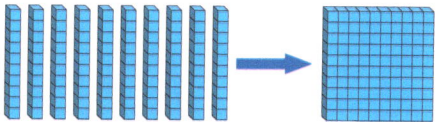

There are 10 tens in
1 hundred.

hundreds place
[lugar de cientos]

3<u>2</u>9

inch [pulgada]

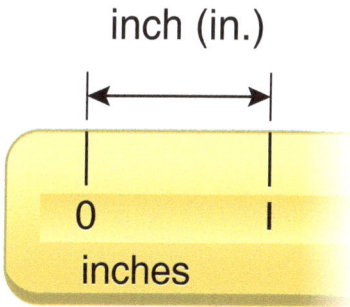

increase [incrementar]

522 ⟶ 532 ⟶ 542

These numbers *increase* by 10.

key [clave]

less than (<) [menor que]

399 < 732

399 is less than 732.

line plot [diagrama lineal]

Pencil Lengths

meter [metro]

meter (m)

There are 100 centimeters in 1 meter.

midnight [medianoche]

Midnight is 12:00 at night.

nickel [moneda de 5¢]

A **nickel** is 5 cents or 5¢.

noon [mediodía]

Noon is 12:00 in the daytime.

octagon [octágono]

8 sides
8 vertices

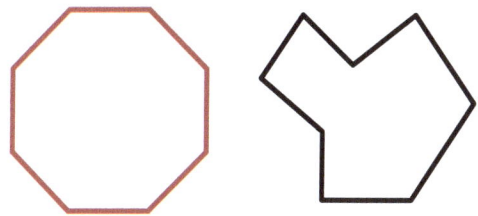

odd [impar]

cannot be shown as equal groups

$1 bill [billete de $1]

$1 bill

open number line
[abrir la línea numérica]

p.m. [p.m.]

 go to sleep

 8:00 p.m.

partial sums [sumas parciales]

		Tens	Ones	
		1	9	
	+	2	4	
10 + 20 =		3	0	⎫ Partial
9 + 4 =		1	3	⎭ Sums
Sum		4	3	

A7

penny   [monedo de 1¢]

A **penny** is 1 cent or 1¢.

---

pentagon   [pentágono]

5 sides
5 vertices

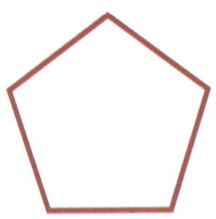 

---

picture graph   [gráfico de imagen]

Favorite Color					
Blue	🙂	🙂			
Green	🙂	🙂	🙂	🙂	
Yellow	🙂	🙂	🙂	🙂	🙂

Each 🙂 = 1 student.

---

polygon   [poligono]

A **polygon** is a closed two-dimensional shape with 3 or more sides.

 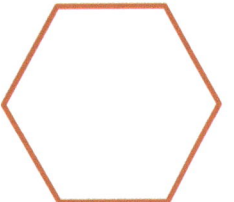

---

quadrilateral   [cuadrilátero]

4 sides
4 vertices

---

quarter   [moneda de 25¢]

A **quarter** is 25 cents or 25¢.

---

quarter past   [y cuarto]

15 minutes after 8 or
quarter past 8

A8

quarter to [menos cuarto]

15 minutes before 8 or **quarter to** 8

R

regroup [reagrupar]

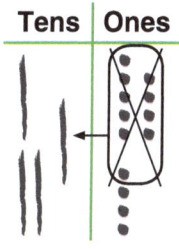

repeated addition
[adición repetida]

$$2 + 2 + 2 + 2$$

rhombus [rombo]

4 sides that are the same length

right angle [ángulo recto]

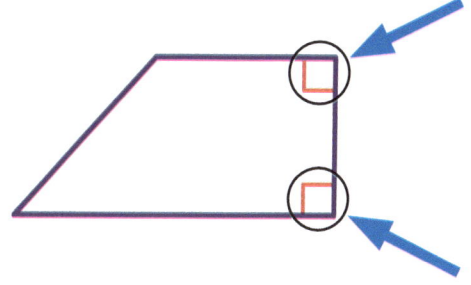

row [fila]

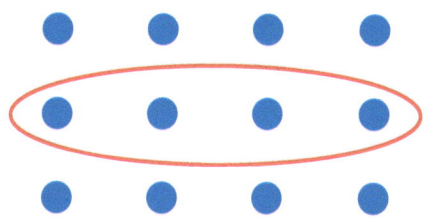

S

side [lado]

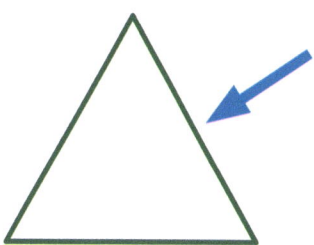

standard form [forma estándar]

329

sum [suma]

$$5 + 3 = 8$$

survey [encuesta]

T

$10 bill [billete de $10]

$10 bill

thirds [tercios]

The square is divided into **thirds**.

thousand [mil]

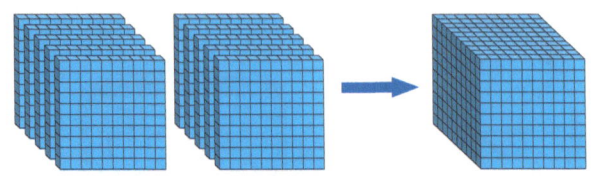

There are 10 hundreds in 1 thousand.

$20 bill [billete de $20]

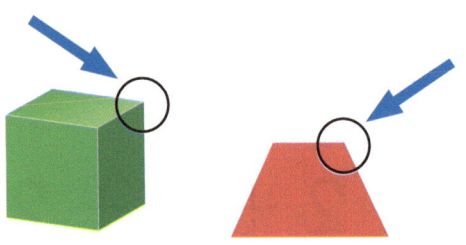

$20 bill

V

vertex [vértice]

W

word form [forma de la palabra]

three hundred twenty-nine

Y

yard [yarda]

yard (yd)

There are 36 inches, or
3 feet, in 1 yard.

Index

Addends, *See also* Addition
    breaking apart, 116–126
    changing order of, 41–46
    definition of, 42

Addition
    within 20, 83–88
    checking subtraction with, 287–292
    choosing strategies for, 133–138, 177–182, 447–452
    of compatible numbers, 442
    using compensation
        with three-digit numbers, 417–422
        with two-digit numbers, 127–132
    using decomposition (breaking addends apart), 116–126
    using doubles strategies, 47–52, 84
    of even and odd numbers, 9–14
    explaining strategies for, 447–452
    of four two-digit numbers, 441–446
    of lengths, 579–584
    using "make a 10" strategy, 59–64, 84
    using mental math, 399–404
    on number line (*See* Number line, adding on)
    order of addends in, 41–46
    using partial sums
        with three-digit numbers, 423–428
        with two-digit numbers, 153–164
    using place value, 115–126
    using regrouping, 165–176
    relationship between subtraction and, 71–76
    repeated, with equal groups, 16–18
    subtraction using, 219–224, 503–508
    summary of strategies for, 447
    of three one-digit numbers, 53–58
    of three two-digit numbers, 183–188
    of three-digit numbers, 411–440
        using compensation, 417–422
        using models, 429–434
        using number line, 411–416
        using partial sums, 423–428
    of two-digit numbers
        using compensation, 127–132
        four, 441–446
        using partial sums, 153–164
        three, 183–188
    word problems solved using
        one-step, 89–94, 189–194
        two-step, 139–144, 189–194

A.M., 717–722

Angles
    definition of, 738
    of polygons, identifying, 737–742
    right, 738–742

Another Way, *Throughout. For example, see:* 20, 60, 110, 178, 208, 294, 406, 468, 676

Apply and Grow: Practice, *In every lesson. For example, see:* 5, 43, 105, 209, 315, 401, 525, 581, 671

Arrays
    definition of, 152
    finding number of objects in, 21–26
    solving word problems using, 27–32

Bar graphs
    making, 637–642
    tally charts compared to, 631, 637
    understanding, 631–636

Bar model, 90
Base ten, 331
Bills, *See* Dollar bills
Breaking apart, *See* Decomposition

Centimeters
    estimating lengths in, 535–540
    measuring lengths in, 523–534

Challenge, *See* Dig Deeper

Chapter Practice, *In every chapter. For example, see:* 35–38, 97–100, 147–150, 257–260, 307–310, 455–458, 573–576, 657–660, 725–728, 781–784

Charts, tally
    bar graphs compared to, 631, 637
    organizing data in, 613–618
    picture graphs compared to, 619, 625

Choose Tools, 531, 549

Clocks, *See* Time

Coins
    combining
        in different ways, 675–680
        to make one dollar, 681–686
    finding total value of, 663–674
    grouping by type, 669–674
    making change from one dollar, 687–692

Columns
    definition of, 152
    in rectangles, 756–760

Common Error, *Throughout. For example, see:* T-30, T-113, T-294, T-338, T-366, T-450, T-492, T-582, T-708, T-734

Common Misconception, T-4, T-190, T-300

Comparing lengths, 565–570
    in word problems, 585–590

Comparing numbers
    using number line, 381–386
    using symbols, 375–380

Compatible numbers, adding, 442

Compensation
    addition using
        with three-digit numbers, 417–422
        with two-digit numbers, 127–132

    subtraction using
        with numbers containing zeros, 498–502
        with three-digit numbers, 479–484
        with two-digit numbers, 237–242

"Count back" strategy
    definition of, 40
    subtraction using, 65–70

"Count on" strategy
    definition of, 40
    subtraction using, 65–70

Counting, skip
    within 120, 351–356
    within 1,000, 357–362, 405–410, 467–472

Cross-Curricular Connections, *In every lesson. For example, see:* T-7, T-81, T-119, T-273, T-329, T-403, T-527, T-601, T-679, T-759

Cubes
    definition of, 750
    drawing, 749–754
    identifying, 749–754

Cumulative Practice, *Throughout. For example, see:* 201–204, 393–396, 607–610, 785–788

Customary units
    estimating lengths in, 553–558
    measuring lengths in, 547–552

Data
    in bar graphs, 631–642
    in line plots, 643–654
    in picture graphs, 619–630
    in tally charts, 613–618

Decade number, *See* Ten

Decomposition
    addition using, 116–126
    subtraction using, 225–236

Define It, *In every chapter. For example, see:* 2, 102, 152, 206, 312, 398, 460, 578, 612, 730

Difference, See Subtraction
Differentiation, see Scaffolding Instruction
Dig Deeper, Throughout. For example, see: 8, 43, 155, 210, 315, 366, 414, 532, 582, 666
Dimes, See also Coins
    value of, 664
Dollar bills
    five ($5), finding total value of, 693–698
    one ($1)
        coins equal to, 681–686
        finding total value of, 693–698
        making change from, 687–692
        value of, 682
    ten ($10), finding total value of, 693–698
Dollar sign ($), 682
Doubles minus 1, addition using, 47–52
Doubles plus 1, addition using, 47–52, 84

E

Edges, of cubes, 750
ELL Support, In every lesson. For example, see: T-2, T-41, T-104, T-156, T-296, T-364, T-485, T-522, T-664, T-730
Equal groups
    definition of, 16
    finding number of objects in, 15–20
Equal shares
    drawing lines showing, 767–778
    identifying lines showing, 761–766
Equal squares, rectangles composed of, 755–760
Equal to symbol (=), 376–380
Equations, definition of, 10
Error Analysis, See You Be the Teacher
Estimating lengths
    in customary units, 553–558
    in metric units, 535–540
Even numbers
    adding, 9–14
    identifying, 3–8
    modeling, 9–14

Explain, Throughout. For example, see: 8, 91, 132, 230, 343, 366, 494, 591, 696, 770
Explore and Grow, In every lesson. For example, see: 41, 103, 153, 207, 263, 313, 461, 523, 579, 663
Expressions, definition of, 42
Extended form of numbers, 331–336

F

Faces, of cubes, 750
Feet
    estimating lengths in, 553–558
    measuring lengths in, 547–552
Five (5), counting by
    within 120, 351–356
    within 1,000, 357–362
Five dollar bills ($5), finding total value of, 693–698
Formative Assessment, Throughout. For example, see: T-6, T-92, T-168, T-240, T-272, T-314, T-372, T-482, T-556, T-628
Fourths
    definition of, 762
    drawing lines showing, 767–778
    identifying lines showing, 761–766

G

Games, In every chapter. For example, see: 34, 96, 196, 256, 388, 454, 516, 572, 656, 780
"Get to 10" strategy, subtraction using, 77–82, 84
Graphs
    bar
        making, 637–642
        tally charts compared to, 631, 637
        understanding, 631–636
    picture
        making, 625–630

tally charts compared to, 619, 625
understanding, 619–624
Greater than symbol (>), 376–380
Groups, equal
definition of, 16
finding number of objects in, 15–20

H

Half past, 712–716
Halves
definition of, 762
drawing lines showing, 767–778
identifying lines showing, 761–766
Hexagons
drawing, 734, 736
identifying, 254, 732–736, 737
Higher Order Thinking, See Dig Deeper
Hour, telling time before and after the, 711–716
Hundred(s) (100), 313–318
adding
using mental math, 399–404
using models, 429–434
using number line, 405–410
in partial sums, 423–428
counting by, within 1,000, 357–362, 405–410, 467–472
definition of, 320
identifying groups of tens as, 313–318
identifying numbers 100 more or 100 less, 369–374
subtracting
using mental math, 461–466
using models, 485–490
using number line, 467–472
understanding place value of, 325–330
Hundred chart, 103, 109, 207, 213

I

Inches
estimating lengths in, 553–558

measuring lengths in, 541–552

L

Learning Target, In every lesson. For example, see: 7, 103, 207, 313, 417, 541, 583, 631, 711
Lengths
adding, on number line, 579–584
comparing, 565–570, 585–590
estimating
in centimeters, 535–540
in customary units, 553–558
in feet, 553–558
in inches, 553–558
in meters, 535–540
in metric units, 535–540
in yards, 553–558
measuring
in centimeters, 523–534
comparing after, 565–570
in customary units, 547–552
in feet, 547–552
in inches, 541–552
making line plots after, 649–654
in meters, 529–534
in metric units, 529–534
using two different units, 559–564
in yards, 547–552
subtracting, on number line, 579–584
in word problems, solving
comparing lengths, 585–590
for missing measurements, 591–596
on number line, 579–584
practicing, 597–602
Less than symbol (<), 376–380
Line plots, making, 643–654
Logic, 23, 540, 558, 772

M

"Make a 10" strategy, addition using, 59–64, 84

Mathematical Practices
    Make sense of problems and persevere in solving them, *Throughout. For example, see:* 3, 89, 139, 219, 281, 316, 411, 628, 698
    Reason abstractly and quantitatively, *Throughout. For example, see:* 117, 185, 230, 265, 377, 446, 599, 665, 755
    Construct viable arguments and critique the reasoning of others, *Throughout. For example, see:* 8, 80, 133, 173, 292, 441, 538, 677, 772
    Model with mathematics, *Throughout. For example, see:* 58, 114, 212, 280, 356, 484, 540, 716, 760
    Use appropriate tools strategically, *Throughout. For example, see:* 6, 124, 177, 299, 322, 369, 464, 549, 637
    Attend to precision, *Throughout. For example, see:* 62, 123, 269, 429, 481, 537, 621, 713, 769
    Look for and make use of structure, *Throughout. For example, see:* 108, 171, 263, 351, 416, 487, 651, 707, 748
    Look for and express regularity in repeated reasoning, *Throughout. For example, see:* 85, 127, 237, 266, 464, 561, 636, 696, 739

Measurement, of lengths, *See* Lengths

Mental math
    addition using, 399–404
    subtraction using, 237, 461–466

Meters
    estimating lengths in, 535–540
    measuring lengths in, 529–534

Metric units
    estimating lengths in, 535–540
    measuring lengths in, 529–534

Midnight, 718

Minus sign (−), 206

Minutes, telling time to nearest five, 705–710

Missing numbers
    in length word problems, 591–596
    using place value to find, 363–368

Model(s)
    addition of three-digit numbers using, 429–434
    bar, 90
    of even and odd numbers, 9–14
    of numbers up to 1,000, 319–324
    part-part-whole, 71, 72
    subtraction using
        of one-digit number from two-digit number, 263–274, 281–286
        of three-digit numbers, 485–490
        of two-digit number from two-digit number, 275–286

Modeling Real Life, *In every lesson. For example, see:* 8, 46, 108, 212, 318, 404, 466, 584, 618, 668

Money, *See also* Coins; Dollar bills
    in word problems, 687–692, 699–704

Multiple Representations, *Throughout. For example, see:* 16, 63, 128, 169, 270, 394, 489, 581, 619, 682

Nickels, *See also* Coins
    value of, 664

Noon, 718

Number(s)
    comparing
        using number line, 381–386
        using symbols, 375–380
    compatible, 442
    even and odd
        identifying, 3–8
        modeling, 9–14
    extended form of, 331–336
    one-digit (*See* One-digit numbers)

representing in different ways, 337–342
standard form of, 331–336
three-digit (*See* Three-digit numbers)
two-digit (*See* Two-digit numbers)
word form of, 331–336

Number line
    adding on
        of lengths, 579–584
        using "make a 10" strategy, 60, 63, 84
        of tens, 103–108
        of tens and hundreds, 405–410
        of tens and ones, 109–114
        of three-digit numbers, 411–416
    comparing numbers using, 381–386
    definition of, 40, 104
    subtracting on
        using addition, 219–224, 503–508
        using "count on" and "count back" strategies, 65–70
        using "get to 10" strategy, 77, 78, 84
        of lengths, 579–584
        of tens, 207–212
        of tens and hundreds, 467–472
        of tens and ones, 213–218
        of three-digit numbers, 473–478

Number Sense, *Throughout. For example, see:* 5, 46, 161, 212, 353, 371, 401, 534, 621, 683

O

Octagons
    drawing, 734
    identifying, 732–736

Odd numbers
    adding, 9–14
    identifying, 3–8
    modeling, 9–14

One(s) (1)
    adding
        breaking addends apart in, 116–126
        using models, 429–434
        using number line, 109–114
        in partial sums, 153–164, 423–428
        in regrouping, 165–176
    counting by
        within 120, 352–356
        within 1,000, 357
    definition of, 320
    identifying numbers 1 more or 1 less, 369–374
    subtracting, using models, 485–490
    understanding place value of, 325–330

One dollar bills ($1)
    coins equal to, 681–686
    finding total value of, 693–698
    making change from, 687–692
    value of, 682

One thousand (1,000)
    modeling and writing numbers up to, 319–324
    skip counting within, 357–362, 405–410, 467–472

One-digit numbers
    adding three, 53–58
    subtracting, from two-digit number, 263–274, 281–286

Open number line, *See* Number line

Open-Ended, 434, 440, 674

Organize It, *In every chapter. For example, see:* 2, 40, 152, 206, 312, 460, 522, 578, 612, 730

P

Partial sums
    with three-digit numbers, 423–428
    with two-digit numbers, 153–164

Part-part-whole model, 71, 72

Patterns, 487, 707, 748, 766

Pennies, *See also* Coins
    value of, 664

Pentagons
    drawing, 734
    identifying, 732–736, 737

Performance Task, *In every chapter. For example, see:* 33, 145, 255, 305, 387, 453, 515, 603, 723, 779

Picture graphs
   making, 625–630
   tally charts compared to, 619, 625
   understanding, 619–624

Place value, *See also* Hundred; One; Ten
   breaking apart addends using, 115–126
   identifying patterns in, 363–368
   representing numbers in different ways with, 337–342
   understanding, 325–330

Plots, line, making, 643–654

P.M., 717–722

Polygons, *See also* specific types
   definition of, 738
   drawing, 743–748
   identifying angles of, 737–742

Practice, *In every lesson. For example, see:* 7–8, 45–46, 157–158, 211–212, 373–374, 465–466, 527–528, 583–584, 617–618, 679–680

Precision, *Throughout. For example, see:* 70, 123, 149, 528, 537, 555, 564, 668, 707, 736

Problem solving, *See* Word problems

Problem Solving Strategy, *Throughout. For example, see:* 90, 142, 193, 250, 303, 586, 594, 700

Problem Types, *Throughout. For example, see:*
   add to,
     change unknown, 50, 92, 114, 191, 410, 422, 455, 630, 746
     result unknown, 11, 88, 126, 284, 362, 432, 496, 579, 758
     start unknown, 91, 192, 408, 426, 453, 593, 700
   compare,
     bigger unknown, 52, 124, 162, 200, 395, 426, 453, 576, 786
     difference unknown, 70, 112, 218, 256, 446, 566, 615, 680, 740, 766
     smaller unknown, 52, 255, 292, 470, 552, 599, 628, 684, 702, 727
   put together,
     addend unknown, 44, 56, 62, 118, 204, 290, 606
     both addends unknown, 76, 453
     total unknown, 18, 56, 138, 174, 284, 441, 515, 570, 700, 786
   take apart,
     addend unknown, 44, 56, 62, 204, 476, 606
     both addends unknown, 76, 478
     total unknown, 83, 243, 490, 514
   take from,
     change unknown, 94, 222, 266, 302, 464, 592, 690
     result unknown, 68, 92, 210, 299, 464, 500, 597, 701, 736, 785
     start unknown, 68, 91, 120, 246, 272, 300, 506, 701

Quadrilaterals
   angles of, 738–742
   drawing, 734, 736
   identifying, 732–736, 737

Quarter past, 712–716

Quarter to, 712–716

Quarters, *See also* Coins
   value of, 664

Reading, *Throughout. For example, see:* T-7, T-87, T-107, T-169, T-279, T-545, T-589, T-635, T-667, T-741

Real World, *See* Modeling Real Life

Reasoning, *Throughout. For example, see:* 14, 111, 215, 227, 407, 469, 511, 599, 615, 665

Rectangles, equal squares in, 755–760

Regrouping
   addition using, 165–176

subtraction using, 263–268
    with numbers containing zeros, 498–502

Repeated addition, of equal groups, 16–18

Repeated Reasoning, 85, 365

Response to Intervention, *Throughout. For example, see:* T-1B, T-43, T-107, T-245, T-317, T-377, T-397B, T-531, T-595, T-661B

Review & Refresh, *In every lesson. For example, see:* 158, 212, 268, 404, 466

Rhombus
    definition of, 744
    drawing, 744

Right angles
    definition of, 738
    identifying, 738–742

Rows
    definition of, 152
    in rectangles, 756–760

S

Scaffolding Instruction, *In every lesson. For example, see:* T-5, T-135, T-185, T-251, T-353, T-401, T-487, T-599, T-615, T-745

Shapes, two-dimensional. *See also specific shapes*
    angles of, 737–742
    drawing, 743–748
    equal shares of
        drawing lines showing, 767–778
        identifying lines showing, 761–766
    identifying types of, 731–736

Shares, *See* Equal shares

Show and Grow, *In every lesson. For example, see:* 4, 42, 154, 208, 264, 314, 400, 524, 580, 664

Sides
    definition of, 732
    identifying number of, 254, 732–736

Skip counting
    within 120, 351–356
    within 1,000, 357–362, 405–410, 467–472

Squares
    definition of, 744
    drawing, 744
    rectangles composed of, 755–760

Standard form of numbers, 331–336

Structure, *Throughout. For example, see:* 20, 55, 114, 218, 330, 374, 416, 478, 584, 677

Subtraction
    within 20, 83–88
    using addition, 219–224, 503–508
    checking with addition, 287–292
    choosing strategies for, 243–248, 293–298, 509–514
    using compensation
        with numbers containing zeros, 498–502
        with three-digit numbers, 479–484
        with two-digit numbers, 237–242
    using "count on" and "count back" strategies, 65–70
    using decomposition (breaking numbers apart), 225–236
    explaining strategies for, 509–514
    using "get to 10" strategy, 77–82, 84
    of lengths, 579–584
    using mental math, 237, 461–466
    using models
        of one-digit number from two-digit number, 263–274, 281–286
        of three-digit numbers, 485–490
        of two-digit number from two-digit number, 275–286
    on number line (*See* Number line, subtracting on)
    using regrouping, 263–268
        with numbers containing zeros, 498–502
    relationship between addition and, 71–76
    summary of strategies for, 293, 509

of three-digit numbers, 473–496
  using compensation, 479–484
  using models, 485–490
  using number line, 473–478
  from numbers containing zeros, 497–502
word problems solved using
  one-step, 89–94, 299–304
  two-step, 249–254, 299–304

Success Criteria, *In every lesson. For example, see:* T-3, T-171, T-219, T-293, T-375, T-447, T-509, T-585, T-631, T-755

Sums, *See also* Addition
  definition of, 42
  partial
    with three-digit numbers, 423–428
    with two-digit numbers, 153–164

Surveys, 614

Symbols
  comparing numbers using, 375–380
  dollar sign ($), 682
  equal to (=), 376–380
  greater than (>), 376–380
  less than (<), 376–380
  minus sign (−), 206
  right angle, 738

T

Tally charts
  bar graphs compared to, 631, 637
  organizing data in, 613–618
  picture graphs compared to, 619, 625

Ten(s) (10)
  adding
    using decomposition, 116–126
    using mental math, 399–404
    using models, 429–434
    using number line, 103–114, 405–410
    in partial sums, 153–164, 423–428
    in regrouping, 165–176
  counting by
    within 120, 351–356
    within 1,000, 357–362, 405–410, 467–472
  definition of, 320
  in "get to 10" strategy, 77–82, 84
  groups of, as hundreds, 313–318
  identifying numbers 10 more or 10 less, 369–374
  in "make a 10" strategy, 59–64, 84
  subtracting
    using decomposition, 231–236
    using mental math, 461–466
    using models, 485–490
    using number line, 467–472
  understanding place value of, 325–330

Ten dollar bills ($10), finding total value of, 693–698

Think and Grow, *In every lesson. For example, see:* 4, 42, 154, 208, 314, 352, 462, 524, 614, 664

Think and Grow: Modeling Real Life, *In every lesson. For example, see:* 6, 44, 106, 210, 266, 366, 402, 464, 526, 666

Thirds
  definition of, 762
  drawing lines showing, 767–778
  identifying lines showing, 761–766

Three-digit numbers
  adding, 411–440
    using compensation, 417–422
    using models, 429–434
    using number line, 411–416
    using partial sums, 423–428
  subtracting, 473–496
    using compensation, 479–484
    using models, 485–490
    using number line, 473–478
    from numbers containing zeros, 497–502
  writing standard, expanded, and word forms of, 331–336

Time, telling
  A.M. and P.M. in, 717–722
  before and after the hour, 711–716

to nearest five minutes, 705–710

Triangles
  angles of, 738–742
  drawing, 734, 736
  identifying, 254, 732–736, 737

Two-digit numbers
  adding
    using compensation, 127–132
    four, 441–446
    using partial sums, 153–164
    three, 183–188
  subtracting
    using compensation, 237–242
    one-digit number from, 263–274, 281–286
    two-digit number from, 275–286

Two-dimensional shapes, *See* Shapes

V

Vertex (vertices)
  of cubes, 750
  definition of, 732
  identifying number of, 254, 732–736

W

Which One Doesn't Belong?, *Throughout. For example, see:* 318, 336, 425, 695, 713

Word form of numbers, 331–336

Word problems, solving
  length
    comparing lengths, 585–590
    for missing measurements, 591–596
    using number line, 579–584
    practicing, 597–602
  money, 699–704
    making change from one dollar, 687–692

  one-step
    using addition, 89–94, 189–194
    using arrays, 27–32
    using subtraction, 89–94, 299–304
  two-step
    using addition, 139–144, 189–194
    using subtraction, 249–254, 299–304

Writing, *Throughout. For example, see:* 132, 176, 286, 481, 502, 567, 602, 636, 733, 739

Y

Yards
  estimating lengths in, 553–558
  measuring lengths in, 547–552

You Be the Teacher, *Throughout. For example, see:* 11, 91, 105, 209, 268, 324, 368, 466, 525, 677

Z

Zero (0), subtraction from numbers containing, 497–502

Reference Sheet

Symbols

+	plus
−	minus
=	equals
>	greater than
<	less than
¢	cent sign
$	dollar sign

Place Value

237

hundreds place   tens place   ones place

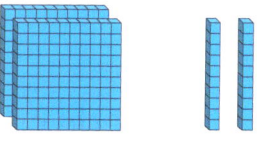

2 flats   3 rods   7 units

Hundreds	Tens	Ones
2	3	7

Money

penny   1¢
100 pennies = $1

nickel   5¢
20 nickels = $1

dime   10¢
10 dimes = $1

quarter   25¢
4 quarters = $1

$1 bill

$5 bill

$10 bill

$20 bill

Time

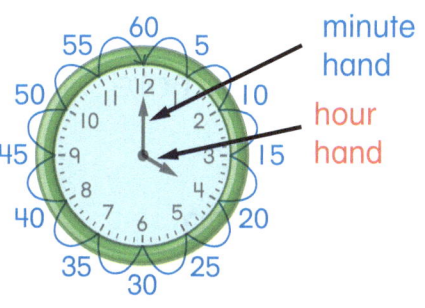

minute hand
hour hand

60 minutes = 1 hour

quarter to

quarter past

half past

Equal Shares

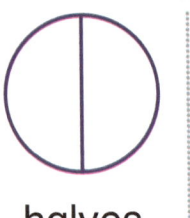
halves

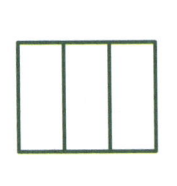
thirds

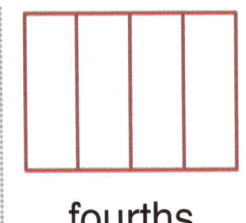
fourths

Length

1 meter = 100 centimeters
1 foot = 12 inches
1 yard = 36 inches
1 yard = 3 feet

Shapes

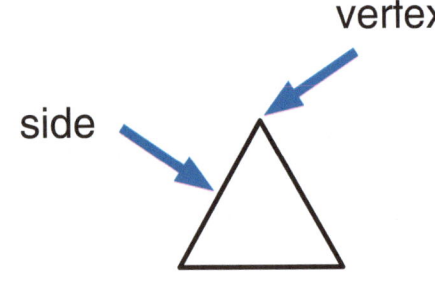

triangles

3 sides
3 vertices

quadrilaterals
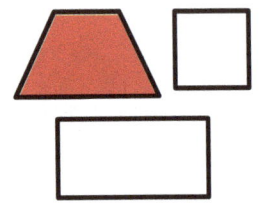
4 sides
4 vertices

pentagons

5 sides
5 vertices

hexagons

6 sides
6 vertices

octagons
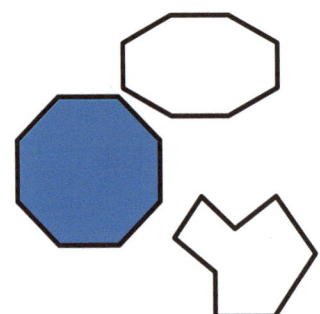
8 sides
8 vertices

A **polygon** is a closed two-dimensional shape with three or more sides. When two sides meet, they form an **angle**.

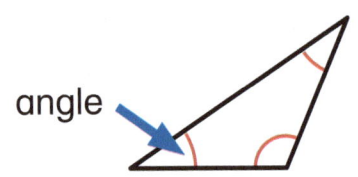
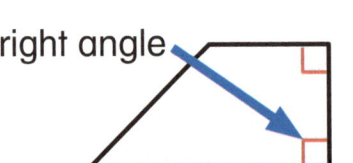

A24

Credits

Chapter 1
1 GerhardvdS10/iStock/Getty Images Plus

Chapter 2
39 Wavebreakmeadia/iStock/Getty Images Plus

Chapter 3
101 LawrenceSawyer/E+/Getty Images

Chapter 4
151 phaitoons/iStock/Getty Images Plus

Chapter 5
205 Herhurricane/iStock/Getty Images Plus

Chapter 6
261 Blend Images/Shutterstock.com

Chapter 7
311 Brent Hofacker/Shutterstock.com

Chapter 8
349 aluxum/iStock/Getty Images Plus

Chapter 9
397 © highwaystarz - stock.adobe.com

Chapter 10
459 HodagMedia/Shutterstock.com

Chapter 11
521 kali9/E+/Getty Images; **547** paulprescott72/iStock/Getty Images Plus

Chapter 12
577 Itsra Sanprasert/Shutterstok.com; **604** Bullet_Chained/iStock/Getty Images Plus; filo/iStock/Getty Images Plus

Chapter 13
611 fstop123/iStock/Getty Images Plus

Chapter 14
661 querbeet/E+/Getty Images; **coins** TokenPhoto/E+/Getty Images; asafta/iStock/Getty Images Plus; Kuzmik_A/iStock/Getty Images Plus; Meral Hydaverdi/Shutterstock.com; **five dollar bill** Studio Araminta/Shutterstock.com

Chapter 15
729 akiyoko/iStock/Getty Images Plus

Cartoon Illustrations: MoreFrames Animation
Design Elements: oksanika/Shutterstock.com; icolourful/Shutterstock.com; Valdis Torms